DATE DUE		

THE STREAM-OF-CONSCIOUSNESS
TECHNIQUE IN THE MODERN NOVEL

Kennikat Press
National University Publications
Literary Criticism Series

General Editor
John E. Becker

THE
STREAM-OF-CONSCIOUSNESS
TECHNIQUE
IN THE
MODERN NOVEL

edited by

ERWIN R. STEINBERG

National University Publications
KENNIKAT PRESS // 1979
Port Washington, N. Y. // London

Manufactured in the United States of America

Published by
Kennikat Press Corp.
Port Washington, N.Y. / London

Library of Congress Cataloging in Publication Data
Main entry under title:

The stream-of-consciousness technique in the modern novel.

(National university publications)

1. English fiction–20th century–History and criticism–Addresses, essays, lectures. 2. Stream of consciousness fiction–Addresses, essays, lectures. 3. Proust, Marcel, 1871–1922–Technique–Addresses, essays, lectures. I. Steinberg, Erwin Ray.
PR888.S76S84   809.3'83   78-21254
ISBN 0-8046-9225-4

CONTENTS

THE STREAM-OF-CONSCIOUSNESS
TECHNIQUE IN THE MODERN NOVEL

ABOUT THE EDITOR

Erwin R. Steinberg is Professor of English and Interdisciplinary Studies at Carnegie-Mellon University. He has published various books and articles in literary journals, and has received numerous awards.

FOREWORD

Leon Edel begins the foreword to his book *The Psychological Novel,
1900-1950* with the statement: "In this essay I have sought to define
what seems to me the most characteristic aspect of twentieth-century
fiction: its inward turning to convey the flow of mental experience—what
has been called the 'stream of consciousness.'"[1] In *The Stream of Consciousness and Beyond in ULYSSES*[2] I examined the development and
use of the stream-of-consciousness technique by James Joyce. This book
deals with the stream-of-consciousness technique more broadly: how it
fits into the history of the modern novel, its sources, the novelists who
developed it, and its impact on modern fiction.

The stream-of-consciousness technique appeared as an identifiable
form and flowered at the high point of what we have come to call the Age
of Modernism. Maurice Beebe, editor of the *Journal of Modern Literature,*
says of that period:

We can see now that Modernism began during the last quarter of the
nineteenth century, reached a crest of creative achievement during the
1920s, and faded at about the time of the Second World War. This period
of more than sixty years, the Age of Modernism, was the time of the great
masters, the myth-builders and world-creators like Yeats and Joyce, Proust
and Mann, Henry James and the early Faulkner. . . .[3]

Most of the major stream-of-consciousness novels appeared between 1915
and 1930; and one of each of the pairs of "great masters" that Beebe lists
wrote important stream-of-consciousness novels during that period: Joyce,

Ulysses (1922); Proust, *Remembrance of Things Past* (1913–1926); and Faulkner, *The Sound and the Fury* (1929) and *As I Lay Dying* (1930). So also did Virginia Woolf (*Mrs. Dalloway*, 1922), and Dorothy Richardson (*Pilgrimage*, 1915–1935).

For the critic or scholar concerned with the novel or with the Age of Modernism, the stream-of-consciousness technique is an important form, the stream-of-consciousness novel an important genre. The readings in this book were collected to answer a series of questions for such a person: What is the stream-of-consciousness technique? What were its literary antecedents? What was the psychological, philosophical, and aesthetic *Weltanschauung* out of which it grew? Who developed it? What did writers and critics think of it at the time? How do we view it now? What impact has it had on the novel?

Some of the essays included in this volume are parts of larger works which the reader may want to investigate further. Some of the headnotes also suggest further readings; and references in the texts and in the footnotes can be used as directions for even wider investigation. Thus, complete in itself as an examination of the stream-of-consciousness technique, this book can also serve as an introduction to a study of other important aspects of modern fiction and the Age of Modernism.

E. R. S.

1

THE STREAM

C. HUGH HOLMAN, ADDISON HIBBARD, AND WILLIAM FLINT THRALL: "The Stream-of-Consciousness Novel," *A Handbook to Literature,* (New York: Odyssey Press, rev. ed., 1960), pp. 471–72.

This short statement about the stream-of-consciousness novel will give the reader a reasonable understanding of the stream-of-consciousness technique, its history, its function, and its practitioners. Before the end of this book the reader will have a much more rigorous definition.

The terms printed in small capitals are defined elsewhere in the handbook (in alphabetical order). For a fuller understanding of this definition, therefore, before proceeding further the reader may want to consult those entries in this particular handbook or in one of the many others available.

Les Lauriers sont coupés, the novel by Edouard Dujardin referred to in the following discussion, was translated by Stuart Gilbert and published as *We'll to the Woods No More* (1938). Since it is referred to frequently in many of the sections which follow, the reader may wish to examine it if he can find a copy. It is of interest as a forerunner of the twentieth-century stream-of-consciousness novel.

HOLMAN, THRALL, AND HIBBARD, *Stream*

The type of PSYCHOLOGICAL NOVEL which takes as its subject matter the uninterrupted, uneven, and endless flow of one or more of its characters. By consciousness in this context is meant the total range of awareness and emotive-mental response of an individual, from the lowest pre-speech level to the highest fully articulated level of rational thought. The assumption is that in the mind of an individual at a given moment his *stream of consciousness* (the phrase originated in this sense with William James) is a mixture of all the levels of awareness, an unending flow of sensations, thoughts, memories, associations, and reflections; if the exact content of the mind ("consciousness") is to be described at any moment, then these varied, disjointed, and illogical elements must find expression in a flow of words, images, and ideas similar to the unorganized flow of the mind. The *stream-of-consciousness novel* uses varied techniques to represent this consciousness adequately. In general, most PSYCHOLOGICAL NOVELS report the flow of conscious and ordered intelligence, as in Henry James, or the flow of memory recalled by association, as in Marcel Proust; but the *stream-of-consciousness novel* tends to concentrate its attention chiefly on the pre-speech, non-verbalized level, where the IMAGE must express the unarticulated response and where the logic of grammar belongs to another world. However differing the techniques employed, the writers of the *stream-of-consciousness novel* seem to share certain common assumptions: (1) that the significant existence of man is to be found in his mental-emotional processes and not in the outside world, (2) that this mental-emotional life is disjointed, illogical, and (3) that a pattern of free psychological association rather than of logical relationship determines the shifting sequence of thought and feeling.

Attempts to concentrate the subject matter of FICTION on the inner consciousness are not new by any means. The earliest impressive example seems to be Laurence Sterne's *Tristram Shandy* (1759–1767), with its motto from Epictetus: "It is not actions, but opinions about actions, which disturb men," and with its application of Locke's psychological theories of association and duration to the functioning of the human mind. Yet Sterne, although he freed the sequence of thought from the rigors of logical organization, did not get beneath the speech level in his portrait of Tristram's consciousness. Henry James, in his PSYCHOLOGICAL NOVELS, too, remained on a consciously articulated level. In a major sense, the present-day *stream-of-consciousness novel* is a product of Freudian psychology with its structure of psychological levels, although it first appeared in *Les Lauriers sont coupés,* by Edouard Dujardin, in 1887, where the INTERIOR MONOLOGUE was used for the first time in the modern sense. Other important users of the INTERIOR MONOLOGUE to create reports on the *stream-of-consciousness* have been Dorothy

Richardson, Virginia Woolf, James Joyce, William Faulkner. The tendency today is to see the *stream-of-consciousness* subject matter and the INTERIOR MONOLOGUE technique as tools to be used in the presentation of character in depth, but not as the exclusive subjects or methods of whole NOVELS. See PSYCHOLOGICAL NOVEL, INTERIOR MONOLOGUE.

2

HEADWATERS AND TRIBUTARIES

JACQUES SOUVAGE, "Narrative Technique In the Novel: The Dramatized Novel, and Point of View," *An Introduction to the Study of the Novel* (Ghent: E. Story–Scientia P.V.B.A., 1965), pp. 36–55.

Souvage traces the history of the "disappearance" of the author and of the growing importance of point of view in the English novel in the nineteenth century and early twentieth centuries. This survey shows where the stream-of-consciousness novel fits in the history of the novel.

The interested reader can find more details in Percy Lubbock, *The Craft of Fiction* (1921), Bernard DeVoto, *The World of Fiction* (1951), and Wayne C. Booth, *The Rhetoric of Fiction* (1961).

Lubbock tells the story through the novels of Henry James. DeVoto carries it further. Booth's treatment deals with "the technique of non-didactic fiction, viewed as the art of communicating with readers—the rhetorical resources available to the writer of epic, novel, or short story as he tries, consciously or unconsciously, to impose his fictional world upon the reader." *The Rhetoric of Fiction* is a central work for anyone interested in the study of the novel.

For the reader who wants to pursue the concept of point of view, James Moffet and Kenneth R. McElhany have edited *Points of View: An Anthology of Short Stories* (1966), in which forty-two stories are ordered "so as to call attention to who the narrator is, when and where he is telling the story, who he is telling it to, what relation to the events he stands in, and what kind of knowledge he claims." The stories are organized under eleven headings: Interior Monologue; Dramatic Monologue; Letter

Narration; Diary Narration; Subjective Narration; Detached Autobiography; Memoir, or Observer Narration; Biography, or Anonymous Narration—Single Character Point of View; Anonymous Narration—Multiple Character Point of View; and Anonymous Narration—No Character Point of View.

A. A. Mendilow in *Time and the Novel* (London: Peter Nevill, 1952) also has some helpful things to say about point of view.

ERWIN R. STEINBERG, "The Sources of the Stream," *The Stream of Consciousness and Beyond in ULYSSES* (Pittsburgh: University of Pittsburgh Press, 1973), pp. 257-76.

This survey of the aesthetics of the nineteenth and early twentieth centuries as seen in statements of painters, authors, and critics provides a further background against which the development of the stream-of-consciousness technique can be understood.

The reader may also wish to consult chapter 2, "Historical Background of the Stream of Consciousness Novel," in *Stream of Consciousness: A Study in Literary Method,* by Melvin J. Friedman (1955). Friedman sees Laurence Sterne as the English author who first "anticipates stream of consciousness."

WILLIAM JAMES, "The Stream of Thought," *The Principles of Psychology* 1 (New York: Henry Holt, 1890): 224-25.

These are the opening-summary-paragraphs of a chapter of some sixty pages in which James begins the "study of the mind from within."

WILLIAM JAMES, "The Stream of Consciousness," *Talks to Teachers on Psychology* (New York: Henry Holt, 1921), pp. 15-21.

In a book published originally in 1899, James outlines his ideas on the psychological stream of consciousness.

SIGMUND FREUD, "Free Association," *The Complete Introductory Lectures on Psychoanalysis* (New York: W. W. Norton, 1966), pp. 106-9.

This statement from a series of lectures delivered by Freud during World War I explains how free association operates not only in dreams but in everyday life.

SIGMUND FREUD, "A Note on the Prehistory of the Technique of Analysis," *Collected Papers,* vol. 5, ed. James Strachey (London: Basic Books, 1953), pp. 101–4.

In this paper, which he published anonymously in 1920, Freud explains that, although the concept of free association had been suggested in a letter by Schiller in 1788 and in "a volume of mystic doggerel verse" by J. J. Garth Wilkinson in 1857, he himself probably first encountered it in an essay entitled "The Art of Becoming an Original Writer in Three Days," written in 1823 by Ludwig Borne. Thus a concept that had an important influence on twentieth-century literature may have had its beginnings in nineteenth-century literature.

The reader will find a useful discussion of the impact of Freud's ideas on the modern novel in Frederick J. Hoffman's *Freudianism and the Literary Mind* (1957).

HENRI BERGSON, "Understanding Reality from Within," *An Introduction to Metaphysics,* trans. T. E. Hulme, (London: Macmillan, 1913), pp. 1–13.

In this statement from a paper first published in 1903 and later reprinted as the opening section of *An Introduction to Metaphysics,* Bergson discusses some of the problems of an author in relating the adventures of a character in a novel and explains the importance of understanding reality "from within, by intuition" rather than by "simple analysis."

HENRI BERGSON, "Duration," *Creative Evolution,* trans. Arthur Mitchell (New York: Henry Holt, 1911), pp. 1–7.

In this passage, the opening pages of *Creative Evolution,* Bergson summarizes the concept of duration. He describes a mental state as "a moving zone which comprises all that we think or feel or will—all, in short, that we are at any given moment." Such states are not distinct, discontinuous, stable elements. Rather, consciousness is a fluid mass in which those states "continue each other in an endless flow"—"a flux of fleeting shades merging into each other."

The interested reader may explore the relationship of Bergson's philosophy with the development of the stream-of-consciousness technique in Shiv K. Kumar's *Bergson and the Stream of Consciousness Novel* (1962), the introduction to which appears later in this volume. A. A. Mendilow considers Bergson's "duration" and other aspects of time in his *Time and the Novel* (1952).

SOUVAGE: *Narrative Technique in the Novel*

Narrative Technique in the "Old" Novel in General. In the "old" novel, the novel of, say, Fielding, Jane Austen, Walter Scott, Charlotte Brontë, Dickens, Thackeray, Trollope, and George Eliot, the story is told by an author who is not only omnipresent and omniscient, but also continually visible to the reader.[1] This is the case, not only with the novels told from the third-person point of view, but also with the majority of the first-person novels, where the narrator partly or completely functions as the author's mouthpiece. (We are here reminded of even such first-person narratives as *Moll Flanders,* where Defoe takes over on many occasions.) As Martin Steinmann, Jr., has remarked, "in the third-person narrative in the old novel"—to confine our attention to novels written from the third-person point of view—"the author is everywhere. Structurally, he makes us feel his presence by such conventions as omniscience, exposition [here to be taken in the sense of "analysis"], and block characterization; stylistically, by such conventions as the vocative case ("Dear reader"), normative words, persuasive definitions, and panoramic narration."[2]

I will now give a few illustrations of what Mr. Steinmann means. Here, to begin with, is Jane Austen again, this time in a passage of generalized psychological analysis from chapter 12 of *Persuasion:*

Who can be in doubt of what followed? When any two young people take it into their heads to marry, they are pretty sure by perseverance to carry their point, be they ever so poor, or ever so imprudent, or ever so little likely to be necessary to each other's ultimate comfort. This may be bad morality to conclude with, but I believe it to be truth; and if such parties succeed, how should a Captain Wentworth and an Anne Elliot, with the advantage of maturity of mind, consciousness of right, and one independent fortune between them, fail of bearing down every opposition?[3]

And here is the narrator of Sir Walter Scott's *The Heart of Midlothian* (1818), appending a moral to his story:

READER—This tale will not be told in vain, if it shall be found to illustrate the great truth, that guilt, though it may attain temporal splendour, can never confer real happiness; that the evil consequences of our crimes long survive their commission, and, like the ghosts of the murdered, for ever haunt the steps of the malefactor; and that the paths of virtue, though seldom those of worldly greatness, are always those of pleasantness and peace.[4]

Next, here is Thackeray's narrator, taking his leave of the reader at the end of *Vanity Fair* (1847-48):

Ah! *Vanitas Vanitatum!* which of us is happy in this world? Which of us has his desire? or, having it, is satisfied?—Come, children, let us shut up the box and the puppets, for our play is played out.[5]

And here Charlotte Brontë's narrator addresses the reader at the very beginning of *Shirley* (1849):

If you think, from this prelude, that anything like a romance is preparing for you, reader, you never were more mistaken. Do you anticipate sentiment, and poetry, and reverie? Do you expect passion, and stimulus, and melodrama? Calm your expectations; reduce them to a lowly standard. Something real, cool, and solid, lies before you; something unromantic as Monday morning. . . .[6]

George Eliot's narrator, commenting on a love scene between Adam Bede and Dinah Morris in chapter 50 of *Adam Bede* (1859), is not so aloof. She takes the line of sentiment:

That is a simple scene, reader. But it is almost certain that you, too, have been in love—perhaps, even, more than once, though you may not choose to say so to all your feminine friends. If so, you will no more think the slight words, the timid looks, the tremulous touches, by which two human souls approach each other gradually, like two little quivering rain-streams, before they mingle into one—you will no more think these things trivial than you will think the first-detected signs of coming spring trivial, though they be but a faint, indescribable something in the air and in the song of the birds, and the tiniest perceptible budding on the hedgerow branches.[7]

And, finally, here is Trollope's narrator at the opening of chapter 2 of *Doctor Thorne* (1858), on one of the many occasions when he is, in the words of Henry James, "betraying a sacred office":

As Dr. Thorne is our hero—or I should rather say my hero, a privilege of selecting for themselves in this respect being left to all my readers—and as Miss Mary Thorne is to be our heroine, a point in which no choice whatsoever is left to any one, it is necessary that they shall be introduced and explained and described in a proper, formal manner. I quite feel that an apology is due for beginning a novel with two long dull chapters full of description. I am perfectly aware of the danger of such a course.[8]

Now, although the above-quoted passages may appear obtrusive when removed from their proper contexts, they are in varying degrees appropriate to, and effective in, the novels in which they occur.[9] In the last analysis some of them are extreme instances of how the novelist may avail himself of the rhetoric of fiction, of the conventions inherent in the art of narrative.

The "Old" Novel versus the "New" or "Dramatized" Novel. Yet, writers of what I have termed the "dramatized" novel and critics reared on Henry James and Percy Lubbock as a rule take strong exception to passages such as the above-quoted, in which the "old" novel abounds. In such passages, they say, the author interposes his own consciousness between his subject and the reader. In short, these passages and, by extension, the novels in which they occur are "undramatic." Mr. Lubbock himself has decided views on the subject, as the following statement from his *The Craft of Fiction* testifies: "The art of fiction does not begin until the novelist thinks of his story as a matter to be *shown*, to be so exhibited that it will tell itself."[10]

All these, in their turn, are assumptions with which those maintaining the cause of the "old" novel are bound to quarrel. Some of its defendants have even fought the new novelists on their own ground. They have pointed out that in many cases the charge of obtrusiveness raised against the old novelists is utterly unfounded. In Fielding's novels *Joseph Andrews, Tom Jones,* and *Amelia,* they have said, it is not the author who narrates the story, but a *mask,* a *second self,* a *persona* of the author. The "Fielding" who narrates *Joseph Andrews,* they have remarked, is quite a different person from the "Fielding" who does the telling in *Tom Jones;* and the "Fielding" who acts as narrator in *Tom Jones* in his turn differs considerably from the "Fielding" who relates the story in *Amelia.* In these three novels, they suggest, Fielding has established an organic relationship between himself, his readers, and his work by creating a *mask,* a *persona,* a *second self.* In *Joseph Andrews, Tom Jones,* and *Amelia* he assumes a role and by so doing achieves an organic relationship with his work and his audience.

Among the names of critics who hold such views we may—to confine ourselves to these few—cite those of Käte Friedemann, Alan Dugald McKillop, Paul Bourget, and Wolfgang Kayser. In her study *Die Rolle des Erzählers in der Epik,* which was published in 1910, Käte Friedemann speaks of the narrator as of "[einen] organischen Bestandteil seines eigenen Kunstwerks."[11] And in his *The Early Masters of English Fiction* Alan Dugald McKillop has stressed the importance of the role of the narrator in *Joseph Andrews* and *Tom Jones:* in *Joseph Andrews,* he says, "it is the narrator who really holds the story together and gives it genuine significance. He keeps the coarser and more extravagant scenes from being taken too seriously; he keeps us amused, not merely disgusted, with Lady Booby, Mrs. Slipslop, and the others. Since he is superior, self-controlled, and playfully ironical, he works and makes for coherence."[12] Moreover, "recent critics have rightly emphasized the role of the narrator [in *Tom Jones*] in keeping the whole story on the comic level, in making certain that we shall not be too tragically concerned for Tom, even when his fortunes are at their lowest."[13] Paul Bourget, the French novelist and literary critic, is even more emphatic in stating that

un roman . . . n'est pas de la vie représentée. C'est de la vie racontée. Les deux définitions sont très différentes. La seconde est, seule, conforme à la nature du genre. Si le roman est de la vie racontée, il suppose un narrateur. . . . Un témoin . . . n'est pas un mirroir impassible, il est un regard qui s'émeut, et l'expression même de ce regard fait partie de ce témoignage.[14]

To Wolfgang Kayser, finally, novel and narrator are by definition coterminous: "Der Roman ist die von einem (fiktiven) persönlichen Erzähler vorgetragene, einen persönlichen Leser einbeziehende Erzählung von Welt, soweit sie als persönliche Erfahrung fassbar wird."[15]

On the other hand, it is little wonder that such modern novelists as Flaubert, Henry James (particularly in his later phase), Dorothy Richardson, James Joyce, Virginia Woolf, Hemingway, Henry Green, and Sartre should have rejected the narrative methods and techniques of the "old" novelists. In fact, as we shall presently discuss at some length, with these modern novelists practically everything tended in the direction of the dramatized novel.

The "Dramatized" Novel. But first I wish to explain what is meant by the term "dramatized novel." For this purpose I will start by broadly defining the dramatic genre as the literary genre which is characterized by scenic presentation. Here, on a stage in front of us, characters enact a plot without interference of any author. In fact, in a play the author may be omnipresent but he is invisible. In a play the story is not told by the author; it is the characters who act it out, who show it for him. And now, simplifying matters, I will say that a novel is "dramatized" to the extent that the novelist, like the dramatist, lets his story tell itself. The novel is "dramatized" in so far as the novelist, instead of telling his story himself, lets his characters take over and show the story for him. In the dramatized novel, scene will increasingly come to take the place of such narrative methods as summary, description, exposition, commentary and character analysis, which were so characteristic of the old novel, as we have seen in our discussion of chapter 1 of *Mansfield Park*. In the process the novelist will efface himself; he may even, as in the novels of Hemingway and of Henry Green, all but disappear. As Bernard DeVoto has remarked, this method of fiction "undertakes to avoid analysis altogether by transferring it from the novel to the reader. In Hemingway, for instance, what the characters do and say is so rigorously selected and forms such a revealing system in itself that the reader is compelled to derive the motives behind it from the action itself."[16] Moreover, not only is there thus placed upon the reader of the modern novel a burden heavier than that which the reader of the traditional novel had to carry; with the disappearance of the novelist from his work and with his relinquishment of the traditional authorial prerogatives—evaluation, judgment, even intrusive comment, etc.—ambiguity and indeterminateness, for better or for worse, also make their entry into the novel.[17]

What chiefly strikes us when we compare the work of these modern novelists with that of their predecessors, is the fact that the work of the former no more evinces that quality of profound moral conviction and assurance which informed the work of the older novelists.[18] This, together with the ever-increasing differentiation of the reading public, which renders it almost impossible for a novelist to identify himself with any audience,[19] accounts—at least partly—for the disappearance of the modern author from his work. Regarded in this light, the "dramatized" novel is the appropriate medium of those novelists who, having neither an established moral code nor a public to whom they might eventually convey such a code, cannot afford to be moralistic or didactic. Moreover, the aesthetic values which in the work of the modern novelists have taken the place of the moral values of the old novelists, also tend in the direction of the dramatized novel. With Flaubert these new values go by the names of dramatic illusion, objectivity, and technique. In his letter to Mademoiselle Leroyer de Chantepie dated March 18, 1857, he writes:

The illusion [of truth in *Madame Bovary*] . . . comes from the very objectivity of the work. It is one of my principles that one must not write oneself into one's work. The artist must be in his work as God is in creation, invisible yet all-powerful; we must sense him everywhere but never see him.

· ·

Then again, Art should rise above personal feeling and emotional susceptibilities! It is time we gave it, through rigid systematization, the exactness of the physical sciences! The chief difficulty for me, however, still remains style, form, that indefinable Beauty arising from the very conception which, as Plato says, is the very splendour of Truth.[20]

With Henry James, as we know, moral values and aesthetic values became almost interchangeable; moreover, he, too, cherished the idea of objectivity for the sake of dramatic illusion. His characteristic method is, perhaps, best to be seen in *The Ambassadors,* where the center of the subject is firmly placed in the consciousness of Strether, the novel's "central intelligence." The subject here is not so much what happens as what Strether, who acts as a "reflector," makes of what happens. As Percy Lubbock has said, the author "does not tell the story of Strether's mind; he makes it tell itself, he dramatizes it."[21] Or, in other words, he has transformed Strether's consciousness into an enacted play.[22] As we know, James relied to an unprecedented extent upon scenic presentation of his materials. This dramatic method he carried to its utmost limit in *The Awkward Age,* which consists of a succession of scenes almost unrelieved with passages of summary, analysis, description, and comment. The preface to the New York edition of the same novel testifies to the great fascination which the scenic method permanently had for Henry James; in its insistence upon the chief advantage of objectivity which the drama has over the novel, it might almost stand for a manifesto of the "dramatized" novel:

. . . The beauty of the conception [of *The Awkward Age*] was in this approximation of the respective divisions of my form to the successive Acts of a Play. . . . The divine distinction of the act of a play—and a greater than any other it easily succeeds in arriving at—was, I reasoned, in its special, its guarded objectivity. This objectivity, in turn, when achieving its ideal, came from the imposed absence of that "going behind," to compass explanations and amplifications, to drag out odds and ends from the "mere" storyteller's great property-shop of aids to illusion: a resource under denial of which it was equally perplexing and delightful, for a change, to proceed. . . .[23]

Joseph Conrad also, in such novels as *Lord Jim, Youth,* and *Chance,* achieved dramatic presentation of his material by creating Marlow, a "permanently involved spectator," who could objectify the material of the narrative while at one further remove Conrad controlled him. With Henry James there started also what Leon Edel regards as the most characteristic movement of twentieth-century fiction: "its inward-turning to convey the flow of mental experience, what has been loosely called the 'stream of consciousness'";[24] this, again, made for dramatization in the novel.[25] In Dorothy Richardson's and Virginia Woolf's work we note the elaboration of highly evolved impressionistic techniques for recording the innermost workings of elusive idiosyncrasies. Next there is James Joyce, who gives what is perhaps the best description of his own method when, echoing Flaubert's statement, he describes the dramatic artist as one who, "like the God of creation, remains within or behind or beyond or above his handiwork . . . paring his fingernails."[26] Molly Bloom's long interior monologue[27] at the end of *Ulysses* affords an apt illustration of the dramatic method as used by Joyce. Here, Molly Bloom's consciousness engaged in silent thought is seen to act itself out almost like an actor on a stage, without her creator mediating:

. . . O and the sea the sea crimson sometimes like fire and the glorious sunsets and the figtrees in the Alameda gardens yes and all the queer little streets and pink and blue and yellow houses and the rosegardens and the jessamine and geraniums and cactuses and Gibraltar as a girl where I was a Flower of the mountain yes when I put the rose in my hair like the Andalusian girls used or shall I wear a red yes and how he kissed me under the Moorish wall and I thought well as well him as another and then I asked him with my eyes to ask again yes and then he asked me would I yes to say yes my mountain flower and first I put my arms around him yes and drew him down to me so he could feel my breasts all perfume yes and his heart was going like mad and yes I said yes I will Yes.[28]

Although it is not possible to dwell here on the achievement of such other innovators as Hemingway and Henry Green, passing reference may perhaps be made to the fictional practice of Sartre, who, in the name of "dogmatic realism," strongly objects to anything that so much as savours of the intervention and presence even of an author in his work and who rejects out of hand the "foolish business of storytelling."[29] Technically speaking, Sartre's method has far-reaching consequences for the treatment of time in the novel. It entails that the action of the novel shall not be foreshortened; nothing in the novel shall be summarized. In other words, with Sartre fictional time and historical time are synonymous:

Ainsi avons-nous appris de Joyce à rechercher une deuxieme espèce de réalisme: le réalisme brut de la subjectivité sans médiation ni distance. Ce qui nous entraîne a professer un troisième réalisme: celui de la temporalité. Si nous plongeons en effet, sans médiation, le lecteur dans une conscience, si nous lui refusons tous les moyens de la survoler, alors il faut lui imposer sans raccourcis le temps de cette conscience. Si je ramasse six mois en une page, le lecteur saute hors du livre.[30]

"Telling" versus "Showing" in the Novel. In his book *The Twentieth-Century Novel: Studies in Technique* Joseph Warren Beach has said that "in a bird's eye view of the English novel from Fielding to Ford, the one thing that will impress . . . more than any other is the disappearance of the author."[31] What this implies we have already considered at length: the disappearance of the author from his work goes hand in hand with critical theories and assumptions to the effect that the novelist should not tell but show, not describe but render. In his epoch-making recent study, *The Rhetoric of Fiction,* Wayne C. Booth has shown how these theories and assumptions which in Henry James's "prefaces" "offer no easy reduction of technique to a simple dichotomy of telling versus showing, no pat rejection of all but James's own methods," have gradually frozen into dogma. Even in Percy Lubbock's *The Craft of Fiction* (1921), Mr. Booth tells us, the process may already be seen to be under way: here, "James's treatment of dozens of literary problems . . . is reduced to the one thing needful: a novel should be made dramatic." We are here reminded of Percy Lubbock's statement that "the art of fiction does not begin until the novelist thinks of his story as a matter to be *shown,* to be so exhibited that it will tell itself." Similarly, Mr. Booth continues, Joseph Warren Beach is ". . . occasionally dogmatic about the author's commentary." However, by 1930 the "legitimate defense of the new" had already "froze[n] into dogma." In Ford Madox Ford's *The English Novel: From the Earliest Days to the Death of Joseph Conrad* we may read the following statements: "The novelist must not, by taking sides, exhibit his preferences. . . . He has . . . to render and not to tell. . . ."[32] After having discussed still other instances of the current practice of

indiscriminately extolling dramatization at the cost of telling,[33] instances such as Caroline Gordon and Allen Tate's *The House of Fiction,* Mr. Booth sets the problem in final perspective. "Instead of comparing fiction unfavorably with music and drama," he asks, "why should we not expect other arts to aspire enviously to the condition of fiction?" Actually, he continues, "neither expectation makes good sense; though we may, in our search for aesthetic constants, find some qualities common to all art, each art thrives when it pursues its own unique possibilities." In recent years several eloquent voices have made themselves heard in defense of the presence of the narrator in the novel. In his essay *Entstehung und Krise des modernen Romans* Wolfgang Kayser has emphatically stated that "der Tod des Erzählers ist der Tod des Romans."[34] W. J. Harvey, in his critical study *The Art of George Eliot,*[35] has vindicated the "omniscient author convention" as used by George Eliot. And Professor Kathleen Tillotson concludes her inaugural lecture, *The Tale and the Teller,* with the statement that "of the two modes [−the narrative and the dramatic−] the novel is the freer form[36]−'independent, elastic, prodigious' as Henry James . . . once called it−and it should not be denied its freedom to include the teller in the tale."[37]

Point of View. This brings us to a discussion of the concept of "point of view," i.e. the position from which the action of the novel is presented.[38] Although the term "point of view" was used as early as July 1866 in modern criticism (*British Quarterly Review* 44, 43-44),[39] it was not until Henry James wrote the prefaces for the New York edition of his novels (1907-9) that it came into its own as a technical term.[40] With Henry James, as we know, the concept of point of view was closely related to the problem of finding a "commanding centre," or "focus" of narration for his novels. The consistent use of a definite point of view he regarded as *the* means through which intensity, vividness, coherence, and economy of treatment could be achieved:

A beautiful infatuation this, always, I think, the intensity of the creative effort to get into the skin of the creature; the act of personal possession of one being by another at its completest−and with the high enhancement, ever, that it is, by the same stroke, the effort of the artist to preserve for his subject that unity, and for his use of it (in other words for the interest he desires to excite) that effect of a *centre,* which most economise its value.[41]

There is no economy of treatment without an adopted, a related point of view, and though I understand, under certain degrees of pressure, a represented community of vision between several parties to the action when it makes for concentration, I understand no breaking-up of the register, no sacrifice of the recording consistency, that doesn't rather scatter and weaken.[42]

Moreover, with Henry James the concept of point of view not infrequently carries overtones of meaning. Nowhere in James is this conception of point of view as something organically related to vision so pronounced as in the celebrated passage in the preface to *The Portrait of a Lady* where James speaks of the "house of fiction" as having "not one window, but a million . . . ; every one of which has been pierced, or is still pierceable, in its vast front, by the need of the individual vision and by the pressure of the individual will." These apertures, he continues, are "but windows at the best, mere holes in a dead wall, disconnected, perched aloft; they are not hinged doors opening straight upon life." Yet they have this distinguishing characteristic that "at each of them stands a figure with a pair of eyes, or at least with a fieldglass, which forms, again and again, for observation, a unique instrument, insuring to the person making use of it an impression distinct from every other." James rounds off this extended simile by identifying the "spreading field, the human scene," with the "choice of subject," and the "pierced aperture, either broad or balconied or slit-like and low-browed," with the "literary form." However, these are, "singly or together, as nothing without the posted presence of the watcher—without, in other words, the consciousness of the artist."[43]

With the publication of Joseph Warren Beach's *The Method of Henry James* (New Haven, 1918)[44] and of Percy Lubbock's *The Craft of Fiction* (1921), the first two critical studies to do justice to the method of Henry James, the concept of point of view became common property.

The following passage from *The Craft of Fiction* conveys some idea of the importance which point of view assumes with Mr. Lubbock: "The whole intricate question of method, in the craft of fiction, I take to be governed by the question of the point of view—the question of the relation in which the narrator stands to the story."[45] In fact, for Mr. Lubbock as for Henry James point of view is the chief means by which the novel can be dramatized, i.e. "be so exhibited that it will tell itself."[46]

In his essay "Point of View in Fiction: The Development of a Critical Concept," from which I have already quoted, Norman Friedman has actually applied the distinction between "telling" and "showing"[47] to the analysis of point of view in fiction, for "point of view provides a *modus operandi* for distinguishing the possible degrees of authorial extinction in the narrative art."[48] He has thus arrived at the following detailed classification of points of view:

1. *Editorial Omniscience.* Here the author's point of view is completely unlimited and the story "may be seen from any or all angles at will." This way of presenting the story is characterized by the "presence of authorial intrusions and generalizations about life, manners, and morals, which may or may not be explicitly related to the story at hand." Examples: *Tom Jones* (Fielding); *War and Peace* (Tolstoy).
2. *Neutral Omniscience.* Differs from Editorial Omniscience only in that the author makes no direct intrusions into the story, but speaks impersonally in the third person. As regards characterization, the author's predominant tendency here is to "describe and explain [his characters] to the reader in his own voice," instead of allowing them to speak and act for themselves. Examples: *Tess of the D'Urbervilles* (Hardy); *Point Counter Point* (Huxley).
3. *"I" as Witness.* Novels written from the first-person point of view, in which the author has delegated his narrative function to a narrator who is not the main character. Here the reader has available to him "only the thoughts, feelings, and perceptions of the witness-narrator; he therefore views the story from what may be called the wandering periphery." Examples: Marlow in *Lord Jim* (Conrad); Overton in *The Way of All Flesh* (Butler); Nick Carraway in *The Great Gatsby* (Scott Fitzgerald). *Somerset Maugham in*
4. *"I" as Protagonist.* Novels written from the first-person point of view, in which the author has shifted the narrative burden to (one of) the chief character(s), viz. the "protagonist-narrator." The "angle of view" here is that of the "fixed center." Example: Pip in *Great Expectations* (Dickens).[49]
5. *Multiple Selective Omniscience.* Here, even the narrator has disappeared from the story: the reader "ostensibly listens to no one [and] the story comes directly through the minds of the characters as it leaves its mark there." The chief difference between this mode of presentation and that of normal omniscience is that "the one renders thoughts, perceptions, and feelings as they occur consecutively and in detail passing through the mind (scene), while the other summarizes and explains them after they have occurred (narrative)." Example: *To the Lighthouse* (Virginia Woolf).
6. *Selective Omniscience.* Instead of being presented directly through the minds of the characters, the story is here conveyed through "the

mind of only one of the characters. Instead, therefore, of being allowed a composite of viewing angles, [the reader] is at the fixed center." Example: *A Portrait of the Artist as a Young Man* (Joyce).

7. *The Dramatic Mode.* Here the author "dispose[s] of mental states altogether." What is here conveyed to the reader is "limited largely to what the characters do and say; their appearance and the setting may be supplied by the author as in stage directions." There is never, however, "any direct indication of what they perceive . . . , what they think, or how they feel." Here the reader "apparently listens to no one but the characters themselves, who move as it were upon a stage; his angle of view is that of the fixed front (third row center), and the distance must always be near (since the presentation is wholly scenic)." Examples: *Hills Like White Elephants* (Hemingway); *The Awkward Age* (Henry James).

8. *The Camera.* This type of point of view Mr. Friedman regards as "the ultimate in authorial exclusion." Here the aim is "to transmit, without apparent selection or arrangement, a 'slice of life' as it passes before the recording medium." An illustration of this mode is provided by the opening section of Christopher Isherwood's novel *Goodbye to Berlin:* "I am a camera with its shutter open, quite passive, recording, not thinking. Recording the man shaving at the window opposite and the woman in the kimono washing her hair. Someday, all this will have to be developed, carefully printed, fixed."

Besides Mr. Friedman's exhaustive classification of points of view, mention should here also be made of a few other classifications which, though they do not enter into the same elaborate detail, may be useful to the critic of the novel.

In his enlightening *Studies in the Narrative Technique of the First-Person Novel*,[50] to which I am much indebted, Bertil Romberg has actually taken Friedman's survey as a starting-point for his own classification of points of view. However, as he regards the first-person novel as "the form in which the author objectifies himself completely in the fiction, by means of the narrator," he has placed it at the very end of his scale, which is as follows: (1) the author is "omniscient, visible and omnipresent"; (2) the author "as a rule renounces his Olympian view and omniscience, and confines himself to the mind(s) of one or more of the characters"; (3) the author "registers and records as a behaviourist observer, a film camera with (apparently) entirely objective reproduction and with no insight into that which is not perceptible to the senses"; (4) the first-person novel.[51]

STEINBERG: *Sources of the Stream*

Wassily Kandinsky has written:

Inner necessity originates from three elements: (1) Every artist, as a creator, has something in him which demands expression (this is the element of personality). (2) Every artist, as a child of his time, is impelled to express the spirit of his age (this is the element of style)—dictated by the period and particular country to which the artist belongs (it is doubtful how long the latter distinction will continue). (3) Every artist, as a servant of art, has to help the cause of art (this is the quintessence of art, which is constant in all ages and among all nationalities).[1]

Let us first quickly acknowledge Joyce's contribution as both a servant and a help to art. By developing the stream-of-consciousness technique so completely and so imaginatively, he made available to the novelists who followed him a very sensitive and very useful method of delineating character and simulating consciousness.

Looking back at that development after the passing of half a century, however, one is tempted to ask questions arising from Kandinsky's first two points. Why Joyce? And why at that particular time? Since the second question is easier to deal with than the first, let us begin with that one.

Perhaps a good place to start would be with Arthur Symons's *The Symbolist Movement in Literature,* which appeared in 1899. According to Mary Colum, it was widely read among university students in Dublin. It is not clear when Joyce read the book. Richard Ellmann suggests 1900. Tindall says flatly 1902, when Yeats introduced Joyce to Symons. (We can be reasonably sure that Joyce did read the book because Mary Colum reports that "he had picked up some of his knowledge of the French symbolists, particularly Mallarmé" from Symons.)[2]

Whether he actually read the book, however, and, if so, when, is not important. I am not trying to prove Joyce derivative. Rather I am trying to show that an important part of his talent was the ability to translate some of the intellectual and aesthetic ideas of his day into imaginative fictional techniques. If he had not met the ideas in Symons's book, he would have heard them from his fellow students in Dublin; and if not in Dublin, then later in Paris. Symons shows us what some of those ideas were.

In his introductory chapter to *The Symbolist Movement,* Symons says, "In speaking to us so intimately, so solemnly, as only religion had hitherto spoken to us, [literature] becomes itself a kind of religion, with all the duties and responsibilities of the sacred ritual." He repeats the prayer of Gérard de Nerval "that I might have the power to create my own universe about me, to govern my dreams instead of enduring them." And he quotes Mallarmé's dictum that "the pure work implies the elocutionary disappearance of the poet."[3] (In the full French text Joyce might also have found "encore la faut-il, pour omettre l'auteur.")[4]

Those ideas, of course, were available elsewhere. In 1857 Gustave Flaubert had written, "An artist must be in his work like God in creation, invisible and all-powerful: he should be everywhere felt, but nowhere seen."[5] And in the preface to *The Picture of Dorian Gray,* published in 1891, Oscar Wilde had written, "The artist is the creator of beautiful things. To reveal art and conceal the artist is art's aim."[6]

It is not surprising, therefore, that in *A Portrait* Joyce should have characterized the girl in the stream who inspired Stephen "To live, to err, to fall, to triumph, to recreate life out of life!" as a "wild angel . . . , the angel of mortal youth and beauty," or that the image he used to describe Stephen's entry into a new way of life should be throwing open "the gates." Thus Joyce is not propounding a new aesthetic principle when he has Stephen tell Lynch, "The artist, like the God of the creation, remains within or behind or beyond or above his handiwork, invisible, refined out of existence, indifferent, paring his fingernails," or when he has Stephen think of himself as "a priest of the eternal imagination, transmuting the daily bread of experience into the radiant body of everlasting life."[7]

What is unusual is the emotional energy with which Joyce manages to infuse the individual images and the extended metaphor by reserving them for the climax of the novel, by clustering them in highly emotional passages, and finally by establishing the explicit parallelism of the two priesthoods. And for the purposes of this study what is even more important, what is also unusual, is the degree that he was able to implement his definition of the artist, the degree to which he was able to refine himself out of existence in the first half of *Ulysses,* to make himself as author invisible by the use of the stream-of-consciousness technique.

There also runs through Symons's *Symbolist Movement in Literature* the awareness that writers were striving for a greater subjectivity, a more explicit reflection of consciousness, that they were attempting to present to their readers their characters' very souls:

Here, then, in this revolt against exteriority, against rhetoric, against a materialistic tradition; in this endeavour to disengage the ultimate essence, the soul, of whatever exists and can be realized by the consciousness; in this dutiful waiting upon every symbol by which the soul of things can be made visible; literature, bowed down by so many burdens, may at last attain liberty, and its authentic speech.

. . . .

"Sincerity and the impression of the moment followed to the letter": that is how [Verlaine] defined his theory of style, in an article written about himself.

. . . .

That the novel should be psychological was a discovery as early as Benjamin Constant, whose *Adolphe* anticipates *Le Rouge et le noir,* that rare, revealing, yet somewhat arid masterpiece of Stendahl. But that psychology could be carried so far into the darkness of the soul, that the flaming walls of the world themselves faded to a glimmer, was a discovery which has been made by no novelist before Huysmans wrote *En route.*

. . . .

Huysmans has found words for even the most subtle and illusive aspects of that inner life which he has come, at last, to apprehend.[8]

Again, it is only a short step to Joyce's attempt to record "what a man says, sees, thinks, and what such seeing, thinking, saying does, to what you Freudians call the subconscious," to Virginia Woolf's expression of interest in "the dark places of psychology," and to her charge to the novelist: "Let us record the atoms as they fall upon the mind in the order in which they fall, let us trace the pattern, however disconnected and incoherent in appearance, which each sight or incident scores upon the consciousness."[9] But again it is the degree to which Joyce was able to recognize the fruitfulness of the approach and to fulfill it that distinguishes him from other novelists.

Joyce may well have encountered the same interest in the impressions of the moment and their impact on consciousness among writers and painters when he was in Paris in 1902 and 1903. Herschel B. Chipp says:

The artists participating in the subjectivist movement of about 1885–1900 may be grouped together only because they all rejected the realist conceptions or art that had prevailed for the preceding generation. . . . The movement was first heralded for the poets in the Symbolist Manifesto (1886) by Jean Moréas (1856–1910). . . . The Symbolist poets, grouped about Stéphane Mallarmé (1842–98), developed theories of art which were to provide an ideological background for the thoughts of many of the artists. . . . Baudelaire's *Culte de moi* was revived; his concern with individuality of expression was transformed into an obsessive concern with the intimate, private world of the self that led to a rejection of the exterior world. . . .

The Symbolist poet Gustave Kahn . . . wrote in *L'Événement*, 1886, that "the essential aim of our art is to objectify the subjective (the externalization of the Idea) instead of subjectifying the objective (nature seen through the ideas of a temperament). Thus we carry the analysis of the Self to the extreme. . . ."

The artists of this movement also wrote essays on their art, sometimes with great perception. . . . Most of them were prolific letter-writers, and they poured out their artistic struggles in the form of lengthy correspondence with their friends.[10]

Joyce should have encountered such discussions in Paris in the cafés, in at least one of which he "argued about literature in French, and when . . . knowledge of that language failed, in Latin," or in later years in Trieste, Paris again, and Zurich.[11] He probably also encountered them in the newspapers and magazines.

The impressionists were interested in sensations well before the symbolist manifesto. A critic wrote in 1875, "Manet paints as he sees, he reproduces the sensation his eye communicates to him."[12] As early as the 1880s, French artists were reading, debating, and trying to put into practice David Sutter's essays on phenomena of vision and the "scientific aesthetics" of Charles Henry, Ogdon N. Rood, and Michel E. Chevreul. The results were evident not only in their impressionistic paintings, but in what they wrote and said. Paul Gauguin, for example, wrote to a friend in 1885: "For a long time the philosophers have considered the phenomena which seem to us supernatural and yet of which we have the *sensation*. Everything is in that word. . . . All our five senses arrive directly *at the brain*, conditioned by an infinity of things which no education can destroy."[13] And Louis Le Bail learned from Pissarro: "Don't work bit by bit but paint everything at once by placing tones everywhere, with brushstrokes of the right color and value, while noticing what is alongside. Use small brushstrokes and try to put down your perceptions immediately. . . . Do not define too closely the outline of things: it is the brushstroke of the right value and color which should produce the drawing."[14] So much did the impressionists' paintings rely for their effect on the individual dab or dot of (often pure) color that they developed theories of retinal fusion and argued over the proper distance from which to view particular canvases.[15]

As late as 1912 Albert Gleizes and Jean Metzinger were writing, "To establish pictoral space, it is necessary to resort to tactile and motor sensations and to all our faculties," and "There is nothing real outside of us, there is nothing real but the coincidence of a sensation and an individual mental tendency. Far be it from us to throw doubt upon the existence of the objects which impinge upon our senses; but it is reasonable that we can only be certain of the image which they produce in our mind."[16]

The intimate world of the self; objectifying the subjective; visual, tactile, and motor sensations; the impact of minute impressions on the eye and mind; building a form from myriad brushstrokes instead of starting with the outline of things—all aspects of the stream-of-consciousness technique as Joyce developed it and as Virginia Woolf described it. Joseph Prescott reminds us that there are intimations of this interest even in *Stephen Hero,* where "we hear that 'Cranly grew used to having sensations and impressions recorded and analysed before him [by Stephen] at the very instant of their apparition.' The introspective habit, illustrated several times in the *Portrait,* is an appropriate base from which Joyce is later to find congenial the internal monologue in Dujardin's *Les Lauriers sont coupés* and the probings of modern psychologists."[17]

The artist himself, it was argued further, must be conscious of sensations and impressions in order that his personality may permeate the work of art. As we have seen, while Joyce was writing *A Portrait,* Gleizes and Metzinger wrote: "To establish pictoral space, it is necessary to resort to tactile and motor sensations and to all our faculties." The rest of the paragraph reads: "It is our entire personality which, contracting or expanding, transforms the plane of the painting. As, reacting, the plane reflects the painter's personality on the understanding of the viewer, pictoral space defines itself: a sensitive pathway between two subjective persons."[18]

In *A Portrait* Joyce wrote:

The simplest epical form is seen emerging out of lyrical literature when the artist prolongs and broods upon himself as the centre of an epical event and this form progresses till the centre of emotional gravity is equidistant from the artist himself and from others. The narrative is no longer purely personal. The personality of the artist passes into the narration itself, flowing round and round the persons and the action like a vital sea.[19]

The cubist's personality "transforms" the painting, whereas the personality of Joyce's artist "passes into the narration." Just as the painter's personality and the viewer's understanding are joined by "a sensitive pathway between two subjective persons," so, for Joyce's artist, "the centre of emotional gravity is equidistant from ... himself and from others."

Through those same years writers and painters also sought to develop new styles—styles appropriate to their subjects as well as personal styles. They wrote and spoke about it frequently. In 1852 Flaubert declared: "What seems beautiful to me, what I should like to write, is a book about nothing, a book dependent on nothing external, which would be held together by the strength of its style, just as the earth, suspended in the void, depends on nothing external for its support; a book which would have almost no subject, or at least in which the subject would be almost invisible, if such a thing is possible."[20] In 1882 Gauguin wrote, "I have sacrificed everything this year, execution, color, for the benefit of style, forcing upon myself something different from what I know how to do. This is, I believe, a transformation which hasn't yet borne its fruits, but which will bear them."[21] In 1910 the futurists, in their technical manifesto, referred to "this truism, unimpeachable and absolute fifty years ago": "that the subject is nothing and that everything lies in the manner of treating it. That is agreed; we, too, admit that."[22] If one thinks of the artists and their paintings, one can trace in his mind's eye the individual struggles for style and how different were the individual styles that the painters developed—Monet, Manet, Dégas, Renoir, Seurat, Van Gogh, Cézanne, Picasso. In Joyce one sees the same sort of struggle to develop a style as, under the early influence of Ibsen, he proceeds from the relative realism of *Dubliners* and *Stephen Hero* through the more subjective and impressionistic *A Portrait of the Artist as a Young Man* to the thoroughly subjective and impressionistic stream-of-consciousness technique in *Ulysses*. Indeed, Joyce told his brother, "Don't talk to me about politics. I am only interested in style."[23] In some ways Joyce's career is reminiscent of that of the French painter Manet a generation earlier, who began as a realist and developed into the father of impressionism.[24]

The symbolists and the impressionists maintained a balance, however between subjectivism and realism. As we can see today, there is nothing "unreal" about the paintings of the impressionists. Symons quoted Huysmans to that effect, for Joyce to read:

In *Là-bas* (1891) . . . he had, indeed realized . . . that "it is essential to preserve the veracity of the document, the precision of detail, the fibrous nervous language of Realism, but it is equally essential to become the well-digger of the soul, and not to attempt to explain what is mysterious by mental maladies. . . . It is essential, in a word, to follow the great road so deeply dug out by Zola, but it is necessary also to trace a parallel pathway in the air, and to grapple with the within and the after, to create, in a word, a spiritual Naturalism."[25]

And as late as the 1920s Monet was saying: "I am simply expending my efforts upon a maximum of appearances in close relation with unknown realities. When one is on the plane of concordant appearances one can not be far from reality, or at least from what we know of it."[26]

Denis Rouart says of the *Water Lilies* that Monet was painting about the time Joyce was finishing *Ulysses,* "Such is the distinctive feature of the last *Water Lilies,* which, while unquestionable representational paintings, yet attain a musicality of form and color sufficient to justify them independently of the subject. This fusion of realism and lyricism was the greatest achievement of Monet's old age, and the fulfillment of his Impressionism."[27] And Kenneth Clark says of the paintings: "This poem takes its point of departure from experience, but the stream of sensation becomes a stream of consciousness. And how does this consciousness become paint? That is the miracle. By a knowledge of each effect so complete that it becomes instinctive, and every movement of the brush is not only a record but also a self-revealing gesture."[28] Except for the references to old age and painting, these remarks would apply as well to Joyce's *Ulysses* as to Monet's *Water Lilies.*

This insistence on realism helps us to see that Joyce's concept of the epiphany was part of the same aesthetic that produced the stream-of-consciousness technique. In *Stephen Hero* Joyce wrote:

Stephen as he passed on his quest heard the following fragment of colloquy out of which he received an impression keen enough to afflict his sensitiveness very severely.
    The Young Lady—(drawling discreetly) . . . O, yes . . . I was . . . at the cha . . . pel . . .

The Young Gentleman—(inaudibly) ... I ... (again inaudibly) ... I ...
The Young Lady—(softly) ... O ... but you're ... ve ... ry ... wick ...
ed. ...

This triviality made him think of collecting many such moments together
in a book of epiphanies. By an epiphany he meant a sudden spiritual
manifestation, whether in the vulgarity of speech or of a gesture or in a
memorable phrase of the mind itself. He believed that it was for the man
of letters to record these epiphanies with extreme care, seeing that they
themselves are the most delicate and evanescent of moments.[29]

Joyce himself wrote a series of such epiphanies.[30] A. Walton Litz says,
"Many of the early *Epiphanies,* written in Paris during the winter and
spring of 1902–03, eventually found their place in the texts of *Stephen
Hero,* the *Portrait,* and *Ulysses,*" and he demonstrates the process.[31]

The impressionists also saw their work as recording "delicate and
evanescent moments." Here are two descriptions by Monet of his attempt
to record a particular series of epiphanies, the first statement from 1890
and the second from 1926:

I am working terribly hard, struggling with a series of different effects
(haystacks), but ... the sun sets so fast that I cannot follow it. ... I am
beginning to work so slowly that I am desperate, but the more I continue,
the more I see that a great deal of work is necessary in order to succeed
in rendering that which I seek: "Instantaneity," especially the "enveloppe,"
the same light spreading everywhere, and more than ever I am dissatisfied
with the easy things that come in one stroke.[32]

· ·

At that time I was painting some haystacks forming a fine group not very
far away. One day I noticed that my light had changed, so I said to my
daughter-in-law, please go to the house and bring another canvas. She
brought it, but in a few minutes it had changed again, then another, and
another was begun! And I painted on each one only when the light was
right. It's quite easy to understand.[33]

Guy de Maupassant also recorded the process:

Last year ... I often followed Claude Monet in his search of impressions.
He was no longer a painter, in truth, but a hunter. He proceeded, followed
by children who carried his canvases, five or six canvases representing the
same subject at different times of day and with different effects.

He took them up and put them aside in turn, following the changes in
the sky. And the painter, before his subject, lay in wait for the sun and

shadows, capturing in a few brushstrokes the ray that fell or the cloud that passed. . . .

I have seen him thus seize a glittering shower of light on the white cliff and fix it in a flood of yellow tones that, strangely, rendered the surprising and fugitive effect of the unseizable and dazzling brilliance. On another occasion he took a downpour beating on the sea in his hands and dashed it on the canvas—and indeed it was the rain he had thus painted.[34]

Joyce and Monet each attempted to record "the most delicate and evanescent of moments" as it flashes across the mind, to capture the "unseizable" in a few impressionistic strokes. Once again we are reminded of Virginia Woolf's statement:

Life is not a series of gig lamps symmetrically arranged; but a luminous halo, a semi-transparent envelope surrounding us from the beginning of consciousness to the end. Is it not the task of the novelist to convey this varying, this unknown and uncircumscribed spirit, whatever aberration or complexity it may display, with as little mixture of the alien and external as possible?[35]

At least one writer, a member of the naturist movement, which opposed symbolist "decadence," had also enunciated the concept of the epiphany before Joyce did (although he did not use the term). At the Naturist Congress in Brussels (1896) a young disciple of Saint-Georges de Bouhélier declared: "A man appears on the scene—he is a mason, or a warrior, or a fisherman. The aim is to take him by surprise in a moment of eternity; the sublime instant when he leans forward to polish a cuirass or cast his net into the water. We know that his attitude at such a moment is in harmony with God."[36] Once again, however, who first enunciated the principle is less important than what Joyce did with it.

As Goldberg indicates, Joyce made the epiphany an important aspect of the stream-of-consciousness technique. After analyzing a passage of Bloom's stream of consciousness from Hades, Goldberg finds:

Clearly this is far from the random, unorganized chaos it was once thought to be. It is certainly no mere record of a stream of passively registered "impressions" or "associations." . . . It is quite deliberately and artistically shaped and rendered. And the basis of organization is clearly the unit of the paragraph, and the paragraph in turn the expression of a separate mental act of apprehension. In short, the real artistic (and dramatic) unit of Joyce's "stream of consciousness" writing is the epiphany. What he renders dramatically are minds engaged in the apprehension of epiphanies—the elements of meaning in apprehended life.[37]

A glance at the passage Goldberg analyzes or at almost any paragraph in "Proteus" or "Lestrygonians" longer than three or four lines is enough to sustain this claim.

Monet's use of the word "instantaneity" also brings us to another problem faced by the stream-of-consciousness writer: that a moment of time is multidimensional, whereas language, in which the writer seeks to present that moment of time, is linear. It was not a new problem, of course. As Gleizes and Metzinger pointed out in 1913, Leonardo da Vinci alluded to "simultaneity" (as many of the painters referred to it) in the fifteenth century:

We know well that the sight, by rapid observations, discovers in one point an infinity of forms; nevertheless it comprehends only one thing at a time. Suppose, reader, that you were to see the whole of this written page at one glance, and were immediately to judge that it is full of different letters; you do not at the same moment know what letters they are, nor what they would say. You must go from one word to another and from line to line if you wish to attain a knowledge of these letters, as you must climb step by step to reach the top of a building, or you will never reach the top.[38]

Writers in the nineteenth century had begun experiments to overcome—or at least to alleviate—the linearity of language. In the famous episode at the fair in *Madame Bovary*, Flaubert alternated back and forth between the lovers and the ceremonies at the fair to approximate simultaneity. Dujardin's use of the internal monologue in *Les Lauriers sont coupés*, in its attempt to simulate what happened in a man's consciousness, could be considered another attempt to come to grips with the problem, as could some of Mallarmé's experiments with typography.[39]

There was also talk before World War I of cubist poetry, which attempted the simultaneity of cubist paintings. Thus Apollinaire's "Lundi rue Christine," written in 1913, "is made up of simultaneous snatches of conversation, overheard, or invented, by the poet in the little Left Bank bar."[40] The ideograms of Apollinaire were also an attempt to adapt cubist techniques to poetry to achieve an effect of simultaneity. Here, for example, is his "Miroir."[41]

<pre>
              DANS
        FLETS   CE
          RE   MI
         LES   ROIR
        SONT   JE
         ME   SUIS
        COM   EN
        NON   Guillaume   CLOS
         ET   Apollinaire   VI
        GES   VANT
         AN   ET
        LES   VRAI
         NE   COM
         GI   ME
        MA   ON
              I
</pre>

Ezra Pound's definition of an image in 1913, with its emphasis on instantaneity, also indicated a concern with the same phenomenon:

An "Image" is that which presents an intellectual and emotional complex in an instant of time. I use the term "complex" rather in the technical sense employed by the newer psychologists, such as Hart, though we might not agree absolutely in our application.

It is the presentation of such a "complex" instantaneously which gives that sense of sudden liberation; that sense of freedom from time limits and space limits; that sense of sudden growth, which we experience in the presence of the greatest works of art.[42]

Through most of the nineteenth century, painters, with their two-dimensional canvases and their ability to simulate a third dimension, did not think that their medium was faced with a problem of simultaneity. Indeed, in 1888 Paul Gauguin wrote of the obvious advantages of multi-dimensional painting over a linear medium like music:

Painting is the most beautiful of all the arts. . . . Like music, it acts on the soul through the intermediary of the senses: harmonious colors correspond to the harmonies of sound. But in painting a unity is obtained which is not possible in music, where the accords follow one another, so that the judgment experiences a continuous fatigue if it wants to reunite the end with the beginning. The ear is actually a sense inferior to the eye. The hearing can only grasp a single sound at a time, whereas the sight takes in everything and simultaneously simplifies it at will.[43]

Seurat's satisfaction with the process of retinal fusion, in which the retina supposedly synthesized the individual dabs or dots of paint which artists applied to their canvases, was another example of how successfully painters felt simultaneity worked for them.

Joyce refers to the problem explicitly in *A Portrait:* "An aesthetic image is presented to us either in space or in time. What is audible is presented in time, what is visible is presented in space."[44] He considers it again in *Ulysses* at the beginning of "Proteus":

Stephen closed his eyes to hear his boots crush crackling wrack and shells. You are walking through it howsomever. I am, a stride at a time. A very short space of time through very short times of space. Five, six, the *nacheinander.* Exactly: and that is the ineluctable modality of the audible. Open your eyes. No. Jesus! If I fell over a cliff that beetles o'er his base, fell through the *nebeneinander* ineluctably. I am getting on nicely in the dark. My ash sword hangs at my side. Tap with it: they do. My two feet in his boots are at the end of his legs, *nebeneinander.* (38:11/37:11)

Thus artists and other writers had worked with the problem of simultaneity before Joyce faced it in attempting to present "what a man says, sees, thinks, and what such seeing, thinking, and saying does, to . . . the subconscious." Once again, however, the measure of Joyce as an artist is not in the initial statement of the problem, but in his responding to a challenge which his predecessors had barely begun to meet, recognizing the promise of what Dujardin and others had started, and developing techniques to simulate multidimensional reality.

It is interesting to note how many of the ideas at the beginning of "Proteus" which Stephen attributes to Aristotle (*maestro di color che sanno*—38:8/37:8) and for which, indeed, there are references in Aristotle were also matters of current concern for the writers and artists at the end of the nineteenth century and the beginning of the twentieth. Take just the opening four lines of the chapter: "Ineluctable modality of the visible: at least that if no more, thought through my eyes. Signatures of all things I am here to read, seaspawn and seawrack, the nearing tide, that rusty boot. Snotgreen, blue-silver, rust: coloured signs." Now here are a series of quotations from and about writers and painters of the period:

> That central secret of the mystics, from Pythagoras onwards, the secret which the Smaragdine Tablet of Hermes betrays in its "As things are below, so are they above"; which Boehme has classed in his teaching of "signatures." (Symons, 1899)[45]

> To discern a form implies, besides the visual function and the faculty of movement, a certain development of the imagination. (Gleizes and Metzinger, 1912)[46]

> Let the forms which [the artist] discerns and the symbols in which he incorporates their qualities be sufficiently remote from the imagination of the vulgar to prevent the truth which they convey from assuming a general character. (Gleizes and Metzinger, 1912)[47]

> The picture will exist ineluctably. [Le tableau existera inéluctablement.] (Apollinaire, 1913)[48]

> [Braque] has taught the aesthetic use of forms so hidden that only certain poets had intimations of them. These luminous signs flare around us, but only a handful of painters have grasped their plastic significance. (Apollinaire, 1913)[49]

> Red, the most powerful of all colors, is the symbol of height, force, and authority; lilac or violet of the solar spectrum, the symbol of coquetry, instability, and weakness. Orange is the image of pride and vanity; blue, that of modesty and candor, etc. (David Sutter, 1880)[50]

> Since plastic form is the basis of all enduring art, and since the creation of intense form is impossible without color, I first determined, by years of color experimentation, the relative spatial relation of the entire color gamut. (Stanton MacDonald Wright, 1916)[51]

Forms and objects as signs and signatures, the ineluctability of visible forms, the signification of colors, the relation between color and form—it is all there. Joyce may have turned to Aristotle for solutions to aesthetic problems, but the problems themselves, and possible solutions to them, had been matters of intense interest to writers and painters for some years before he became a writer and continued to be while he was writing *Ulysses.* Stephen's experiment at the beginning of "Proteus" and Joyce's development of the stream-of-consciousness technique reflected clearly the aesthetic interests of the times.

Also relevant to this discussion is the interest among novelists of the second half of the nineteenth century in point of view. The obviously intrusive author who spoke directly to the reader was rejected, and many writers insisted on the importance of telling their story from the point of view of one of the characters involved, even to the point of having one of the characters tell the story. I need only mention here the novels of Joseph Conrad and Henry James as the most obvious examples. Percy Lubbock in *The Craft of Fiction,* Melvin J. Friedman in *Stream of Consciousness: A Study in Literary Method,* Leon Edel in *The Psychological Novel, 1900-1950,* and Wayne Booth in *The Rhetoric of Fiction* have all told this story and discussed its meaning too well for me to repeat it here.[52] The painters, of course, from the early impressionists to the late cubists (that is, from Joyce's birth to the completion of *Ulysses*) also wrote and talked about point of view and undertook endless experiments in point of view on their canvases. Once again, Joyce's development of the stream-of-consciousness technique, a technique for viewing the world through the eyes and mind of a particular character, was a culminating and fulfilling step in a long trend.

We should also note movements parallel to those in aesthetics among the sciences, philosophy, psychology, music, and the popular arts. Indeed, many claim that new discoveries in science around the turn of the century gave new direction and new thrust to the aesthetics of the day. As a result of the discoveries of men like Thompson, Planck, and Rutherford,

The generation that grew to manhood about 1900 realized that the ground which their forebears had confidently trod was now giving way beneath their own feet; reality was everywhere breaking up into elusive, impalpable fragments. Disbelief in the solidity of the world—formerly the subject of paradoxical discussions on the part of philosophers, or of wild conjectures by more or less unbalanced individuals—became an actual issue, an urgent, crucial, and compelling problem. The intellectual conceptions which for centuries had been man's stay and support in hours of doubt and trial, now suddenly collapsed, encumbering the path of progress with their debris.[53]

Wassily Kandinsky remembered that when Rutherford and Soddy reported the radioactive disintegration of the atom in 1903 there was a "terrific impact, comparable to the end of the world. . . . All things became flimsy, with no strength or certainty. I would hardly have been surprised if the stones had risen in the air and disappeared. To me, science had been destroyed. In its place—a mere delusion, guesswork."[54]

George Bernard Shaw has one of his characters in *Too True to Be Good* (1932) make much the same statement:

Yes, sir: the universe of Isaac Newton, which has been an impregnable citadel of modern civilization for three hundred years, has crumbled like the walls of Jericho before the criticism of Einstein. Newton's universe was the stronghold of rational Determinism: the stars in their orbits obeyed immutably fixed laws; and when we turned from surveying their vastness to study the infinite littleness of the atoms, there too we found the electrons in their orbits obeying the same universal laws. Every moment of time dictated and determined the following moment, and was itself dictated and determined by the moment that came before it. Everything was calculable: everything happened because it must: the commandments were erased from the tables of the law; and in their place came the cosmic algebra: the equations of the mathematicians. Here was my faith: here I found my dogma of infallibility: I, who scorned alike the Catholic with his vain dream of responsible Free Will, and the Protestant with his pretence of private judgment. And now—now—what is left of it? The orbit of the electron obeys no law: it chooses one path and rejects another: it is as capricious as the planet Mercury, who wanders from his road to warm his hands at the sun. All is caprice: the calculable world has become incalculable: Purpose and Design, the pretexts for all the vilest superstitions, have risen from the dead to cast down the mighty from their seats and put paper crowns on presumptuous fools.[55]

Armand Siegel explains the impact this way:

The impact of the success of science, or what amounts to the same thing for purposes of this discussion, its *intensity* as a functioning social institution, may also help to resolve the following paradox: That art seemed less alienated by the mechanistic, literal theories of earlier eras of science than it is by the seemingly more cautious operational theories of the current era. Although a man was represented as a sort of elaborate clockwork by the science of the nineteenth century, this was not so disturbing, in view of the extent to which this earlier science fell short of precisely implementing this picture, as the modern description, which is in less literal terms but is far more advanced in its empirical progress.[56]

At the very time, then, that aesthetics had become interested in exploring below the surface of reality, in questioning traditional materialism, science exploded that reality and that materialism and to the short strokes, dabs, and dots of the impressionists added invisible particles and waves. Once again reality proved to be not palpable and solid in outline but hidden, evanescent, mysterious—like the fleeting, darting, suggestive sensations, images, and perceptions in the flow of consciousness.

There were similar tendencies in philosophy and psychology. Bergson's ideas, as we know from Wyndham Lewis's *Time and Western Man* and from Shiv K. Kumar's *Bergson and the Stream of Consciousness Novel*, were important in developing many of the concepts behind the stream-of-consciousness technique.[57] The philosopher-psychologist William James devoted an important section of his major work, *The Principles of Psychology* (1890), to the stream of consciousness. An important tool for the German psychologists for the ten years before and ten years after the turn of the century was introspection. Before World War I, T. E. Hulme was telling artists to place themselves "inside the object instead of surveying it from outside."[58] Joyce may not have read about or discussed the works or specific ideas of any of these men, but they were very much part of the intellectual world in which he lived.

Joyce did know something, however, about C. G. Jung and Sigmund Freud, whose explorations into depth psychology made an important impact on the intellectual life of Europe after the turn of the century. Jung published a study on word association in 1913, and Freud's entire theory was based on free association. In 1920 Freud published (anonymously) *A Note on the Prehistory of the Technique of Analysis* in which he noted recommendations to writers on the use of free association by Schiller (1788), by J. J. Garth Wilkinson (1857), who was a physician, a poet, and a Swedenborgian mystic, and by Ludwig Börne, whom Freud had read as a boy.[59] "The Art of Becoming an Original Writer in Three Days," an essay written by Börne in 1823 and published in the first volume of the 1962 edition of his collected works, ends:

And here follows the practical application that was promised. Take a few sheets of paper and for three days on end write down, without fabrication or hypocrisy, everything that comes into your head. Write down what you think of yourself, of your wife, of the Turkish war, of Goethe, of Fonk's trial, of the Last Judgment, of your superiors—and when three days have passed you will be quite out of your senses with astonishment at the new and unheard-of thoughts you have had. This is the art of becoming an original writer in three days.[60]

Again, whether or not Joyce read any of the documents of the psycho-analytic movement, with its interest in free association, dream symbols, and other processes of the mind, it was part of the world which made the stream-of-consciousness technique possible.

Music also contributed to the stream-of-consciousness technique, particularly the Wagnerian concept of the leitmotif: "*In Ulysses* . . . Joyce constructs, as Wagner had done in the *Ring,* a major, an all-inclusive work resting upon carefully placed leitmotifs as upon steel reinforcements. There are more than 150 motifs in the book, and of its 786 pages," says William Blisset, "I have found fewer than fifty without the sounding of at least one."[61] Blisset's analysis of the impact of Wagner on the symbolists and on Joyce's works is particularly thorough. Clive Bell, just before the publication of *Ulysses,* also saw the reflections of jazz in that novel:

In literature Jazz manifests itself both formally and in content. Formally its distinctive characteristic is the familiar one—syncopation. It has given us a ragtime literature which flouts traditional rhythms and sequences and grammar and logic. . . . In prose I think Mr. Joyce will serve as a perhaps not very good example. . . . In his later publications Mr. Joyce does deliberately go to work to break up the traditional sentence, throwing overboard sequence, syntax, and, indeed most of those conventions which men habitually employ for the exchange of precise ideas. Effectually and with a will he rags the literary instrument.[62]

There were also reverberations between jazz and the films—and Sergei Eisenstein's discussion of the relationship between film and jazz techniques contains phrases and concepts we have encountered elsewhere: "repetition of identical elements . . . the intensity of contrast"; "several perspectives, simultaneously employed"; "A man enters his environment— the environment is seen through his eyes"; "intricate synthesis."[63] Joyce, of course, was interested in the film, at least commercially, and may have been influenced by techniques in the newly developing popular art.[64] Eisenstein made his first film in 1920, while Joyce was writing *Ulysses.*

The concept of montage as it developed in the films is reminiscent of both Joyce's use of the epiphany and Pound's definition of the image. In Eisenstein's *The Film Sense* appear such statements as:

Two film pieces of any kind, placed together, inevitably combine into a new concept, a new quality, arising out of that juxtaposition.

The juxtaposition of two separate shots by splicing them together resembles not so much a simple sum of one shot plus another shot—as
it does a *creation.*

. . . .

A work of art, understood dynamically, is just this process of arranging
images in the feelings and mind of the spectator. It is this that constitutes the peculiarity of a truly vital work of art and distinguishes it
from a lifeless one.

. . . .

Before the inner vision, before the perception of the creator, hovers a
given image, emotionally embodying his theme. The task that confronts
him is to transform this image into a few basic *partial representations*
which, in their combination and juxtaposition, shall evoke in the consciousness and feelings of the spectator, reader, or auditor, that same
initial general image which originally hovered before the creative artist.[65]

The last statement sounds much like T. S. Eliot's concept of the objective
correlative, enunciated in 1919: "The only way of expressing emotion in
the form of art is by finding an 'objective correlative'; in other words, a
set of objects, a situation, a chain of events which shall be the formula
of that *particular* emotion; such that when the external facts, which must
terminate in sensory experience, are given, the emotion is immediately
evoked."[66] The similarity of Eisenstein's concept of the image and
Eliot's concept of the objective correlative thus shows the latter also to
be related to Joyce's concept of the epiphany.

Finally, we must come to the other question raised at the beginning
of the chapter: why Joyce? One answer may be, as we shall see in the next
chapter, that it was partly a matter of personality. A simpler answer is
that at least two people very close to Joyce used the interior monologue,
a special form of the stream-of-consciousness technique—one quite consciously as an experiment in writing, the other quite unconsciously, but
regularly in her letters. In the diary of Joyce's younger brother, Stanislaus,
which Joyce read regularly, is a long passage on the working of the mind,
a passage too long to quote here except in part:

The mind "sees," that is is conscious of the image the eye reflects for it,
and says continually within itself: "This is a road, the Malahide Rd. I
know it well now that I see it. There are high broken hedges on both
sides of it, and a few trees. Where the road branches an irregular dwelling-
house with an orchard about it, sidles [?] to an arm and before pointing

the bifurcation, is an old gate entrance. There is a young fellow on the opposite side going in the same direction as I am"; thinking not in sentences as in a book, but thought succeeding thought without utterance like harmonies in music, while conveying a more definite impression to the mind.[67]

Phillip Herring also says, "Those letters of Nora [Joyce's wife] which survive are written in a style so strikingly similar to Molly's interior monologue that she probably surpasses Edouard Dujardin in importance as a stylistic influence on the 'Penelope' episode." He then quotes part of a letter from Nora in support of his contention:

My darling Jim since I left Trieste I am continually thinking about you how are you getting on without me or do you miss me at all. I am dreadfully lonely for you I am quite tired of Ireland already well I arrived in Dublin on Monday night your father charley Eva Florrie were at the Station all looking very well we all went on to Finn's Hotel I stayed two nights.[68]

Why Joyce? And why at that particular time? He had models—from members of his family and in literature already written. And the times conspired to provide him with the philosophy and psychology and aesthetics necessary to develop the stream-of-consciousness technique. But other people had those same models and lived in the same times; so ultimately, as we shall see, the answer must be: because he was Joyce.

JAMES: *Stream of Thought*

We now begin our study of the mind from within. Most books start with sensations, as the simplest mental facts, and proceed synthetically, constructing each higher stage from those below it. But this is abandoning the empirical method of investigation. No one ever had a simple sensation by itself. Consciousness, from our natal day, is of a teeming multiplicity of objects and relations, and what we call simple sensations are results of discriminative attention, pushed often to a very high degree. It is astonishing what havoc is wrought in psychology by admitting at the outset apparently innocent suppositions, that nevertheless contain a flaw. The bad consequences develop themselves later on, and are irremediable, being woven through the whole texture of the work. The notion that sensations, being the simplest things, are the first things to take up in psychology is one of these suppositions. The only thing which psychology has a right to postulate at the outset is the fact of thinking itself, and that must first be taken up and analyzed. If sensations then prove to be amongst the elements of the thinking, we shall be no worse off as respects them than if we had taken them for granted at the start.

The first fact for us, then, as psychologists, is that thinking of some sort goes on. I use the word "thinking," in accordance with what was said on p. 186, for every form of consciousness indiscriminately. If we could say in English "it thinks," as we say "it rains" or "it blows," we should be stating the fact most simply and with the minimum of assumption. As we cannot, we must simply say that thought goes on.

Five Characters in Thought. How does it go on? We notice immediately five important characters in the process, of which it shall be the duty of the present chapter to treat in a general way:

1. Every thought tends to be part of a personal consciousness.
2. Within each personal consciousness thought is always changing.
3. Within each personal consciousness thought is sensibly continuous.
4. It always appears to deal with objects independent of itself.
5. It is interested in some parts of these objects to the exclusion of others, and welcomes or rejects—*chooses* from among them, in a word—all the while.

In considering these five points successively, we shall have to plunge *in medias res* as regards our vocabulary, and use psychological terms which can only be adequately defined in later chapters of the book. But every one knows what the terms mean in a rough way; and it is only in a rough way that we are now to take them. This chapter is like a painter's first charcoal sketch upon his canvas, in which no niceties appear.

JAMES: *Stream of Consciousness*

I said a few minutes ago that the most general elements and workings of the mind are all that the teacher absolutely needs to be acquainted with for his purposes.

Now the *immediate* fact which psychology, the science of mind, has to study is also the most general fact. It is the fact that in each of us, when awake (and often when asleep), *some kind of consciousness is always going on.* There is a stream, a succession of states, or waves, or fields (or whatever you please to call them), of knowledge, of feeling, of desire, of deliberation, etc., that constantly pass and repass, and that constitute our inner life. The existence of this stream is the primal fact, the nature and origin of it form the essential problem, of our science. So far as we class the states or fields of consciousness, write down their several natures, analyze their contents into elements, or trace their habits of succession, we are on the descriptive or analytic level. So far as we ask where they come from or why they are just what they are, we are on the explanatory level.

In these talks with you, I shall entirely neglect the questions that come up on the explanatory level. It must be frankly confessed that in no fundamental sense do we know where our successive fields of consciousness come from, or why they have the precise inner constitution which they do have. They certainly follow or accompany our brain states, and of course their special forms are determined by our past experiences and education. But, if we ask just *how* the brain conditions them, we have not the remotest inkling of an answer to give; and, if we ask just how the education moulds the brain, we can speak but in the most abstract, general, and conjectural terms. On the other hand, if we should say that they are due to a spiritual being called our Soul, which reacts on our brain states by these peculiar forms of spiritual energy, our words would be familiar enough, it is true; but I think you will agree that they would offer little genuine explanatory meaning. The truth is that we really *do not know* the answers to the problems on the explanatory level, even though in some directions of inquiry there may be promising speculations to be found. For our present purposes I shall therefore dismiss them entirely, and turn to mere description. This state of things was what I had in mind when, a moment ago, I said there was no "new psychology" worthy of the name.

We have thus fields of consciousness—that is the first general fact; and the second general fact is that the concrete fields are always complex. They contain sensations of our bodies and of the objects around us, memories of past experiences and thoughts of distant things, feelings of satisfaction and dissatisfaction, desires and aversions, and other emotional conditions, together with determinations of the will, in every variety of permutation and combination.

In most of our concrete states of consciousness all these different classes of ingredients are found simultaneously present to some degree, though the relative proportion they bear to one another is very shifting. One state will seem to be composed of hardly anything but sensations, another of hardly anything but memories, etc. But around the sensation, if one considers carefully, there will always be some fringe of thought or will, and around the memory some margin or penumbra of emotion or sensation.

In most of our fields of consciousness there is a core of sensation that is very pronounced. You, for example, now, although you are also thinking and feeling, are getting through your eyes sensations of my face and figure, and through your ears sensations of my voice. The sensations are the *centre* or *focus,* the thoughts and feelings the *margin,* of your actually present conscious field.

On the other hand, some object of thought, some distant image, may have become the focus of your mental attention even while I am speaking—your mind, in short, may have wandered from the lecture; and, in that case, the sensations of my face and voice, although not absolutely vanishing from your conscious field, may have taken up there a very faint and marginal place.

Again, to take another sort of variation, some feeling connected with your own body may have passed from a marginal to a focal place, even while I speak.

The expressions "focal object" and "marginal object," which we owe to Mr. Lloyd Morgan, require, I think, no further explanation. The distinction they embody is a very important one, and they are the first technical terms which I shall ask you to remember.

In the successive mutations of our fields of consciousness, the process by which one dissolves into another is often very gradual, and all sorts of inner rearrangements of contents occur. Sometimes the focus remains but little changed, while the margin alters rapidly. Sometimes the focus alters, and the margin stays. Sometimes focus and margin change places. Sometimes, again, abrupt alterations of the whole field occur. There can seldom be a sharp description. All we know is that, for the most part, each field has a sort of practical unity for its possessor, and that from this practical point of view we can class a field with other fields similar to it, by calling it a state of emotion, of perplexity, of sensation, of abstract thought, of volition, and the like.

Vague and hazy as such an account of our stream of consciousness may be, it is at least secure from positive error and free from admixture of conjecture or hypothesis. An influential school of psychology, seeking to avoid haziness of outline, has tried to make things appear more exact and scientific by making the analysis more sharp. The various fields of consciousness, according to this school, result from a definite number of perfectly definite elementary mental states, mechanically associated into a mosaic or chemically combined. According to some thinkers—Spencer, for example, or Taine—these resolve themselves at last into little elementary psychic particles or atoms of "mind-stuff," out of which all the more immediately known mental states are said to be built up. Locke introduced this theory in a somewhat vague form. Simple "ideas" of sensation and reflection, as he called them, were for him the bricks of which our mental architecture is built up. If I ever have to refer to this theory again, I shall refer to it as the theory of "ideas." But I shall try to steer clear of it altogether. Whether it be true or false, it is at any rate only conjectural; and, for your practical purposes as teachers, the more unpretending conception of the stream of consciousness, with its total waves or fields incessantly changing, will amply suffice.*

*In the light of some of the expectations that are abroad concerning the "new psychology," it is instructive to read the unusually candid confession of its founder Wundt, after his thirty years of laboratory-experience:

"The service which it (the experimental method) can yield consists essentially in perfecting our inner observation, or rather, as I believe, in making this really possible, in any exact sense. Well, has our experimental self-observation, so understood, already accomplished aught of importance? No general answer to this question can be given, because in the unfinished state of our science, there is, even inside of the experimental lines of inquiry, no universally accepted body of psychologic doctrine. . . ."

. . . .

"In such a discord of opinions (comprehensible enough at a time of uncertain and groping development), the individual inquirer can only tell for what views and insights he himself has to thank the newer methods. And if I were asked in what for me the worth of experimental observation in psychology has consisted, and still consists, I should say that it has given me an entirely new idea of the nature and connection of our inner processes. I learned in the achievements of the sense of might to apprehend the fact of creative mental synthesis. . . . From my inquiry into time-relations, etc., . . . I attained an insight into the close union of all those psychic functions usually separated by artificial abstractions and names, such as ideation, feeling, will; and I saw the indivisibility and inner homogeneity, in all its phases, of the mental life. The chronometric study of association-processes finally showed me that the notion of distinct mental "images" [reproducirten Vorstellungen] was one of those numerous self-deceptions which are no sooner stamped in a verbal term than they forthwith thrust non-existent fictions into the place of the reality. I learned to understand an "idea" as a process no less melting and fleeting than an act of feeling or of will, and I comprehended the older doctrine of association of "ideas" to be no longer tenable. . . . Besides all this, experimental observation yielded much other information about the span of consciousness, the rapidity of certain processes, the exact numerical value of certain psycho-physical data, and the like. But I hold all these more special results to be relatively insignificant by-products, and by no means the important thing." (Philosophische Studien, x. 121-24)

The whole passage should be read. As I interpret it, it amounts to a complete espousal of the vaguer conception of the stream of thought, and a complete renunciation of the whole business, still so industriously carried on in text-books, of chopping up "the mind" into distinct units of composition or function, numbering these off, and labelling them by technical names.

FREUD: *Free Association*

If I ask someone to tell me what occurs to him in response to a particular element of a dream, I am asking him to surrender himself to free association *while keeping an idea in mind as a starting-point.* This calls for a special attitude of the attention which is quite different from reflection and which excludes reflection. Some people achieve this attitude with ease; others show an incredibly high degree of clumsiness when they attempt it. There is, however, a higher degree of freedom of association: that is to say, I may drop the insistence on keeping an initial idea in mind and only lay down the sort or kind of association I want—I may, for instance, require the experimenter to allow a proper name or a number to occur to him freely. What then occurs to him would presumably be even more arbitrary and more indeterminable than with our own technique. It can be shown, however, that it is always strictly determined by important internal attitudes of mind which are not known to us at the moment at which they operate—which are as little known to us as the disturbing purposes of parapraxes and the provoking ones of chance actions.

I and many others after me have repeatedly made such experiments with names and numbers thought of at random, and a few of these have been published.[1] Here the procedure is to produce a series of associations to the name which has emerged; these latter associations are accordingly no longer completely free but have a link, like the associations to the elements of dreams. One continues doing this until one finds the impulse exhausted. But by then light will have been thrown both on the motive and the meaning of the random choice of the name. These experiments always lead to the same result; reports on them often cover a wealth of material and call for extensive expositions. The associations to *numbers* chosen at random are perhaps the most convincing; they run off so quickly and proceed with such incredible certainty to a hidden goal that the effect is really staggering. I will give you only one example of an analysis like this of a name, since dealing with it calls for a conveniently small amount of material.

In the course of treating a young man I had occasion to discuss this topic, and mentioned the thesis that, in spite of an apparently arbitrary choice, it is impossible to think of a name at random which does not turn out to be closely determined by the immediate circumstances, the characteristics of the subject of experiment, and his situation at the moment. Since he was sceptical, I suggested that he should make an experiment of the kind himself on the spot. I knew that he carried on particularly numerous relationships of every kind with married women and girls, so I thought he would have a specially large choice open to him if it were to be a woman's name that he was asked to choose. He agreed to this. To my astonishment, or rather, perhaps, to his, no avalanche of women's names broke over me; he remained silent for a moment and then admitted that only a single name had come into his head and none other besides: "Albine."—How curious! But what does that name mean to you? How many "Albines" do you know?—Strange to say, he knew no one called "Albine" and nothing further occurred to him in response to the name. So it might be thought that the analysis had failed. But not at all: it was already complete, and no further associations were needed. The man had an unusually fair complexion and in conversation during the treatment I had often jokingly called him an albino. We were engaged at the time in determining the feminine part of his constitution. So it was he himself who was this "Albine," the woman who was the most interesting to him at the moment.

In the same way tunes that come into one's head without warning turn out to be determined by and to belong to a train of thought which has a right to occupy one's mind though without one's being aware of its activity. It is easy to show then that the relation to the tune is based on its text or its origin. But I must be careful not to extend this assertion to really musical people, of whom, as it happens, I have had no experience. It may be that for such people the musical content of the tune is what decides its emergence. The earlier case is certainly the commoner one. I know of a young man, for instance, who was positively persecuted for a time by the tune (incidentally a charming one) of Paris's song in [Offenbach's] *La belle Hélène*, till his analysis drew his attention to a contemporary competition in his interest between an "Ida" and a "Helen."[2]

If then things that occur to one quite freely are determined in this way and form parts of a connected whole, we shall no doubt be justified in concluding that things that occur to one with a single link—namely their link with the idea which serves as their starting-point—cannot be any less determined. Investigation shows, in fact, that, apart from the link we have given them with the initial idea, they are found to be dependent as well on groups of strongly emotional thoughts and interests, "complexes," whose participation is not known at the moment—that is to say, is unconscious.

The occurrence of ideas with links of this kind has been the subject of very instructive experimental researches, which have played a notable part in the history of psycho-analysis. The school of Wundt has introduced what are known as association-experiments, in which a *stimulus word* is called out to the subject and he has the task of replying to it as quickly as possible with any *reaction* that occurs to him. It is then possible to study the interval that passes between the stimulus and the reaction, the nature of the answer given as a reaction, possible errors when the same experiment is repeated later, and so on. The Zürich school, led by Bleuler and Jung, found the explanation of the reactions that followed in the association-experiment by getting the subjects to throw light on their reactions by means of subsequent associations, if those reactions had shown striking features. It then turned out that these striking reactions were determined in the most definite fashion by the subject's complexes. In this manner Bleuler and Jung built the first bridge from experimental psychology to psycho-analysis.

FREUD: *Note on the Prehistory of Analysis*[1]

A recent book by Havelock Ellis (so justly admired for his researches into sexual science, and an eminent critic of psycho-analysis), which bears the title of *The Philosophy of Conflict* (1919), includes an essay on "Psycho-Analysis in Relation to Sex." The aim of this essay is to show that the writings of the creator of analysis should be judged not as a piece of scientific work but as an artistic production. We cannot but regard this view as a fresh turn taken by resistance and as a repudiation of analysis, even though it is disguised in a friendly, indeed in too flattering a manner. We are inclined to meet it with a most decided contradiction.

It is not, however, with a view to contradicting him on this point that we are now concerned with Havelock Ellis's essay, but for another reason. His wide reading has enabled him to bring forward an author who practised and recommended free association as a technique, though for purposes other than ours, and thus has a claim to be regarded as a forerunner of psycho-analysis.

In 1857, Dr. J. J. Garth Wilkinson, more noted as a Swedenborgian mystic and poet than a physician, published a volume of mystic doggerel verse written by what he considered "a new method," the method of "Impression."

"A theme is chosen or written down," he stated; "as soon as this is done the first impression upon the mind which succeeds the act of writing the title is the beginning of the evolution of that theme, no matter how strange or alien the word or phrase may seem." "The first mental movement, the first word that comes" is "the response to the mind's desire for the unfolding of the subject." It is continued by the same method, and Garth Wilkinson adds: "I have always found it lead by an infallible instinct into the subject." The method was, as Garth Wilkinson viewed it, a kind of exalted *laissez-faire*, a command to the deepest unconscious instincts to express themselves. Reason and will, he pointed out, are left aside; you trust to "an influx," and the faculties of the mind are "directed to ends they know not of." Garth Wilkinson, it must be clearly understood, although he was a physician, used this method for religious and literary, and never for scientific or medical ends; but it is easy to see that essentially it is the method of psycho-analysis applied to oneself, and it is further evidence how much Freud's method is an artist's method.

Those who are familiar with psycho-analytic literature will recall at this point the interesting passage in Schiller's correspondence with Körner[2] in which (1788) the great poet and thinker recommends anyone who desires to be productive to adopt the method of free association. It is to be suspected that what is alleged to be Garth Wilkinson's new technique had already occurred to the minds of many others and that its systematic application in psycho-analysis is not evidence so much of Freud's artistic nature as of his conviction, amounting almost to a prejudice, that all mental events are completely determined. It followed from this view that the first and most likely possibility was that a free association would be related to the subject designated; and this was confirmed by experience in analysis except in so far as too great resistances made the suspected connection unrecognizable.

Meanwhile it is safe to assume that neither Schiller nor Garth Wilkinson had in fact any influence on the choice of psycho-analytic technique. It is from another direction that there are indications of a personal influence at work.

A short time ago in Budapest Dr. Hugo Dubowitz drew Dr. Ferenczi's attention to a short essay covering only four and a half pages, by Ludwig Börne. This was written in 1823 and was reprinted in the first volume of the 1862 edition of his collected works. It is entitled "The Art of Becoming an Original Writer in Three Days" and shows the familiar stylistic features of Jean Paul, of whom Börne was at that time a great admirer. He ends the essay with the following sentences:

And here follows the practical application that was promised. Take a few sheets of paper and for three days on end write down, without fabrication or hypocrisy, everything that comes into your head. Write down what you think of yourself, of your wife, of the Turkish War, of Goethe, of Fonk's trial, of the Last Judgment, of your superiors—and when three days have passed you will be quite out of your senses with astonishment at the new and unheard-of thoughts you have had. This is the art of becoming an original writer in three days.

When Professor Freud came to read this essay of Börne's, he brought forward a number of facts that may have an important bearing on the question that is under discussion here as to the prehistory of the psychoanalytic use of free associations. He said that when he was fourteen he had been given Börne's works as a present, that he still possessed the book now, fifty years later, and that it was the only one that had survived from his boyhood. Börne, he said, had been the first author into whose writings he had penetrated deeply. He could not remember the essay in question, but some of the others that were contained in the same volume—such as "A Tribute to the Memory of Jean Paul," "The Artist in Eating," and "The Fool at the White Swan Inn"—kept on recurring to his mind for no obvious reason over a long period of years. He was particularly astonished to find expressed in the advice to the original writer some opinions which he himself had always cherished and vindicated. For instance: "A disgraceful cowardliness in regard to thinking holds us all back. The censorship of governments is less oppressive than the censorship exercised by public opinion over our intellectual productions." (Moreover there is a reference here to a "censorship," which reappears in psycho-analysis as the dream-censorship.) "It is not lack of intellect but lack of character that prevents most writers from being better than they are. . . . Sincerity is the source of all genius, and men would be cleverer if they were more moral. . . ."

Thus it seems not impossible that this hint may have brought to light the fragment of cryptomnesia which in so many cases may be suspected to lie behind apparent originality.

BERGSON: *Understanding Reality*

A comparison of the definitions of metaphysics and the various conceptions of the absolute leads to the discovery that philosophers, in spite of their apparent divergencies, agree in distinguishing two profoundly different ways of knowing a thing. The first implies that we move round the object; the second that we enter into it. The first depends on the point of view at which we are placed and on the symbols by which we express ourselves. The second neither depends on a point of view nor relies on any symbol. The first kind of knowledge may be said to stop at the *relative;* the second, in those cases where it is possible, to attain the *absolute.*

Consider, for example, the movement of an object in space. My perception of the motion will vary with the point of view, moving or stationary, from which I observe it. My expression of it will vary with the systems of axes, or the points of reference, to which I relate it; that is, with the symbols by which I translate it. For this double reason I call such motion *relative:* in the one case, as in the other, I am placed outside the object itself. But when I speak of an *absolute* movement, I am attributing to the moving object an interior and, so to speak, states of mind; I also imply that I am in sympathy with those states, and that I insert myself in them by an effort of imagination. Then, according as the object is moving or stationary, according as it adopts one movement or another, what I experience will vary. And what I experience will depend neither on the point of view I may take up in regard to the object, since I am inside the object itself, nor on the symbols by which I may translate the motion, since I have rejected all translations in order to possess the original. In short, I shall no longer grasp the movement from without, remaining where I am, but from where it is, from within, as it is in itself. I shall possess an absolute.

Consider, again, a character whose adventures are related to me in a novel. The author may multiply the traits of his hero's character, may make him speak and act as much as he pleases, but all this can never be equivalent to the simple and indivisible feeling which I should experience if I were able for an instant to identify myself with the person of the hero himself. Out of that indivisible feeling, as from a spring, all the words, gestures, and actions of the man would appear to me to flow naturally. They would no longer be accidents which, added to the idea I had already formed of the character, continually enriched that idea, without ever completing it. The character would be given to me all at once, in its entirety, and the thousand incidents which manifest it, instead of adding themselves to the idea and so enriching it, would seem to me, on the contrary, to detach themselves from it, without, however, exhausting it or impoverishing its essence. All the things I am told about the man provide me with so many points of view from which I can observe him. All the traits which describe him, and which can make him known to me only by so many comparisons with persons or things I know already, are signs by which he is expressed more or less symbolically. Symbols and points of view, therefore, place me outside him; they give me only what he has in common with others, and not what belongs to him and to him alone. But that which is properly himself, that which constitutes his essence, cannot be perceived from without, being internal by definition, nor be expressed by symbols, being incommensurable with everything else. Description, history, and analysis leave me here in the relative. Coincidence with the person himself would alone give me the absolute.

It is in this sense, and in this sense only, that *absolute* is synonymous with *perfection*. Were all the photographs of a town, taken from all possible points of view, to go on indefinitely completing one another, they would never be equivalent to the solid town in which we walk about. Were all the translations of a poem into all possible languages to add together their various shades of meaning and, correcting each other by a kind of mutual retouching, to give a more and more faithful image of the poem they translate, they would yet never succeed in rendering the inner meaning of the original. A representation taken from a certain point of view, a translation made with certain symbols, will always remain imperfect in comparison with the object of which a view has been taken, or which the symbols seek to express. But the absolute, which is the object and not its representation, the original and not its translation, is perfect, by being perfectly what it is.

It is doubtless for this reason that the *absolute* has often been identified with the *infinite*. Suppose that I wished to communicate to someone who did not know Greek the extraordinarily simple expression that a passage in Homer makes upon me; I should first give a translation of the lines, I should then comment on my translation, and then develop the commentary; in this way, by piling up explanation on explanation, might approach nearer and nearer to what I wanted to express; but should never quite reach it. When you raise your arm, you accomplish a movement of which you have, from within, a simple perception; but for me, watching it from the outside, your arm passes through one point then through another, and between these two there will be still other points; so that, if I began to count, the operation would go on for ever. Viewed from the inside, then, an absolute is a simple thing; but looked at from the outside, that is to say, relatively to other things, it becomes in relation to these signs which express it, the gold coin for which we never seem able to finish giving small change. Now, that which lends itself at the same time both to an indivisible apprehension and to an inexhaustible enumeration is, by the very definition of the word, an infinite.

It follows from this that an absolute could only be given in an *intuition,* whilst everything else falls within the province of *analysis.* By intuition is meant the kind of *intellectual sympathy* by which one places oneself within an object in order to coincide with what is unique in it and consequently inexpressible. Analysis, on the contrary, is the operation which reduces the object to elements already known, that is, to elements common both to it and other objects. To analyze, therefore, is to express a thing as a function of something other than itself. All analysis is thus a translation, a development into symbols, a representation taken from successive points of view from which we note as many resemblances as possible between the new object which we are studying and others which we believe we know already. In its eternally unsatisfied desire to embrace the object around which it is compelled to turn, analysis multiplies without end the number of its points of view in order to complete its always incomplete representation, and ceaselessly varies its symbols that it may perfect the always imperfect translation. It goes on, therefore, to infinity. But intuition, if intuition is possible, is a simple act.

Now, it is easy to see that the ordinary function of positive science is analysis. Positive science works, then, above all, with symbols. Even the most concrete of the natural sciences, those concerned with life, confine themselves to the visible form of living beings, their organs and anatomical elements. They make comparisons between these forms, they reduce the more complex to the more simple; in short, they study the workings of life in what is, so to speak, only its visual symbol. If there exists any means of possessing a reality absolutely instead of knowing it relatively, of placing oneself within it instead of looking at it from outside points of view, of having the intuition instead of making the analysis: in short, of seizing it without any expression, translation, or symbolic representation—metaphysics is that means. *Metaphysics, then, is the science which claims to dispense with symbols.*

There is one reality, at least, which we all seize from within, by intuition and not by simple analysis. It is our own personality in its flowing time—our self which endures. We may sympathise intellectually with nothing else, but we certainly sympathise with our own selves. When I direct my attention inward to contemplate my own self (supposed for the moment to be inactive), I perceive at first, as a crust solidified on the surface, all the perceptions which come to it from the material world. These perceptions are clear, distinct, juxtaposed or juxtaposable one with another; they tend to group themselves into objects. Next, I notice the memories which more or less adhere to these perceptions and which serve to interpret them. These memories have been detached, as it were, from the depth of my personality, drawn to the surface by the perceptions which resemble them; they rest on the surface of my mind without being absolutely myself. Lastly, I feel the stir of tendencies and motor habits—a crowd of virtual actions, more or less firmly bound to these perceptions and memories. All these clearly defined elements appear more distinct from me, the more distinct they are from each other. Radiating, as they do, from within outwards, they form collectively the surface of a sphere which tends to grow larger and lose itself in the exterior world. But if I draw myself in from the periphery towards the centre, if I search in the depth of my being that which is most uniformly, most constantly and most enduringly myself, I find an altogether different thing.

There is, beneath these sharply cut crystals and this frozen surface, a continuous flux which is not comparable to any flux I have ever seen. There is a succession of states, each of which announces that which follows and contains that which precedes it. They can, properly speaking, only be said to form multiple states when I have already passed them and turn back to observe their track. Whilst I was experiencing them, they were so solidly organized, so profoundly animated with a common life, that I could not have said where any one of them finished or where another commenced. In reality, no one of them begins or ends, but all extend into each other.

This inner life may be compared to the unrolling of a coil, for there is no living being who does not feel himself coming gradually to the end of his role; and to live is to grow old. But it may just as well be compared to a continual rolling up, like that of a thread on a ball, for our past follows us, it swells incessantly with the present that it picks up on its way; and consciousness means memory.

But actually it is neither an unrolling nor a rolling up, for these two similes evoke the idea of lines and surfaces whose parts are homogeneous and superposable on one another. Now, there are no two identical moments in the life of the same conscious being. Take the simplest sensation, suppose it constant, absorb in it the entire personality: the consciousness which will accompany this sensation cannot remain identical with itself for two consecutive moments, because the second moment always contains, over and above the first, the memory that the first has bequeathed to it. A consciousness which could experience two identical moments would be a consciousness without memory. It would die and be born again continually. In what other way could one represent unconsciousness?

It would be better, then, to use as a comparison the myriad-tinted spectrum, with its insensible gradations leading from one shade to another. A current of feeling which passed along the spectrum, assuming in turn the tint of each of its shades, would experience a series of gradual changes, each of which would announce the one to follow and would sum up those which preceded it. Yet even here the successive shades of the spectrum always remain external one to another. They are juxtaposed; they occupy space. But pure duration, on the contrary, excludes all idea of juxtaposition, reciprocal externality, and extension.

Let us, then, rather, imagine an infinitely small elastic body, contracted, if it were possible, to a mathematical point. Let this be drawn out gradually in such a manner that from the point comes a constantly lengthening line. Let us fix our attention not on the line as a line, but on the action by which it is traced. Let us bear in mind that this action, in spite of its duration, is indivisible if accomplished without stopping, that if a stopping point is inserted, we have two actions instead of one, that each of these separate actions is then the indivisible operation of which we speak, and that it is not the moving action itself which is divisible, but, rather, the stationary line it leaves behind it as its track in space. Finally, let us free ourselves from the space which underlies the movement in order to consider only the movement itself, the act of tension or extension; in short, pure mobility. We shall have this time a more faithful image of the development of our self in duration.

However, even this image is incomplete, and indeed, every comparison will be insufficient, because the unrolling of our duration resembles in some of its aspects the unity of an advancing movement and in others the multiplicity of expanding states; and, clearly, no metaphor can express one of these two aspects without sacrificing the other. If I use the comparison of the spectrum with its thousand shades, I have before me a thing already made, whilst duration is continually "in the making." If I think of an elastic which is being stretched, or of a spring which is extended or relaxed, I forget the richness of colour, characteristic of duration that is lived, to see only the simple movement by which consciousness passes from one shade to another. The inner life is all this at once: variety of qualities, continuity of progress, and unity of direction. It cannot be represented by images.

But it is even less possible to represent it by *concepts,* that is by abstract, general, or simple ideas. It is true that no image can reproduce exactly the original feeling I have of the flow of my own conscious life. But it is not even necessary that I should attempt to render it. If a man is incapable of getting for himself the intuition of the constitutive duration of his own being, nothing will ever give it to him, concepts no more than images.

BERGSON: *Duration*

The existence of which we are most assured and which we know best is unquestionably our own, for of every other object we have notions which may be considered external and superficial, whereas, of ourselves, our perception is internal and profound. What, then, do we find? In this privileged case, what is the precise meaning of the word "exist"? Let us recall here briefly the conclusions of an earlier work.

I find, first of all, that I pass from state to state. I am warm or cold, I am merry or sad, I work or I do nothing, I look at what is around me, or I think of something else. Sensations, feelings, volitions, ideas—such are the changes into which my existence is divided and which color it in turns. I change, then, without ceasing. But this is not saying enough. Change is far more radical than we are at first inclined to suppose.

For I speak of each of my states as if it formed a block and were a separate whole. I say indeed that I change, but the change seems to me to reside in the passage from one state to the next: of each state, taken separately, I am apt to think that it remains the same during all the time that it prevails. Nevertheless, a slight effort of attention would reveal to me that there is no feeling, no idea, no volition which is not undergoing change every moment; if a mental state ceased to vary, its duration would cease to flow. Let us take the most stable of internal states, the visual perception of a motionless external object. The object may remain the same, I may look at it from the same angle, in the same light; nevertheless the vision I now have of it differs from that which I have just had, even if only because the one is an instant older than the other. My memory is there, which conveys something of the past into the present. My mental state, as it advances on the road of time, is continually swelling with the duration which it accumulates: it goes on increasing—rolling upon itself, as a snowball on the snow. Still more is this the case with states more deeply internal, such as sensations, feelings, desires, etc., which do not correspond, like a simple visual perception, to an unvarying external object. But it is expedient to disregard the uninterrupted change, and to notice it only when it becomes sufficient to impress a new attitude on the body, a new direction on the attention. Then, and then only, we find that our state has changed. The truth is that we change without ceasing, and that the state itself is nothing but change.

This amounts to saying that there is no essential difference between passing from one state to another and persisting in the same state. If the state which "remains the same" is more varied than we think, on the other hand the passing from one state to another resembles, more than we imagine, a single state being prolonged; the transition is continuous. But, just because we close our eyes to the unceasing variation of every psychical state, we are obliged, when the change has become so considerable as to force itself on our attention, to speak as if a new state were placed alongside the previous one. Of this new state we assume that it remains unvarying in its turn, and so on endlessly. The apparent discontinuity of the psychical life is then due to our attention being fixed on it by a series of separate acts: actually there is only a gentle slope; but in following the broken line of our acts of attention, we think we perceived separate steps. True, our psychic life is full of the unforeseen. A thousand incidents arise, which seem to be cut off from those which precede them, and to be disconnected from those which follow. Discontinuous though they appear, however, in point of fact they stand out against the continuity of a background on which they are designed, and to which indeed they owe the intervals that separate them; they are the beats of the drum which break forth here and there in the symphony. Our attention fixes on them because they interest it more, but each of them is borne by the fluid mass of our whole psychical existence. Each is only the best illuminated point of a moving zone which comprises all that we feel or think or will—all, in short, that we are at any given moment. It is this entire zone which in reality makes up our state. Now, states thus defined cannot be regarded as distinct elements. They continue each other in an endless flow.

But, as our attention has distinguished and separated them artificially, it is obliged next to reunite them by an artificial bond. It imagines, therefore, a formless *ego*, indifferent and unchangeable, on which it threads the psychic states which it has set up as independent entities. Instead of a flux of fleeting shades merging into each other, it perceives distinct and, so to speak, *solid* colors, set side by side like the beads of a necklace; it must perforce then suppose a thread, also itself solid, to hold the beads together. But if this colorless substratum is perpetually colored by that which covers it, it is for us, in its indeterminateness, as if it did not exist, since we only perceive what is colored, or, in other words psychic states. As a matter of fact, this substratum has no reality; it is merely a symbol intended to recall unceasingly to our consciousness the artificial character of the process by which the attention places clean-cut states side by side, where actually there is a continuity which unfolds. If our existence were composed of separate states with an impassive ego to unite them, for us there would be no duration. For an ego which does not change does not *endure,* and a psychic state which remains the same so long as it is not replaced by the following state does not *endure* either. Vain, therefore, is the attempt to range such states beside each other on the ego supposed to sustain them: never can these solids strung upon a solid make up that duration which flows. What we actually obtain in this way is an artificial imitation of the internal life, a static equivalent which will lend itself better to the requirements of logic and language, just because we have eliminated from it the element of real time. But, as regards the psychical life unfolding beneath the symbols which conceal it, we readily perceive that time is just the stuff it is made of.

There is, moreover, no stuff more resistant nor more substantial. For our duration is not merely one instant replacing another; if it were, there would never be anything but the present—no prolonging of the past into the actual, no evolution, no concrete duration. Duration is the continuous progress of the past which gnaws into the future and which swells as it advances. And as the past grows without ceasing, so also there is no limit to its preservation. Memory, as we have tried to prove,[1] is not a faculty of putting away recollections in a drawer, or of inscribing them in a register. There is no register, no drawer; there is not even, properly speaking, a faculty, for a faculty works intermittently, when it will or when it can, whilst the piling up of the past upon the past goes on without relaxation. In reality, the past is preserved by itself, automatically. In its entirety, probably, it follows us at every instant; all that we have felt, thought, and willed from our earliest infancy is there, leaning over the present which is about to join it, pressing against the portals of consciousness that would fain leave it outside. The cerebral mechanism is arranged just so as to drive back into the unconscious almost the whole of this past, and to admit beyond the threshold only that which can cast light on the present situation or further the action now being prepared— in short, only that which can give *useful* work. At the most, a few superfluous recollections may succeed in smuggling themselves through the half-open door. These memories, messengers from the unconscious, remind us of what we are dragging behind us unawares. But, even though we may have no distinct idea of it, we feel vaguely that our past remains present to us. What are we, in fact, what is our *character*, if not the condensation of the history that we have lived from our birth—nay, even before our birth, since we bring with us prenatal dispositions? Doubtless we think with only a small part of our past, but it is with our entire past, including the original bent of our soul, that we desire, will, and act. Our past, then, as a whole, is made manifest to us in its impulse; it is felt in the form of tendency, although a small part of it only is known in the form of idea.

From this survival of the past it follows that consciousness cannot go through the same state twice. The circumstances may still be the same, but they will act no longer on the same person, since they find him at a new moment of his history. Our personality, which is being built up each instant with its accumulated experience, changes without ceasing. By changing it prevents any state, although superficially identical with another, from ever repeating it in its very depth. That is why our duration is irreversible. We could not live over again a single moment, for we should have to begin by effacing the memory of all that had followed. Even could we erase this memory from our intellect, we could not from our will.

Thus our personality shoots, grows, and ripens without ceasing. Each of its moments is something new added to what was before. We may go further: it is not only something new, but something unforeseeable. Doubtless, my present state is explained by what was in me and by what was acting on me a moment ago. In analyzing it I should find no other elements. But even a superhuman intelligence would not have been able to foresee the simple indivisible form which gives to these purely abstract elements their concrete organization. For to foresee consists of projecting into the future what has been perceived in the past, or of imagining for a later time a new grouping, in a new order, of elements already perceived. But that which has never been perceived, and which is at the same time simple, is necessarily unforeseeable. Now such is the case with each of our states, regarded as a moment in a history that is gradually unfolding: it is simple, and it cannot have been already perceived, since it concentrates in its indivisibility all that has been perceived and what the present is adding to it besides. It is an original moment of a no less original history.

The finished portrait is explained by the features of the model, by the nature of the artist, by the colors spread out on the palette; but, even with the knowledge of what explains it, no one, not even the artist, could have foreseen exactly what the portrait would be, for to predict it would have been to produce it before it was produced—an absurd hypothesis which is its own refutation. Even so with regard to the moments of our life, of which we are the artisans. Each of them is a kind of a creation. And just as the talent of the painter is formed or deformed—in any case, is modified—under the very influence of the works he produces, so each of our states, at the moment of its issue, modifies our personality, being indeed the new form that we are just assuming. It is then right to say that what we do depends on what we are; but it is necessary to add also that we are, to a certain extent, what we do, and that we are creating ourselves continually. This creation of self by self is the more complete, the more one reasons on what one does. For reason does not proceed in such matters as in geometry, where impersonal premises are given once for all, and an impersonal conclusion must perforce be drawn. Here, on the contrary, the same reasons may dictate to different persons, or to the same person at different moments, acts profoundly different, although equally reasonable. The truth is that they are not quite the same reasons, since they are not those of the same person, nor of the same moment. That is why we cannot deal with them in the abstract, from outside, as in geometry, nor solve for another the problems by which he is faced in life. Each must solve them from within, on his own account. But we need not go more deeply into this. We are seeking only the precise meaning that our consciousness gives to this word "exist," and we find that, for a conscious being, to exist is to change, to change is to mature, to mature is to go on creating oneself endlessly. . . .

3

DISCOVERIES AND EXPLORERS

VIRGINIA WOOLF, "Modern Fiction," *The Common Reader,* (New York: Harcourt, Brace, 1925), pp. 150–59.

By 10 April 1919, when this essay appeared in the *Times Literary Supplement* under the title of "Modern Novels," nine episodes of James Joyce's *Ulysses* had appeared in the *Little Review.* In the essay Mrs. Woolf, herself a pioneer in the use of the stream-of-consciousness technique, says that H. G. Wells, Arnold Bennett, and John Galsworthy are disappointing "because they are concerned not with the spirit but with the body" ("materialists" she calls them). She then goes on to explain how modern writers like James Joyce—and presumably herself—are "concerned at all costs to reveal the flickerings of that innermost flame which flashes its messages to the brain."

VIRGINIA WOOLF, "On Dorothy Richardson, James Joyce, and *Ulysses,*" *A Writer's Diary,* ed. Leonard Woolf (New York: Harcourt, Brace, 1954), pp. 22, 46, 48–49.

In the privacy of her own diary, Virginia Woolf, although certain that *Ulysses* is a work of genius, is less complimentary to Joyce's writing than she is in public. She also discusses her ideas for "a new form" for a novel in language different from the language she uses in "Modern Fiction."

ARTHUR POWER, "James Joyce on Modern Literature," *Conversations with James Joyce,* ed. Clive Hart (New York: Barnes & Noble, 1974), pp. 73–75.

Arthur Power remembers a conversation with Joyce in which Joyce explained the difference between "classical" and "modern" literature. Although Joyce's language is more abstract than Virginia Woolf's, in this statement he says much of what she said in "Modern Fiction." Instead of speaking of "the ordinary mind on the ordinary day" receiving "a myriad impressions" as she did, he speaks of "jugs, and pots and plates, back- streets and blowsy living-rooms inhabited by blowsy women" and of exploring "the hidden world, those undercurrents which flow beneath the apparently firm surface."

STANISLAUS JOYCE, "On the Stream of Consciousness," in Robert Scholes and Richard M. Kain, *The Workshop of Daedalus,* (Evanston: Northwestern University Press, 1965), pp. 78–79.

James Joyce told Djuna Barnes, "In *Ulysses* I have recorded, simul- taneously, what a man says, sees, thinks, and what such seeing, thinking, saying does, to what you Freudians call the subconscious"; and in *Finne- gans Wake* he wrote, ". . . the steady monologuy of the interiors; the pardonable confusion for which some blame the cudgel and more blame the soot. . . ." But beyond what Power reported there is no record of any extended statement by Joyce, either in speech or in writing, on the stream-of-consciousness technique. Stanislaus Joyce, James's younger brother, however, did write such a statement in his diary; and we know that James read that diary. Readers may also want to examine a passage of stream-of-consciousness writing in Stanislaus's diary which may have been one of the models Joyce used: Stanislaus Joyce, *The Dublin Diary of Stanislaus Joyce,* ed. George Harris Healey (Ithaca: Cornell University Press, 1962), pp. 108–10.

DOROTHY RICHARDSON, "Autobiographical Sketch," in Stanley J. Kunitz, ed., *Authors Today and Yesterday* (New York: H. W. Wilson, 1933), p. 562.

Dorothy Richardson is widely credited with being one of the innova- tors of the stream-of-consciousness technique. In this statement she dis- cusses consciousness, how an author presents—or represents—it, and what that technique of presentation or representation should be called. Al- though this statement and the one following were written thirty years after Miss Richardson began writing *Pilgrimage,* they tell us a good deal about what she was trying to do in those early days.

DOROTHY RICHARDSON, foreword to *Pilgrimage* 1 (New York: Alfred A. Knopf, 1938), : 9–12.

The thirteen novels in the *Pilgrimage* series have been republished in four paperbound volumes: *Pilgrimage 1 (Pointed Roofs; Backwater; Honeycomb); Pilgrimage 2 (The Tunnel; Interim); Pilgrimage 3 (Deadlock; Revolving Lights; The Trap); Pilgrimage 4 (Oberland; Dawn's Left Hand; Clear Horizon; Dimple Hill; March Moonlight).*

The series originally appeared as twelve novels. In his introduction to *Pilgrimage 1* Walter Allen says, *"March Moonlight,* hitherto unpublished in book form, stands as a coda, as the rounding-off and summation of all that has gone before." In *Pilgrimage,* Allen says, Dorothy Richardson set herself the task of rendering "current existence as reflected in the consciousness of her heroine."

MARCEL PROUST, "A Little Cake Releases a Hidden Memory," *Swann's Way,* trans. C. K. Scott Montcrief, *Remembrance of Things Past* (New York: Random House, 1941), 1: 33–36.

At the beginning of Proust's long novel, the narrator describes how a taste unexpectedly triggers the memory of a long forgotten experience. This episode—the tasting of the "petite madeleine"—is the one most frequently referred to by critics discussing Proust's method.

MARCEL PROUST, "The Principle of Involuntary Memory," prologue to *Contre Sainte-Beuve, On Arts and Literature,* trans. Sylvia Townsend Warner (New York: Meridian Books, 1958), pp. 19–26.

In this essay Proust describes the occurrence in his own life which must have served as the original for the episode of the madeleine in *Swann's Way.* He then goes on to describe how involuntary memory works and explains why it is superior to intellect.

WOOLF: *Modern Fiction*

In making any survey, even the freest and loosest, of modern fiction it is difficult not to take it for granted that the modern practice of the art is somehow an improvement upon the old. With their simple tools and primitive materials, it might be said, Fielding did well and Jane Austen even better, but compare their opportunities with ours! Their master-pieces certainly have a strange air of simplicity. And yet the analogy between literature and the process, to choose an example, of making motor cars scarcely holds good beyond the first glance. It is doubtful whether in the course of the centuries, though we have learnt much about making machines, we have learnt anything about making literature. We do not come to write better; all that we can be said to do is to keep moving, now a little in this direction, now in that, but with a circular tendency should the whole course of the track be viewed from a sufficiently lofty pinnacle. It need scarcely be said that we make no claim to stand, even momentarily, upon that vantage ground. On the flat, in the crowd, half blind with dust, we look back with envy to those happier warriors, whose battle is won and whose achievements wear so serene an air of accomplishment that we can scarcely refrain from whispering that the fight was not so fierce for them as for us. It is for the historian of literature to decide; for him to say if we are now beginning or ending or standing in the middle of a great period of prose fiction, for down in the plain little is visible. We only know that certain gratitudes and hostilities inspire us; that certain paths seem to lead to fertile land, others to the dust and the desert; and of this perhaps it may be worth while to attempt some account.

Our quarrel, then, is not with the classics, and if we speak of quarrelling with Mr. Wells, Mr. Bennett, and Mr. Galsworthy it is partly that by the mere fact of their existence in the flesh their work has a living, breathing, every-day imperfection which bids us take what liberties with it we choose. But it is also true that, while we thank them for a thousand gifts, we reserve our unconditional gratitude for Mr. Hardy, for Mr. Conrad, and in a much lesser degree for the Mr. Hudson, of *The Purple Land, Green Mansions,* and *Far Away and Long Ago.* Mr. Wells, Mr. Bennett, and Mr. Galsworthy have excited so many hopes and disappointed them so persistently that our gratitude largely takes the form of thanking them for having shown us what they might have done but have not done; what we certainly could not do, but as certainly, perhaps, do not wish to do. No single phrase will sum up the charge or grievance which we have to bring against a mass of work so large in its volume and embodying so many qualities, both admirable and the reverse. If we tried to formulate our meaning in one word we should say that these three writers are materialists. It is because they are concerned not with the spirit but with the body that they have disappointed us, and left us with the feeling that the sooner English fiction turns its back upon them, as politely as may be, and marches, if only into the desert, the better for its soul. Naturally, no single word reaches the centre of three separate targets. In the case of Mr. Wells it falls notably wide of the mark. And yet even with him it indicates to our thinking the fatal alloy in his genius, the great clod of clay that has got itself mixed up with the purity of his inspiration. But Mr. Bennett is perhaps the worst culprit of the three, inasmuch as he is by far the best workman. He can make a book so well constructed and solid in its craftsmanship that it is difficult for the most exacting of critics to see through what chink or crevice decay can creep in. There is not so much as a draught between the frames of the windows, or a crack in the boards. And yet—if life should refuse to live there? That is a risk which the creator of *The Old Wives' Tale,* George Cannon, Edwin Clayhanger, and hosts of other figures, may well claim to have surmounted. His characters live abundantly, even unexpectedly, but it remains to ask how do they live, and what do they live for? More and more they seem to us, deserting even the well-built villa in the Five Towns, to spend their time in some softly padded first-class railway carriage, pressing bells and buttons innumerable; and the destiny to which they travel so luxuriously becomes more and more unquestionably an eternity of bliss spent in the very best hotel in Brighton. It can scarcely be said of Mr. Wells that he is a materialist in the sense that he takes too much delight in the solidity of his fabric. His mind is too generous in its sympathies to allow him to spend much time in making things shipshape and substantial. He is a materialist from sheer goodness of heart, taking upon his shoulders the work that ought to have been discharged by government officials, and in the plethora of his ideas and facts scarcely having leisure to realize, or forgetting to think important, the crudity and coarseness of his human beings. Yet what more damaging criticism can there be both of his earth and of his Heaven than that they are to be inhabited here and hereafter by his Joans and his Peters? Does not the inferiority of their natures tarnish whatever institutions and ideals may be provided for them by the generosity of their creator? Nor, profoundly though we respect the integrity and humanity of Mr. Galsworthy, shall we find what we seek in his pages.

If we fasten, then, one label on all these books, on which is one word, "materialists," we mean by it that they write of unimportant things; that they spend immense skill and immense industry making the trivial and the transitory appear the true and enduring.

We have to admit that we are exacting, and, further, that we find it difficult to justify our discontent by explaining what it is that we exact. We frame our question differently at different times. But it reappears most persistently as we drop the finished novel on the crest of a sigh—Is it worth while? What is the point of it all? Can it be that owing to one of those little deviations which the human spirit seems to make from time to time Mr. Bennett has come down with his magnificent apparatus for catching life just an inch or two on the wrong side? Life escapes; and perhaps without life nothing else is worth while. It is a confession of vagueness to have to make use of such a figure as this, but we scarcely better the matter by speaking, as critics are prone to do, of reality. Admitting the vagueness which afflicts all criticism of novels, let us hazard the opinion that for us at this moment the form of fiction most in vogue more often misses than secures the thing we seek. Whether we call it life or spirit, truth or reality, this, the essential thing, has moved off, or on, and refuses to be contained any longer in such ill-fitting vestments as we provide. Nevertheless, we go on perseveringly, conscientiously, constructing our two and thirty chapters after a design which more and more ceases to resemble the vision in our minds. So much of the enormous labour of proving the solidity, the likeness to life, of the story is not merely labour thrown away but labour misplaced to the extent of obscuring and blotting out the light of the conception. Examine for a moment an ordinary mind on an ordinary day. The mind receives a myriad impressions—trivial, fantastic, evanescent, or engraved with the sharpness of steel. From all sides they come, an incessant shower of innumerable atoms; and as they fall, as they shape themselves into the life of Monday or Tuesday, the accent falls differently from of old; the moment of importance came not here but there; so that if a writer were a free man and not a slave, if he could write what he chose, not what he must, if he could base his work upon his own feeling and not upon convention, there would be no plot, no comedy, no tragedy, no love interest or catastrophe in the accepted style, and perhaps not a single button sewn on as the Bond Street tailors would have it. Life is not a series of gig lamps symmetrically arranged; but a luminous halo, a semi-transparent envelope surrounding us from the beginning of consciousness to the end. Is it not the task of the novelist to convey this varying, this unknown and uncircumscribed spirit, whatever aberration or complexity it may display, with as little mixture of the alien and external as possible? We are not pleading merely for courage and sincerity; we are suggesting that the proper stuff of fiction is a little other than custom would have us believe it.

It is, at any rate, in some such fashion as this that we seek to define the quality which distinguishes the work of several young writers, among whom Mr. James Joyce is the most notable, from that of their predecessors. They attempt to come closer to life, and to preserve more sincerely and exactly what interests and moves them, even if to do so they must discard most of the conventions which are commonly observed by the novelist. Let us record the atoms as they fall upon the mind in the order in which they fall, let us trace the pattern, however disconnected and incoherent in appearance, which each sight or incident scores upon the consciousness. Let us not take it for granted that life exists more fully in what is commonly thought big than in what is commonly thought small. Any one who has read *The Portrait of the Artist as a Young Man* or, what promises [written April 1919] to be a far more interesting work, *Ulysses,* now appearing in the *Little Review,* will have hazarded some theory of this nature as to Mr. Joyce's intention. On our part, with such a fragment before us, it is hazarded rather than affirmed; but whatever the intention of the whole there can be no question but that it is of the utmost sincerity and that the result, difficult or unpleasant as we may judge it, is undeniably important. In contrast with those whom we have called materialists Mr. Joyce is spiritual; he is concerned at all costs to reveal the flickerings of that innermost flame which flashes its messages through the brain, and in order to preserve it he disregards with complete courage whatever seems to him adventitious, whether it be probability, or coherence or any other of these signposts which for generations have served to support the imagination of a reader when called upon to imagine what he can neither touch nor see. The scene in the cemetery, for instance, with its brilliancy, its sordidity, its incoherence, its sudden lightning flashes of significance, does undoubtedly come so close to the quick of the mind that, on a first reading at any rate, it is difficult not to acclaim a masterpiece. If we want life itself here, surely we have it. Indeed, we find ourselves fumbling rather awkwardly if we try to say what else we wish, and for what reason a work of such originality yet fails to compare, for we must take high examples, with *Youth* or *The Mayor of Casterbridge.* It fails because of the comparative poverty of the writer's mind, we might say simply and have done with it. But it is possible to press a little further and wonder whether we may not refer our sense of being in a bright yet narrow room, confined and shut in, rather than enlarged and set free, to some limitation imposed by the method as well as by the mind. Is it the method that inhibits the creative power? Is it due to the method that we feel neither jovial nor magnanimous, but centred in a self which, in spite of its tremor of susceptibility, never embraces or creates what is outside itself and beyond? Does the emphasis laid, perhaps didactically, upon indecency, contribute to the effect of something angular and isolated? Or is it merely that in any effort of such originality it is much easier, for contemporaries especially, to feel what it lacks than to name what it gives? In any case it is a mistake to stand outside examining "methods." Any method is right, every method is right, that expresses what we wish to express, if we are writers; that brings us closer to the novelist's intention if we are readers. This method has the merit of bringing us closer to what we were prepared to call life itself; did not the reading of *Ulysses* suggest how much of life is excluded or ignored, and did it not come with a shock to open *Tristram Shandy* or even *Pendennis* and be by them convinced that there are not only other aspects of life, but more important ones into the bargain.

However this may be, the problem before the novelist at present, as we suppose it to have been in the past, is to contrive means of being free to set down what he chooses. He has to have the courage to say that what interests him is no longer "this" but "that": out of "that" alone must he construct his work. For the moderns "that," the point of interest, lies very likely in the dark places of psychology. At once, therefore, the accent falls a little differently; the emphasis is upon something hitherto ignored; at once a different outline of form becomes necessary, difficult for us to grasp, incomprehensible to our predecessors. No one but a modern, perhaps no one but a Russian, would have felt the interest of the situation which Tchekov has made into the short story which he calls "Gusev." Some Russian soldiers lie ill on board a ship which is taking them back to Russia. We are given a few scraps of their talk and some of their thoughts; then one of them dies and is carried away; the talk goes on among the others for a time, until Gusev himself dies, and looking "like a carrot or a radish" is thrown overboard. The emphasis is laid upon such unexpected places that at first it seems as if there were no emphasis at all; and then, as the eyes accustom themselves to twilight and discern the shapes of things in a room we see how complete the story is, how profound, and how truly in obedience to his vision Tchekov has chosen this, that, and the other, and placed them together to compose something new. But it is impossible to say "this is comic," or "that is tragic," nor are we certain, since short stories, we have been taught, should be brief and conclusive, whether this, which is vague and inconclusive, should be called a short story at all.

The most elementary remarks upon modern English fiction can hardly avoid some mention of the Russian influence, and if the Russians are mentioned one runs the risk of feeling that to write of any fiction save theirs is waste of time. If we want understanding of the soul and heart where else shall we find it of comparable profundity? If we are sick of our own materialism the least considerable of their novelists has by right of birth a natural reverence for the human spirit. "Learn to make yourself akin to people. . . . But let this sympathy be not with the mind—for it is easy with the mind—but with the heart, with love towards them." In every great Russian writer we seem to discern the features of a saint, if sympathy for the sufferings of others, love towards them, endeavour to reach some goal worthy of the most exacting demands of the spirit constitute saintliness. It is the saint in them which confounds us with a feeling of our own irreligious triviality, and turns so many of our famous novels to tinsel and trickery. The conclusions of the Russian mind, thus comprehensive and compassionate, are inevitably, perhaps, of the utmost sadness. More accurately indeed we might speak of the inconclusiveness of the Russian mind. It is the sense that there is no answer, that if honestly examined life presents question after question which must be left to sound on and on after the story is over in hopeless interrogation that fills us with a deep, and finally it may be with a resentful, despair. They are right perhaps; unquestionably they see further than we do and without our gross impediments of vision. But perhaps we see something that escapes them, or why should this voice of protest mix itself with our gloom? The voice of protest is the voice of another and an ancient civilisation which seems to have bred in us the instinct to enjoy and fight rather than to suffer and understand. English fiction from Sterne to Meredith bears witness to our natural delight in humour and comedy, in the beauty of earth, in the activities of the intellect, and in the splendour of the body. But any deductions that we may draw from the comparison of two fictions so immeasurably far apart are futile save indeed as they flood us with a view of the infinite possibilities of the art and remind us that there is no limit to the horizon, and that nothing—no "method," no experiment, even of the wildest— is forbidden, but only falsity and pretence. "The proper stuff of fiction" does not exist; everything is the proper stuff of fiction, every feeling, every thought; every quality of brain and spirit is drawn upon; no perception comes amiss. And if we can imagine the art of fiction come alive and standing in our midst, she would undoubtedly bid us break her and bully her, as well as honour and love her, for so her youth is renewed and her sovereignty assured.

WOOLF: *Dorothy Richardson, James Joyce, and "Ulysses"*

Monday, January 26th [1920]

The day after my birthday; in fact I'm 38, well, I've no doubt I'm a great deal happier than I was at 28; and happier today than I was yesterday having this afternoon arrived at some idea of a new form for a new novel. Suppose one thing should open out of another—as in an unwritten novel—only not for 10 pages but 200 or so—doesn't that give the looseness and lightness I want; doesn't that get closer and yet keep form and speed, and enclose everything, everything? My doubt is how far it will enclose the human heart—Am I sufficiently mistress of my dialogue to net it there? For I figure that the approach will be entirely different this time: no scaffolding; scarcely a brick to be seen; all crepuscular, but the heart, the passion, humour, everything as bright as fire in the mist. Then I'll find room for so much—a gaiety—an inconsequence—a light spirited stepping at my sweet will. Whether I'm sufficiently mistress of things—that's the doubt; but conceive (?) *Mark on the Wall, K. G.* and *Unwritten Novel* taking hands and dancing in unity. What the unity shall be I have yet to discover; the theme is a blank to me; but I see immense possibilities in the form I hit upon more or less by chance two weeks ago. I suppose the danger is the damned egotistical self; which ruins Joyce and Richardson to my mind: is one pliant and rich enough to provide a wall for the book from oneself without its becoming, as in Joyce and Richardson, narrowing and restricting? My hope is that I've learnt my business sufficiently now to provide all sorts of entertainments. Anyhow, I must still grope and experiment but this afternoon I had a gleam of light. Indeed, I think from the ease with which I'm developing the unwritten novel[1] there must be a path for me there.

Wednesday, August 16th [1922]

I should be reading *Ulysses,* and fabricating my case for and against. I have read 200 pages so far—not a third; and have been amused, stimulated, charmed, interested, by the first 2 or 3 chapters—to the end of the cemetery scene; and then puzzled[,] bored, irritated, and disillusioned by a queasy undergraduate scratching his pimples. And, Tom,[2] great Tom, thinks this on a par with *War and Peace!* An illiterate, underbred book it seems to me; the book of a self taught working man, and we all know how distressing they are, how egotistic, insistent, raw, striking, and ultimately nauseating. When one can have the cooked flesh, why have the raw? But I think if you are anaemic, as Tom is, there is a glory in blood. Being fairly normal myself I am soon ready for the classics again. I may revise this later. I do not compromise my critical sagacity. I plant a stick in the ground to mark page 200.

Wednesday, September 6th [1922]

I finished *Ulysses* and think it a mis-fire. Genius it has, I think; but of the inferior water. The book is diffuse. It is brackish. It is underbred, not only in the obvious sense, but in the literary sense. A first rate writer, I mean, respects writing too much to be tricky; startling; doing stunts. I'm reminded all the time of some callow board school boy, full of wits and powers, but so self-conscious and egotistical that he loses his head, becomes extravagant, mannered, uproarious, ill at ease, makes kindly people feel sorry for him and stern ones merely annoyed; and one hopes he'll grow out of it; but as Joyce is 40 this scarcely seems likely. I have not read it carefully; and only once; and it is very obscure; so no doubt I have scamped the virtue of it more than is fair. I feel that myriads of tiny bullets pepper one and spatter one; but one does not get one deadly wound straight in the face—as from Tolstoy, for instance; but it is entirely absurd to compare him with Tolstoy.

Thursday, September 7th [1922]

Having written this, L. put into my hands a very intelligent review of *Ulysses*, in the American *Nation;* which, for the first time, analyses the meaning; and certainly makes it very much more impressive than I judged. Still I think there is virtue and some lasting truth in first impressions; so I don't cancel mine. I must read some of the chapters again. Probably the final beauty of writing is never felt by contemporaries; but they ought, I think, to be bowled over; and this I was not. Then again, I had my back up on purpose; then again I was over stimulated by Tom's praises.

Thursday, September 26th [1922]

Wittering. Morgan came on Friday; Tom on Saturday. My talk with Tom deserves writing down, but won't get it for the light fading; and we cannot write talk down either, as was agreed at Charleston the other day. There was a good deal of talk about *Ulysses*. Tom said, "He is a purely literary Writer. He is founded upon Walter Pater with a dash of Newman." I said he was virile—a he-goat; but didn't expect Tom to agree. Tom did though; and said he left out many things that were important. The book would be a landmark, because it destroyed the whole of the nineteenth century. It left Joyce himself with nothing to write another book on. It showed up the futility of all the English styles. He thought some of the writing beautiful. But there was no "great conception"; that was not Joyce's intention. He thought that Joyce did completely what he meant to do. But he did not think that he gave a new insight into human nature —said nothing new like Tolstoy. Bloom told one nothing. Indeed, he said, this new method of giving the psychology proves to my mind that it doesn't work. It doesn't tell as much as some casual glance from outside often tells. I said I had found *Pendennis* more illuminating in this way. (The horses are now cropping near my window; the little owl calling, and so I write nonsense.) So we go on to S. Sitwell, who merely explores his sensibility—one of the deadly crimes as Tom thinks: to Dostoievsky— the ruin of English literature, we agreed; Singe [sic] a fake; present state disastrous, because the form don't fit, to his mind not even promising well; he said that one must now be a very first rate poet to be a poet at all: When there were great poets, the little ones caught some of the glow, and were not worthless. Now there's no great poet.

POWER: *Joyce on Modern Literature*

—[T]o my mind [classical literature] is a form of writing which contains little or no mystery, commented Joyce, and since we are surrounded by mystery it has always seemed to me inadequate. It can deal with facts very well, but when it has to deal with motives, the secret currents of life which govern everything, it has not the orchestra, for life is a complicated problem. It is no doubt flattering and pleasant to have it presented in an uncomplicated fashion, as the classicists pretend to do, but it is an intellectual approach which no longer satisfies the modern mind, which is interested above all in subtleties, equivocations, and the subterranean complexities which dominate the average man and compose his life. I would say that the difference between classical literature and modern literature is the difference between the objective and the subjective: classical literature represents the daylight of human personality while modern literature is concerned with the twilight, the passive rather than the active mind. We feel that the classicists explored the physical world to its limit, and we are now anxious to explore the hidden world, those undercurrents which flow beneath the apparently firm surface. But as our education was based on the classical, most of us have a fixed idea of what literature should be, and not only literature but also of what life should be. And so we moderns are accused of distortion; but our literature is no more distorted than classical literature is. All art in a sense is distorted in that it must exaggerate certain aspects to obtain its effect and in time people will accept this so-called modern distortion, and regard it as the truth. Our object is to create a new fusion between the exterior world and our contemporary selves, and also to enlarge our vocabulary of the subconscious as Proust has done. We believe that it is in the abnormal that we approach closer to reality. When we are living a normal life we are living a conventional one, following a pattern which has been laid out by other people in another generation, an objective pattern imposed on us by the church and state. But a writer must maintain a continual struggle against the objective: that is his function. The eternal qualities are the imagination and the sexual instinct, and the formal life tries to suppress both. Out of this present conflict arise the phenomena of modern life.

—In my Mabbot Street scene I approached reality closer in my opinion than anywhere else in the book except perhaps for moments in the last chapter. Sensation is our object, heightened even to the point of hallucination. You described Plutarch's account of Antony as concise, imaginative, and clear. In my opinion it is more concise than clear or imaginative; what is really imaginative is the contrary to what is concise and clear.

—Also in regard to environment, or "background" to use a literary term, the background of the classicists and romantics is unreal for the majority of men. It has no relation to the lives that most of us live and to the surroundings which enclose them:

> *Ordure amons, ordure nous assuit;*
> *Nous deffuyons onneur, il nous deffuit,*
> *En ce bordeau ou tenons nostre estat.*

as Villon puts it. If we are to paint the twilight of the human personality we must darken the landscape also. Idealism is a pleasant bauble, but in these days of overwhelming reality it no longer interests us, or even amuses. We regard it as a sort of theatrical drop-scene. Most lives are made up like the modern painter's themes, of jugs, and pots and plates, back-streets and blowsy living-rooms inhabited by blowsy women, and of a thousand daily sordid incidents which seep into our minds no matter how we strive to keep them out. These are the furniture of our life, which you want to reject for some romantic and flimsy drop-scene.

—I admit I prefer my illusion, I said.

—There you are mistaken, said Joyce, for the fact of things as they are is far more exciting. Eliot has a mind which can appreciate and express both and by placing one in contrast to the other he has obtained striking effects. It is true that one cannot shed the past completely and one must take both worlds into consideration, but the hidden or subconscious world is the most exciting and the modern writer is far more interested in the potential than in the actual—in the unexplored and hallucinatory even—than in the well-trodden romantic or classical world.

STANISLAUS JOYCE: *On the Stream of Consciousness*

My mind used to have a very disputacious turn when I was younger. I used to take up some opinion that pleased me and in my mind argue with some figmentary opponent something in this way: Concerning the idea of education. See there is a man going alone along the Malahide Rd. Supposing he has nothing great on his mind, he is not ~~in love~~ a lover in the expectation of plenty like the farmer that hanged himself, supposing he has no great trouble, his only child has not died, he has not lost all his money, supposing, too, he is not a philosopher, what is he thinking about? Nothing, you say. But how does one decide, how do I decide what is the probable right answer? I cast about in my memory to try if I can find there what I think about in similar circumstances. Then it seems to me that only in a dreamless sleep is there nothing in the living mind. If you still persist, for argument sake in holding that there is nothing in his mind, I think I can convince you this way. His eyes are open and if he is not blind he sees. Yes, he sees, you say but his mind is silent. But listen. If you hold a glass before the scene he is passing, will it not reflect it more truly than the retina of his eye? Does the glass, then, "see"?

Words crossed out appear so in the diary.

Seeing implies consciousness, and you cannot in seriousness pretend to doubt ~~it~~ with that tag of scepticism, that the glass is not conscious, for we believe for reasons almost innumerable that it is not, ~~our reason being~~ for the reasons, for instance, that men by taking thought have made it what it is, a glass, and as it was made just so it remains, nor does it ever move itself, nor reflect things in the manner it chooses but as they are presented to it, nor reflect only such things as it chooses, nor has it showed any signs that are even of life, neither grew nor was capable of growth, reproduced nor was capable of reproducing. But the mind "sees," that is is conscious of the image the eye reflects for it, and says continually within self: "This is a road, the Malahide Rd. I know it well now that I see it. There are high broken hedges on both sides of it, and a few trees. Where the road branches an irregular dwelling-house with an orchard about it, sidles [?] to an arm and before pointing the bifurcation, is an old gate entrance. There is a young man fellow on the opposite side going in the same direction as I am"; thinking not in sentences as in a book, but thought succeeding thought without utterance like harmonies in music, while conveying a more definite impression to the mind. ~~But~~ Now it seems to me that the right purpose of education is to make these impressions and thoughts and judgments distinct, intelligible and definite. Such an education, you say, would make a man very silent and self-centered. It would, to a certain degree, but in that succession of thoughts there would ~~be~~ come impressions that would be beautiful and imaginative, original or witty or brilliant thoughts that would not be kept silent, and judgments that would remain as precious things kept bravely in the mind, that linking wit and brilliancy and imagination, would influence a mind seeing beauty and remembering happiness, would refine and mold it to a free and potent nobility.—Such thinking seems to me vain and vulgar, as if I were showing off to a spectator also figmentary. ~~It would have been better for instance to spend~~ It seems vulgar because, except the last, it was thought easily and with a secret distrust of its logic and yet passed. It would have been better to spend time and call the eye, for instance, a conscious glass. It is stupid, too, for I make my interlocutor stupid to make an argument in the first place and then the easier to beat him. Uncle Willie said to me, "You with Socratic mind." He didn't believe himself, or reserved the right not to believe himself and to think his own mind better than Socratic; but he was right in a way. There is something feebly Socratic in its style. I like my leisure and can use it, my mind gives me ordinary fare for pleasure, but how cumbrously my brain moves in its shell. I see the road I go plainly, the bare hedges and trees and lush Spring colours, but I do not see one step before or after. But for the light of the conscious glass my mind is dark. How many are like me?

RICHARDSON: *Autobiographical Sketch*

There is but little to tell of me. My childhood and youth were passed, in secluded surroundings, in late-Victorian England. Day-school linked me with "the world," upon which I was thrown when, in my seventeenth year, my home broke up. Some of my impressions of what is implied in the capacious term are set down in *Pilgrimage*, not yet complete. This book was begun in 1913. Its first chapter, *Pointed Roofs*, appeared in 1915. [Its tenth, in 1931.]

... What do I think of the term "Stream of Consciousness" as applied, in England, to the work of several modern novelists? Just this: that amongst the company of useful labels devised to meet the exigencies of literary criticism it stands alone, isolated by its perfect imbecility. The transatlantic amendment "Interior Monologue" tho rather more inadequate than even a label has any need to be, at least carries a meaning.

Definitions of consciousness vary from school to school and are necessarily as incomplete as definitions of life. The only satisfactory definition of a man's consciousness is his life. And this, superficially regarded, does seem to exhibit a sort of stream-line. But his consciousness sits stiller than a tree. "The mind" may be, or may become, anything from a rag-bag to a madhouse. It may wobble continuously or may be more or less steadily focused. But its central core, luminous point (call it what you will, its names are legion), tho more or less continuously expanding from birth to maturity, remains stable, one with itself thruout life.

We all date our personal existence from our first conscious awareness of reality outside ourselves. And this awareness is direct and immediate, *preceding* instruction as to the nature of the realities by which we are surrounded. Instruction and experience can enrich and deepen but can never outdo or replace this first immediate awareness. It recurs, in different forms, thruout life.

Literature is a product of this stable human consciousness, enriched by experience and capable of deliberate, concentrated contemplation. Is not this consciousness the sole link between reader and writer? The writer's (and the reader's) brain may be "on fire," his imagination may construct this and that, but the contemplative center remains motionless. Does not the power and the charm of all literature, from the machine-made product to the "work of art," from the book which amuses or instructs to the one which remakes the world and ourselves (*why* do we recognize it?) reside in its ability to rouse and to concentrate the reader's contemplative consciousness?

The process may go forward in the form of a conducted tour, the author leading, visible and audible, all the time. Or the material to be contemplated may be thrown on the screen, the author out of sight and hearing; present, if we seek him, only in the attitude towards reality, inevitably revealed: subtly by his accent, obviously by his use of adjective, epithet, and metaphor. But whatever be the means by which the reader's collaboration is secured, a literary work, for reader and writer alike, remains essentially an adventure of the stable contemplative human consciousness.

. . . I have tried to answer your question. And if, to what I have already written, is added the fact of the survival and increase, in the writer, of wonder and of joy (many other strong emotions competing but never quite prevailing) I shall have responded also, in essentials, to your suggestion that I should supply biographical material.

RICHARDSON: *Foreword to Pilgrimage*

Although the translation of the impulse behind his youthful plan for a tremendous essay on *Les Forces humaines* makes for the population of his great cluster of novels with types rather than with individuals, the power of a sympathetic imagination, uniting him with each character in turn, gives to every portrait the quality of a faithful self-portrait, and his treatment of backgrounds, contemplated with an equally passionate interest and themselves, indeed, individual and unique, would alone qualify Balzac to be called the father of realism.

Less deeply concerned with the interplay of human forces, his first English follower portrays with complete fidelity the lives and adventures of inconspicuous people, and for a while, when in the English literary world it began its career as a useful label, realism was synonymous with Arnold Bennett.

But whereas both Balzac and Bennett, while representing, the one in regard to a relatively concrete and coherent social system, the other in regard to a society already showing signs of disintegration, the turning of the human spirit upon itself, may be called realists by nature and unawares, their immediate successors possess an articulate creed. They believe themselves to be substituting, for the telescopes of the writers of romance whose lenses they condemn as both rose-coloured and distorting, mirrors of plain glass.

By 1911, though not yet quite a direct supply of documentary material for the dossiers of the *cause cèlébre,* Man versus conditions impeached as the authors of his discontent, realist novels are largely explicit satire and protest, and every form of conventionalized human association is being arraigned by biographical and autobiographical novelists.

Since all these novelists happened to be men, the present writer, proposing at this moment to write a novel and looking round for a contemporary pattern, was faced with the choice between following one of her regiments and attempting to produce a feminine equivalent of the current masculine realism. Choosing the latter alternative, she presently set aside, at the bidding of a dissatisfaction that revealed its nature without supplying any suggestion as to the removal of its cause, a considerable mass of manuscript. Aware, as she wrote, of the gradual falling away of the preoccupations that for a while had dictated the briskly moving script, and of the substitution, for these inspiring preoccupations, of a stranger in the form of contemplated reality having for the first time in her experience its own say, and apparently justifying those who acclaim writing as the surest means of discovering the truth about one's own thoughts and beliefs, she had been at the same time increasingly tormented, not only by the failure, of this now so independently assertive reality, adequately to appear within the text, but by its revelation, whencesoever of a hundred faces, any one of which, the moment it was entrapped within the close mesh of direct statement, summoned its fellows to disqualify it.

In 1913, the opening pages of the attempted chronicle became the first chapter of *Pilgrimage,* written to the accompaniment of a sense of being upon a fresh pathway, an adventure so searching and, sometimes, so joyous as to produce a longing for participating not quite the same as a longing for publication, whose possibility, indeed, as the book grew, receded to vanishing point.

To a publisher, nevertheless, at the bidding of Mr. F. D. Beresford, the book was ultimately sent. By the time it returned, the second chapter was partly written and the condemned volume, put away and forgotten, would have remained in seclusion but for the persistence of the same kind friend, who acquired and sent it to Edward Garnett, then reading from Messrs. Duckworth. In 1915, the covering title being at the moment in use elsewhere, it was published as *Pointed Roofs*.

The lonely track, meanwhile, had turned out to be a populous highway. Amongst those who had simultaneously entered it, two figures stood out. One a woman mounted upon a magnificently caparisoned charger, the other a man walking, with eyes devoutly closed, weaving as he went a rich garment of new words wherewith to clothe the antique dark material of his engrossment.

News came from France of one Marcel Proust, said to be producing an unprecedentedly profound and opulent reconstruction of experience focused from within the mind of a single individual, and, since Proust's first volume had been published and several others written by 1913, the France of Balzac now appeared to have produced the earliest adventurer.

Finally, however, the role of pathfinder was declared to have been played by a venerable gentleman, a charmed and charming high priest of nearly all the orthodoxies, inhabiting a softly lit enclosure he mistook, until 1914, for the universe, and celebrated by evolving, for the accommodation of his vast tracts of urbane commentary, a prose style demanding, upon the first reading, a perfection of sustained concentration akin to that which brought it forth, and bestowing, again upon the first reading, the recreative delights peculiar to this form of spiritual exercise.

And, while, indeed, it is possible to claim for Henry James, keeping the reader incessantly watching the conflict of human forces through the eye of a single observer, rather than taking him, before the drama begins, upon a tour amongst the properties, or breaking in with descriptive introductions of the players as one by one they enter his enclosed resounding chamber where no plant grows and no mystery pours in from the unheeded stars, a far from inconsiderable technical influence, it was nevertheless not without a sense of relief that the present writer recently discovered, in *Wilhelm Meister,* the following manifesto:

In the novel, reflections and incidents should be featured; in drama, character and action. The novel must proceed slowly, and the thought-processes of the principal figure must, by one device or another, hold up the development of the whole. . . . The hero of the novel must be acted upon, or, at any rate, not himself the principal operator. . . . Grandison,

Clarissa, Pamela, the Vicar of Wakefield, and Tom Jones himself, ever
where they are not acted upon, are still retarding personalities and all the
incidents are, in a certain measure, modelled according to their thoughts

Phrases began to appear, formulae devised to meet the exigencies o
literary criticism. "The Stream of Consciousness" lyrically led the way
to be gladly welcomed by all who could persuade themselves of the
possibility of comparing consciousness to a stream. Its transatlantic
successors, "Interior Monologue" and "Slow-motion Photography,"
may each be granted a certain technical applicability leaving them, to
this extent, unhampered by the defects of their qualities.

Lives in plenty have been devoted to the critic's exacting art and a
lifetime might be spent in engrossed contemplation of the movement
of its continuous ballet. When the dancers tread living boards, the board
will sometimes be heard to groan. The present writer groans, gently and
resignedly, beneath the reiterated tap-tap accusing her of feminism, o
failure to perceive the value of the distinctively masculine intelligence
of pre-War sentimentality, of post-war Freudianity. But when her work
is danced upon for being unpunctuated and therefore unreadable, she i
moved to cry aloud. For here is truth.

Feminine prose, as Charles Dickens and James Joyce have delightfully
shown themselves to be aware, should properly be unpunctuated, moving
from point to point without formal obstructions. And the author o
Pilgrimage must confess to an early habit of ignoring, while writing, the
lesser of the stereotyped system of signs, and, further, when finally
sprinkling in what appeared to be necessary, to a small unconscious de
parture from current usage. While meeting approval, first from the friend
who discovered and pointed it out to her, then from an editor who wel
comed the article she wrote to elucidate and justify it, and recently, by
the inclusion of this article in a text-book for students of journalism and
its translation into French, the small innovation, in further complicating
the already otherwise sufficiently complicated task of the official
reader, helped to produce the chaos for which she is justly reproached

For the opportunity, afforded by the present publishers, of eliminating
this source of a reputation for creating avoidable difficulties, and o
assembling the scattered chapters of *Pilgrimage* in their proper relation
ship, the author desires here to express her gratitude and, further, to offe
to all those readers who have persisted in spite of every obstacle, a
heart-felt apology.

PROUST: *A Little Cake*

And so it was that, for a long time afterwards, when I lay awake at
night and revived old memories of Combray, I saw no more of it than
this sort of luminous panel, sharply defined against a vague and shadowy
background, like the panels which a Bengal fire or some electric sign
will illuminate and dissect from the front of a building the other parts of
which remain plunged in darkness: broad enough at its base, the little
parlour, the dining-room, the alluring shadows of the path along which
would come M. Swann, the unconscious author of my sufferings, the
hall through which I would journey to the first step of that staircase, so
hard to climb, which constituted, all by itself, the tapering "elevation"
of an irregular pyramid; and, at the summit, my bedroom, with the little
passage through whose glazed door Mamma would enter; in a word, seen
always at the same evening hour, isolated from all its possible surroundings, detached and solitary against its shadowy background, the bare
minimum of scenery necessary (like the setting one sees printed at the
head of an old play, for its performance in the provinces) to the drama of
my undressing, as though all Combray had consisted of but two floors
joined by a slender staircase, and as though there had been no time there
but seven o'clock at night. I must own that I could have assured any ques-
tioner that Combray did include other scenes and did exist at other hours
than these. But since the facts which I should then have recalled would
have been prompted only by an exercise of the will, by my intellectual
memory, and since the pictures which that kind of memory shews us of
the past preserve nothing of the past itself, I should never have had any
wish to ponder over this residue of Combray. To me it was in reality all
dead.

Permanently dead? Very possibly.

There is a large element of hazard in these matters, and a second
hazard, that of our own death, often prevents us from awaiting for any
length of time the favours of the first.

I feel that there is much to be said for the Celtic belief that the
souls of those whom we have lost are held captive in some inferior being,
in an animal, in a plant, in some inanimate object, and so effectively
lost to us until the day (which to many never comes) when we happen
to pass by the tree or to obtain possession of the object which forms
their prison. Then they start and tremble, they call us by our name,
and as soon as we have recognised their voice the spell is broken. We

have delivered them: they have overcome death and return to shar
our life.

And so it is with our own past. It is a labour in vain to attempt t
recapture it: all the efforts of our intellect must prove futile. The pas
is hidden somewhere outside the realm, beyond the reach of intellec
in some material object (in the sensation which that material object wi
give us) which we do not suspect. And as for that object, it depends o
chance whether we come upon it or not before we ourselves must di

Many years had elapsed during which nothing of Combray, save wha
was comprised in the theatre and the drama of my going to bed ther
had any existence for me, when one day in winter, as I came home, m
mother, seeing that I was cold, offered me some tea, a thing I did n
ordinarily take. I declined at first, and then, for no particular reasor
changed my mind. She sent out for one of those short, plump little cak
called "petites madeleines," which look as though they had been moulde
in the fluted scallop of a pilgrim's shell. And soon, mechanically, wear
after a dull day with the prospect of a depressing morrow, I raised to m
lips a spoonful of the tea in which I had soaked a morsel of the cake. N
sooner had the warm liquid, and the crumbs with it, touched my palat
than a shudder ran through my whole body, and I stopped, intent upo
the extraordinary changes that were taking place. An exquisite pleasur
had invaded my senses, but individual, detached, with no suggestion c
its origin. And at once the vicissitudes of life had become indifferer
to me, its disasters innocuous, its brevity illusory—this new sensatio
having had on me the effect which love has of filling me with a preciou
essence; or rather this essence was not in me, it was myself. I had cease
now to feel mediocre, accidental, mortal. Whence could it have con
to me, this all-powerful joy? I was conscious that it was connected wit
the taste of tea and cake, but that it infinitely transcended those savour
could not, indeed, be of the same nature as theirs. Whence did it come
What did it signify? How could I seize upon and define it?

I drink a second mouthful, in which I find nothing more than in th
first, a third, which gives me rather less than the second. It is time t
stop; the potion is losing its magic. It is plain that the object of my ques
the truth, lies not in the cup but in myself. The tea has called up in m
but does not itself understand, and can only repeat indefinitely with
gradual loss of strength, the same testimony; which I, too, cann
interpret, though I hope at least to be able to call upon the tea for
again and to find it there presently, intact and at my disposal, for m

inal enlightenment. I put down my cup and examine my own mind.
t is for it to discover the truth. But how? What an abyss of uncertainty
ɥhenever the mind feels that some part of it has strayed beyond its own
ᵇorders; when it, the seeker, is at once the dark region through which it
ᵌust go seeking, where all its equipment will avail it nothing. Seek?
ᵈore than that: create. It is face to face with something which does not
ᵒ far exist, to which it alone can give reality and substance, which it
lone can bring into the light of day.

And I begin to ask myself what it could have been, this unremembered
ᵗate which brought with it no logical proof of its existence, but only the
ᵉnse that it was happy, that it was a real state in whose presence other
ᵗates of consciousness melted and vanished. I decide to attempt to
ᵌake it reappear. I retrace my thoughts to the moment at which I drank
ᵗe first spoonful of tea. I find again the same state, illuminated by no
ᶦesh light. I compel my mind to make one further effort, to follow
ᵌd recapture once again the fleeting sensation. And that nothing may
ᵗterrupt it in its course I shut out every obstacle, every extrane-
ᵇus idea, I stop my ears and inhibit all attention to the sounds
ᵛhich come from the next room. And then feeling that my mind is
ᵍowing fatigued without having any success to report, I compel it for a
ᵺange to enjoy that distraction which I have just denied it, to think of
ᵗher things, to rest and refresh itself before the supreme attempt. And
ᵺen for the second time I clear an empty space in front of it. I place
ᵫ position before my mind's eye the still recent taste of that first mouth-
ᵾl, and I feel something start within me, something that leaves its resting-
ᵘace and attempts to rise, something that has been embedded like an
ᵫchor at a great depth; I do not know yet what it is, but I can feel it
ᵌounting slowly; I can measure the resistance, I can hear the echo of
ᵍeat spaces traversed.

Undoubtedly what is thus palpitating in the depths of my being must
ᵇe the image, the visual memory which, being linked to that taste, has
ᶦied to follow it into my conscious mind. But its struggles are too far off,
ᵒo much confused; scarcely can I perceive the colourless reflection in
ᵛhich are blended the uncapturable whirling medley of radiant hues,
ᵌd I cannot distinguish its form, cannot invite it, as the one possible
ᵗterpreter, to translate to me the evidence of its contemporary, its
ᵗseparable paramour, the taste of cake soaked in tea; cannot ask it to
ᵺform me what special circumstance is in question, of what period in my
ᵫst life.

Will it ultimately reach the clear surface of my consciousness, thi
memory, this old, dead moment which the magnetism of an identica
moment has travelled so far to importune, to disturb, to raise up out o
the very depths of my being? I cannot tell. Now that I feel nothing, i
has stopped, has perhaps gone down again into its darkness, from whic
who can say whether it will ever rise? Ten times over I must essay the task
must lean down over the abyss. And each time the natural laziness whic
deters us from every difficult enterprise, every work of importance, ha
urged me to leave the thing alone, to drink my tea and to think merel
of the worries of to-day and of my hopes for to-morrow, which le
themselves be pondered over without effort or distress of mind.

And suddenly the memory returns. The taste was that of the littl
crumb of madeleine which on Sunday mornings at Combray (because o
those mornings I did not go out before church-time), when I went to say
good day to her in her bedroom, my aunt Léonie used to give me, dippin
it first in her own cup of real or of lime-flower tea. The sight of the littl
madeleine had recalled nothing to my mind before I tasted it; perhap
because I had so often seen such things in the interval, without tastin
them, on the trays in pastry-cooks' windows, that their image had dissoci
ated itself from those Combray days to take its place among others mor
recent; perhaps because of those memories, so long abandoned and put ou
of mind, nothing now survived, everything was scattered; the forms o
things, including that of the little scallop-shell pastry, so richly sensua
under its severe, religious folds, were either obliterated or had been s
long dormant as to have lost the power of expansion which would hav
allowed them to resume their place in my consciousness. But when fror
a long-distant past nothing subsists, after the people are dead, after th
things are broken and scattered, still, alone, more fragile, but with mor
vitality, more unsubstantial, more persistent, more faithful, the smel
and taste of things remain poised a long time, like souls, ready to remin
us, waiting and hoping for their moment, amid the ruins of all the res
and bear unfaltering, in the tiny and almost impalpable drop of thei
essence, the vast structure of recollection.

And once I had recognized the taste of the crumb of madeleine soake
in her decoction of lime-flowers which my aunt used to give (althoug
I did not yet know and must long postpone the discovery of why thi
memory made me so happy), immediately the old grey house upon th
street, where her room was , rose up like the scenery of a theatre to attac
itself to the little pavilion, opening on to the garden, which had bee

uilt out behind it for my parents (the isolated panel which until that moment had been all that I could see); and with the house the town, from morning to night and in all weathers, the Square where I was sent before luncheon, the streets along which I used to run errands, the country roads we took when it was fine. And just as the Japanese amuse themselves by filling a porcelain bowl with water and steeping in it little crumbs of paper which until then are without character or form, but the moment they become wet, stretch themselves and bend, take on colour and dis-tinctive shape, become flowers or houses or people, permanent and recog-nisable, so in that moment all the flowers in our garden and in M. Swann's park, and the water-lilies on the Vivonne and the good folk of the village and their little dwellings and the parish church and the whole of Com-bray and of its surroundings, taking their proper shapes and growing solid, sprang into being, town and gardens alike, from my cup of tea.

PROUST: *Principle of Involuntary Memory*

Every day I set less store on intellect. Every day I see more clearly that if the writer is to repossess himself of some part of his impressions, get to something personal, that is, and to the only material of art, he must put it aside. What intellect restores to us under the name of the past, is not the past. In reality, as soon as each hour of one's life has died, it embodies itself in some material object as do the souls of the dead in certain folk-stories, and hides there. There it remains captive, captive for ever, unless we should happen on the object, recognise what lies within, call it by its name, and so set it free. Very likely we may never happen on the object (or the sensation, since we apprehend every object as sensation) that it hides in; and thus there are hours of our life that will never be resuscitated: for this object is so tiny, so lost in the world, and there is so little likelihood that we shall come across it.

Several summers of my life were spent in a house in the country. I thought of those summers from time to time, but they were not them-selves. They were dead, and in all probability they would always remain so. Their resurrection, like all these resurrections, hung on a mere chance. One snowy evening, not long ago, I came in half frozen, and had sat down in my room to read by lamplight, and as I could not get warm my old cook offered to make me a cup of tea, a thing I never drink. And as chance would have it, she brought me some slices of dry toast. I dipped the toast

in the cup of tea and as soon as I put it in my mouth and felt its softene
texture, all flavoured with tea, against my palate, something came ove
me—the smell of geraniums and orange-blossoms, a sensation of extra
ordinary radiance and happiness; I sat quite still, afraid that the slightes
movement might cut short this incomprehensible process which was takin
place in me, and concentrated on the bit of sopped toast which seeme
responsible for all these marvels; then suddenly the shaken partitions i
my memory gave way, and into my conscious mind there rushed th
summers I had spent in the aforesaid house in the country, with the
early mornings, and the succession, the ceaseless onset, of happy hou
in their train. And then I remembered. Every morning, when I wa
dressed, I went down to my grandfather in his bedroom, where he had ju
woken up and was drinking his tea. He soaked a rusk in it, and gave me th
rusk to eat. And when those summers were past and gone, the taste of
rusk soaked in tea was one of the shelters where the dead hours—dead a
far as intellect knew—hid themselves away, and where I should certainl
never have found them again if, on that winter's evening when I came i
frozen from the snow, my cook had not offered me the potion to which
by virtue of a magic past I knew nothing about, their resurrection wa
plighted.

But as soon as I had tasted the rusk, a whole garden, up till then vagu
and dim, mirrored itself, with its forgotten walks and all their urns wit
all their flowers, in the little cup of tea, like those Japanese flowers whic
do not re-open as flowers until one drops them into water. In the sam
way, many days in Venice, which intellect had not been able to give bac
were dead for me until last year, when crossing a courtyard I came to
stand-still among the glittering uneven paving-stones. The friends I wa
with feared I might have wrenched my ankle, but I waved to them to g
on, and that I would catch up with them. Something of greater importanc
engaged me, I still did not know what it was, but in the depth of my bein
I felt the flutter of a past that I did not recognise; it was just as I set foo
on a certain paving-stone that this feeling of perplexity came over m
I felt an invading happiness, I knew that I was going to be enriched by tha
purely personal thing, a past impression, a fragment of life in unsullie
preservation (something we can only know in preservation, for while w
live in it, it is not present in the memory, since other sensation
accompany and smother it) which asked only that it should be set fre
that it should come and augment my wealth of life and poetry. But
did not feel that I had the power to free it. No, intellect could have dor

nothing for me at such a moment! Trying to put myself back into the same state, I retraced my steps a little so that I might come afresh to those uneven shining paving-stones. It was the same sensation underfoot that I had felt on the smooth, slightly uneven pavement of the baptistry of Saint Mark's. The shadow which had lain that day on the canal where a gondola waited for me, and all the happiness, all the wealth of those hours—this recognised sensation brought them hurrying after it, and that very day came alive for me.

It is not merely that intellect can lend no hand in these resurrections; these past hours will only hide themselves away in objects where intellect has not tried to embody them. The objects which you have consciously tried to connect with certain hours of your life, these they can never take shelter in. What is more, if something else should resuscitate those hours, the objects called back with them will be stripped of their poetry.

I remember how once when I was travelling by train I strove to draw impressions from the passing landscape, I wrote about the little country churchyard while it was still passing before my eyes, I noted down the bright bars of sunlight on the trees, the wayside flowers like those in *Le Lys dans la vallée*. Since then, calling to mind those trees streaked with light and that little churchyard, I have often tried to conjure up that day, that day itself, I mean, not its pallid ghost. I could never manage it, and I had lost all hope of doing so, when at lunch, not long ago, I let my spoon fall on my plate. And then it made the same noise as the hammers of the linesmen did that day, tapping on the wheels when the train halted at stations. The burning blinded hour when that noise rang out instantly came back to me, and all that day in its poetry—except for the country churchyard, the trees streaked with light, and the Balzacian flowers, gained by deliberate observation and lost from the poetic resurrection.

Now and again, alas, we happen on the object, and the lost sensation thrills in us, but the time is too remote, we cannot give a name to the sensation, or call on it, and it does not come alive. As I was walking through a pantry the other day, a piece of green canvas plugging a broken window-pane made me stop dead and listen inwardly. A gleam of summer crossed my mind. Why? I tried to remember. I saw wasps in a shaft of sunlight, a smell of cherries came from the table—I could not remember. For a moment I was like those sleepers who wake up in the dark and do not know where they are, who ask their bodies to give them a bearing as to their whereabouts, not knowing what bed, what house, what part of the world, which year of their life they are in. For a moment I hesitated like this, groping round the square of green canvas to discover the time and the place where my scarcely awakened memory would find itself at home. All the sensations of my life, confused, or known, or forgotten, I was hesitating among all of them at once; this only lasted a minute. Soon I saw nothing more; my memory had fallen asleep again for ever.

How often during our walks have not my friends known me to halt like this at the turning-off of an avenue, or beside a clump of trees, and ask them to leave me alone for a minute. Nothing came of it. I shut my eyes and made my mind a blank to recruit fresh energies for my pursuit of the past, then suddenly re-opened them, all in an attempt to see those same trees as if for the first time, I could not tell where I had seen them. I could recognise their shapes and their grouping, their outline seemed to have been traced from some beloved drawing that trembled in my heart. But I could tell no more of them, and they themselves seemed by their artless passionate attitude to say how sorry they felt not to be able to make themselves clear, not to be able to tell me the secret that they well knew I could not unriddle. Ghosts of a dear past, so dear that my heart beat to bursting, they held out powerless arms to me, like the ghosts that Aeneas met in the underworld. Was it in the walks near the town of my happy childhood, was it only in that imagined country where, later on, I dreamed that Mamma was so ill, close to a lake and in a forest where it was light all night long, a dream country only but almost as real as the country of my childhood which was already no more than a dream? I should never know more of it. And I had to rejoin my friends who were waiting for me at the turn of the road, with the anguish of turning my back for ever on a past I might see no more, of disowning the dead who held out their powerless fond arms to me, and seemed to say, Recall us to life. And before I fell into step and into conversation with my friends, I again turned round for a moment to cast a less and less discerning glance towards the receding crooked line of mutely expressive trees still undulating before my eyes.

Compared with this past, this private essence of ourselves, the truths of intellect seem scarcely real at all. So, and above all from the time when our vitality begins to dwindle, it is to whatever may help us to re-cover this past that we resort, even though this should entail being very ill-understood by intellectual people who do not know that the artist lives to himself, that the absolute value of what he sees means nothing to him and that his scale of values is wholly subjective. A nauseating musical show put on by a provincial company, or a ball that people of taste would laugh at, may be far more quickening to his memories, far more relevant to the nature of what he dreams of and dwells on, than a brilliant performance at the Opera House or an ultra-elegant evening party in the Faubourg Saint-Germain. A railway time-table with its names of stations where he loves to fancy himself getting out of the train on an autumn evening when the trees are already stripped of their leaves and the bracing air is full of their rough scent, or a book that means nothing to people of discrimination but is full of names he has not heard since he was a child, can be worth incommensurably more to him than admirable philosophical treatises, so that people of discrimination will remark that for a man of talent he has very stupid likings.

Perhaps it will cause surprise that I, who make light of the intellect, should have devoted the following few pages precisely to some of those considerations that intellect, in contradiction to the platitudes that we hear said or read in books, suggests to us. At a time when my days may be numbered (and besides, are we not all in the same case?) it is perhaps very frivolous of me to undertake an intellectual exercise. But if the truths of intellect are less precious than those secrets of feeling that I was talking about just now, yet in one way they too have their interest. A writer is not only a poet; in our imperfect world where master-pieces are no more than the ship-wrecked flotsam of great minds, even the greatest writers of our century have cast a net of intellect round jewels of feeling which only here or there show through it. And if one believes that on this important point one hears the best among one's contemporaries making mistakes, there comes a time when one shakes off one's indolence and feels the need to speak out. Sainte-Beuve's method is not, at first sight, such an important affair. But perhaps in the course of these pages we may be led to realise that it touches on very important intellectual problems, and on what is perhaps for an artist the greatest of all; this relative inferiority of the intellect which I spoke of at the beginning. Yet all the same, it is intellect we must call on to establish this inferiority. Because if intellect does not deserve the crown of crowns, only intellect is able to award it. And if intellect only ranks second in the hierarchy of virtues, intellect alone is able to proclaim that the first place must be given to instinct.

4

CELEBRANTS AND ORACLES

MAY SINCLAIR, "The Novels of Dorothy Richardson," *The Egoist* 5 (April 1918): 57–59.

May Sinclair, a British novelist, was an early admirer of the work of Dorothy Richardson. In 1919 she published *Mary Olivier*, in which she used the technique she analyzes in this essay on the first three novels in Miss Richardson's *Pilgrimage.*

J. MIDDLETON MURRY, "The Break-up of the Novel," *Discoveries* (London: W. W. Collins Sons, 1924), pp. 131-52.

Murry, the husband of Katherine Mansfield, a writer sometimes associated with the stream-of-consciousness technique, was an important British editor and critic. *The Dictionary of National Biography* says of him, "When he was appointed editor of the *Athenaeum* in 1919, at the age of thirty, he was a key figure and perhaps then the leading figure of the post-war literary generation which included T. S. Eliot, Aldous Huxley, and D. H. Lawrence." In this essay, written in March 1922, he discusses what had by then clearly become a new departure in the novel.

ETHEL WALLACE HAWKINS, "The Stream-of-Consciousness Novel," *Atlantic Monthly* 138 (September 1926): 356–60.

Although the first major American experiment with the stream-of-consciousness technique was not to appear until 1929, with William Faulkner's *The Sound and the Fury*, Americans were very much aware of the new directions of the stream-of-consciousness novel, as this essay shows.

The reader may also wish to read Edouard Dujardin's *Le Monologue intérieur: Son apparition, ses origines, sa place dans l'oeuvre de James Joyce* (Paris: Albert Messein, 1931).

SINCLAIR: *Novels of Dorothy Richardson*

I do not know whether this article is or is not going to be a criticism, for so soon as I begin to think what I shall say I find myself criticizing criticism, wondering what is the matter with it and what, if anything, can be done to make it better, to make it alive. Only a live criticism can deal appropriately with a live art. And it seems to me that the first step towards life is to throw off the philosophic cant of the nineteenth century. I don't mean that there is no philosophy of Art, or that if there has been there is to be no more of it; I mean that it is absurd to go on talking about realism and idealism, or objective and subjective art, as if the philosophies were sticking where they stood in the eighties.

In those days the distinction between idealism and realism, between subjective and objective was important and precise. And so long as the ideas they stand for had importance and precision those words were lamps to the feet and lanterns to the path of the critic. Even after they had begun to lose precision and importance they still served him as useful labels for the bewildering phenomena of the arts.

But now they are beginning to give trouble; they obscure the issues. Mr. J. B. Beresford in his admirable introduction to *Pointed Roofs* confesses to having felt this trouble. When he read it in manuscript he decided that it "was realism, was objective." When he read it in typescript he thought: "This . . . is the most subjective thing I have ever read." It is evident that when first faced with the startling "newness" of Miss Richardson's method, and her form, the issues did seem a bit obscure to Mr. Beresford. It was as if up to one illuminating moment he had been obliged to think of methods and forms as definitely objective or definitely subjective. His illuminating moment came with the third reading, when *Pointed Roofs* was a printed book. The book itself gave him the clue to his own trouble, which is my trouble, the first hint that criticism up till now has been content to think in *clichés,* missing the new trend of the philosophies of the twentieth century. All that we know of reality at first hand is given to us through contacts in which those interesting distinctions are lost. Reality is thick and deep, too thick and too deep, and at the same time too fluid to be cut with any convenient carving-knife. The novelist who would be close to reality must confine himself to this knowledge at first hand. He must, as Mr. Beresford says, simply "plunge in." Mr. Beresford says that Miss Richardson is the first novelist who has plunged in. She has plunged so neatly and quietly that even admirers of her performance might remain unaware of what it is precisely that she has done. She has disappeared while they are still waiting for the splash. So that Mr. Beresford's introduction was needed.

When I first read *Pointed Roofs* and *Backwater* and *Honeycomb* I too thought, like Mr. Beresford, that Miss Richardson has been the first to plunge. But it seems to me rather that she has followed, independently perhaps unconsciously, a growing tendency to plunge. As far back as the eighties the de Goncourts plunged completely, finally, in *Soeur Philomène* *Germinie Lacerteux*, and *Les Frères Zemgann*. Marguerite Audoux plunged in the best passages of *Marie Claire*. The best of every good novelist's best work is a more or less sustained immersion. The more modern the novelist the longer his capacity to stay under. Miss Richardson has no plunged deeper than Mr. James Joyce in his *Portrait of the Artist as a Young Man*.

By imposing very strict limitations on herself she has brought her art her method, to a high pitch of perfection, so that her form seems to be newer than it perhaps is. She herself is unaware of the perfection of her method. She would probably deny that she has written with any deliberate method at all. She would say: "I only know there are certain things mustn't do if I was to do what I wanted." Obviously, she must not interfere; she must not analyse or comment or explain. Rather less obviously she must not tell a story or handle a situation or set a scene; she must avoid drama as she avoids narration. And there are some things she must not be. She must not be the wise, all-knowing author. She must be Miriam Henderson. She must not know or divine anything that Miriam does not know or divine; she must not see anything that Miriam does not see. She has taken Miriam's nature upon her. She is not concerned, in the way that other novelists are concerned with character. Of the persons who move through Miriam's world you know nothing but what Miriam knows. Miriam is mistaken, well, she and not Miss Richardson is mistaken. Miriam is an acute observer, but she is very far from seeing the whole of these people. They are presented to us in the same vivid but fragmentary way in which they appeared to Miriam, the fragmentary way in which people appear to most of us. Miss Richardson has only imposed on herself th conditions that life imposes on us all. And if you are going to quarrel with those conditions you will not find her novels satisfactory. But your satisfaction is not her concern. And I find it impossible to reduce to intelligible terms this satisfaction that I feel. To me these three novels show an art and method and form carried to punctilious perfection. Yet I have heard other novelists say that they have no art and no method and no form, and that it is this formlessness that annoys them. They say that they have no beginning and no middle and no end, and that to have form a novel must have an end, and a beginning and a middle. We have come to words that in more primitive times would have been blows on this subject. There is a certain plausibility in what they say, but it depends on what constitutes a beginning and a middle and an end. In this series there is no drama, no situation, no set scene. Nothing happens. It is just life going on and on. It is Miriam Henderson's stream of consciousness going on and on. And in neither is there any grossly discernible beginning or middle or end.

In identifying herself with this life, which is Miriam's stream of consciousness, Miss Richardson produces her effect of being the first, of getting closer to reality than any of our novelists who are trying so desperately to get close. No attitude or gesture of her own is allowed to come between her and her effect. Whatever her sources and her raw material, she is concerned and we ought to be concerned solely with the finished result, the work of art. It is to Miriam's almost painfully acute senses that we owe what in any other novelist would be called the "portraits" of Miriam's mother, of her sister Harriet, of the Corries and Joey Banks in *Honeycomb,* of the Miss Pernes and Julia Doyle, and the North London school-girls in *Backwater,* of Fräulein Pfaff and Mademoiselle, of the Martins and Emma Bergmann and Ulrica and "the Australian" in *Pointed Roofs.* The mere "word-painting" is masterly.

. . Miriam noticed only the hoarse, hacking laugh of the Australian. Her eyes flew up the table and fixed her as she sat laughing, her chair drawn back, her knees crossed—tea was drawing to an end. The detail of her terrifyingly stylish ruddy-brown frieze dress, with its Norfolk jacket bodice and its shiny leather belt, was hardly distinguishable from the dark background made by the folding doors. But the dreadful outline of her shoulders was visible, the squarish oval of her face shone out—the wide forehead from which the wiry black hair was combed to a high puff, the red eyes, black now, the long, straight nose, the wide, laughing mouth with the enormous teeth.

And so on all round the school tea-table. It looks easy enough to "do" until you try it. There are thirteen figures round that table, and each is drawn with the first few strokes, and so well that you see them all and never afterwards can you mistake or confuse them.

You look at the outer world through Miriam's senses, and it is as if you had never seen it so vividly before. Miriam in *Backwater* is on the top of a bus, driving from North London to Piccadilly:

On the left a tall grey church was coming towards them, spindling up into the sky. It sailed by, showing Miriam a circle of little stone pillars-built into its spire. Plumy trees streamed by, standing large and separate on moss-green grass railed from the roadway. Bright, white-faced houses with pillared porches shone through from behind them and blazed white above them against the blue sky. Wide side streets opened, showing high balconied houses. The side streets were feathered with trees and ended mistily.

Away ahead were edges of clean, bright masonry in profile, soft tufted heads of trees, bright green in the clear light. At the end of the vista the air was like pure saffron-tinted mother-of-pearl.

Or this "interior" from *Honeycomb:*

. . . the table like an island under the dome of the low-hanging rose-shaded lamp, the table-centre thickly embroidered with beetles' wings, the little dishes stuck about, sweets, curiously crusted brown almonds, sheeny grey-green olives; the misty beaded glass of the finger bowls—Venetian glass from the shop in Regent street—the four various wine glasses at each right hand, one on a high thin stem, curved and fluted like a shallow tulip, filled with hock; and floating in the warmth amongst all these things the strange, exciting, dry sweet fragrance coming from the mass of mimosa, a forest of little powdery blossoms, little stiff grey—the arms of railway signals at junctions—Japanese looking leaves—standing as if it were growing, in a shallow bowl under the rose-shaded lamp.

It is as if no other writers had ever used their senses so purely and with so intense a joy in their use.

This intensity is the effect of an extreme concentration on the thing seen or felt. Miss Richardson disdains every stroke that does not tell. Her novels are novels of an extraordinary compression and of an extenuation more extraordinary still. The moments of Miriam's consciousness pass one by one, or overlapping; moments tense with vibration, moments drawn out fine, almost to snapping-point. On one page Miss Richardson seems to be accounting for every minute of Miriam's time. On another she passes over events that might be considered decisive with the merest slur of reference. She is not concerned with the strict order of events in time. Chapter 3 of *Pointed Roofs* opens with an air of extreme decision and importance: "Miriam was practising on the piano in the larger of the two English bedrooms," as if something hung on her practising. But no, nothing hangs on it, and if you want to know on what day she is practising you have to read on and back again. It doesn't matter. It is Miriam's consciousness that is going backwards and forwards in time. The time it goes in is unimportant. On the hundredth page out of three hundred and twelve pages, Miriam has been exactly two weeks in Hanover. Nothing has happened but the infinitely little affairs of the school, the practising, the *vorspielen,* the English lesson, the *raccommodage,* the hair-washing. At the end of the book Fräulein Pfaff is on the station platform, gently propelling Miriam "up three steps into a compartment marked *Damen-Coupé.* It smelt of biscuits and wine." Miriam has been no more than six months in Hanover. We are not told and Miriam is not told, but we know, as Miriam knows, that she is going because Pastor Labmann has shown an interest in Miriam very disturbing to Fräulein Pfaff's interest in him. We are not invited to explore the tortuous mind of the pious, sentimental, secretly hysterical Fräulein; but we know, as Miriam knows, that before she can bring herself to part with her English governess she must persuade herself that it is Miriam and not Mademoiselle who is dismissed because she is an unwholesome influence.

In this small world where nothing happens "that dreadful talk with Gertrude," and Fräulein's quarrel with the servant Anna, the sound of her laugh and her scream, "Ja, Sie Können Ihre paar Groschen haben! Ihre paar Groschen!" and Miriam's vision of Mademoiselle's unwholesomeness, stand out as significant and terrifying; they *are* terrifying, they *are* significant; through them we know Gertrude, we know Fräulein Pfaff, we know Mademoiselle as Miriam knows them, under their disguises.

At the end of the third volume, *Honeycomb,* there is, apparently, a break with the design. Something does happen. Something tragic and terrible. We are not told what it is; we know, as Miriam knows, only by inference. Miriam is sleeping in her mother's room.

Five o'clock. Three more hours before the day began. The other bed was still. "It's going to be a magnificent day," she murmured, pretending to stretch and yawn again. A sigh reached her. The stillness went on and she lay for an hour tense and listening. Someone else must know. . . . At the end of the hour a descending darkness took her suddenly. She woke from it to the sound of violent language, furniture being roughly moved, a swift, angry splashing of water . . . something breaking out, breaking through the confinements of this little furniture-filled room . . . the best gentlest thing she knew openly despairing at last.

Here Miss Richardson "gets" you as she gets you all the time—she never misses once—by her devout adhesion to her method, by the sheer depth of her plunge. For this and this alone is the way things happen. What we used to call the "objective" method is a method of after-thought, of spectacular reflection. What has happened has happened in Miriam's bedroom, if you like; but only by reflection. The first-hand, intimate, and intense reality of the happening is in Miriam's mind, and by presenting it thus and not otherwise Miss Richardson seizes reality alive. The intense rapidity of the seizure defies you to distinguish between what is objective and what is subjective either in the reality presented or the art that presents.

Nothing happens. In Miriam Henderson's life there is, apparently, nothing to justify living. Everything she ever wanted was either withheld or taken from her. She is reduced to the barest minimum on which it is possible to support the life of the senses and the emotions at all. And yet Miriam is happy. Her inexhaustible passion for life is fed. Nothing happens, and yet everything that really matters is happening; you are held breathless with the anticipation of its happening. What really matters is a state of mind, the interest or the ecstasy with which we close with life. It can't be explained. To quote Mr. Beresford again: "explanation in this connexion would seem to imply knowledge that only the mystics can faintly realize." But Miss Richardson's is a mysticism apart. It is compatible with, it even encourages such dialogue as this:

"Tea," smiled Eve serenely.
"All right, I'm coming, damn you, aren't I?"
"Oh, Mimmy!"
"Well, damn *me*, then. Somebody in the house must swear. I say, Eve!"
"What?"
"Nothing, only I *say*."
"Um."

It is not wholly destroyed when Miriam eats bread and butter—thus:

> When she began at the hard thick edge there always seemed to be tender places on her gums, her three hollow teeth were uneasy and she had to get through worrying thoughts about them—they would get worse as the years went by, and the little places in the front would grow big and painful and disfiguring. After the first few mouthfuls of solid bread a sort of padding seemed to take place and she could go on forgetful.

This kind of thing annoys Kensington. I do not say that it really matters, but that it is compatible with what really matters. Because of such passages it is a pity that Miss Richardson could not use the original title of her series: "Pilgrimage," for it shows what she is really after. Each book marks a stage in Miriam's pilgrimage. We get the first hint of where she is going to in the opening of the tenth chapter of *Pointed Roofs:* "Into all the gatherings at Waldstrasse the outside world came like a presence. It removed the sense of pressure, of being confronted and challenged. Everything that was said seemed to be incidental to it, like remarks dropped in a low tone between individuals at a great conference." In *Backwater* the author's intention becomes still clearer. In *Honeycomb* it is transparently clear:

> Her room was a great square of happy light . . . happy, happy. She gathered up all the sadness she had ever known and flung it from her. All the dark things of the past flashed with a strange beauty as she flung them out. The light had been there all the time; but she had known it only at moments. Now she knew what she wanted. Bright mornings, beautiful bright rooms, a wilderness of beauty all round her all the time— at any cost.

And yet not that:

> Something that was not touched, that sang far away down inside the gloom, that cared nothing for the creditors and could get away down and down into the twilight far away from the everlasting accusations of humanity. . . . Deeper down was something cool and fresh—endless—an endless garden. In happiness it came up and made everything in the world into a garden. Sorrow blotted it out; but it was always there, waiting and looking on. It had looked on in Germany and had loved the music and the words and the happiness of the German girls, and at Banbury Park, giving her no peace until she got away.
> And now it had come to the surface and was with her all the time.

There are two essays of Rémy de Gourmont in *Promenades littéraires,* one on "L'Originalité de Maeterlinck," one on "La Leçon de Saint Antoine." Certain passages might have been written concerning the art of Dorothy Richardson.

Si la vie en soi est un bienfait, et il faut l'accepter comme telle, ou la nier, la fait même de vivre le contient tout entier, et les grands mouvements de la sensibilité, loin de l'enricher, l'appauvrissent au contraire, en concentrant sur quelques partis de nous-mêmes, envahies au hasard par la destinée, l'effort d'attention qui serait plus uniformement reparti sur l'ensemble de notre conscience vitale. De ce point de vue une vie où il semblerait ne rien se passer que d'elementaire et quotidien serait mieux remplié qu'une autre vie riche en apparence d'incidents et d'aventures.... Il y a peut-être un sentiment nouveau a créer, celui de l'amour de la vie pour la vie elle-même, abstraction faite des grandes joies qu'elle ne donne pas à tous, et qu'elle ne donne peut-être à personne.... Notre paradis, c'est la journée qui passe, la minute qui s'envole, le moment qui n'est déjà plus. Telle est la leçon de Saint Antoine.

MURRY: *Break-up of the Novel*

In the years 1913-14 three significant books, calling themselves novels, made an unobtrusive and independent appearance. In France, Marcel Proust published *Du Côté de chez Swann,* in America, the Irishman, James Joyce, published *A Portrait of the Artist as a Young Man,* in England, Dorothy Richardson published *Pointed Roofs.* These books had points of outward resemblance. Each was in itself incomplete, a foretaste of sequels to come. Each was autobiographical and, within the necessary limits of individuality, autobiographical in the same new and peculiar fashion. They were attempts to record immediately the growth of a consciousness. Immediately; without any effort at mediation by means of an interposed plot or story. All three authors were trying to present the content of their consciousness as it was before it had been reshaped in obedience to the demands of practical life; they were exploring the strange limbo where experiences once conscious fade into unconsciousness. The method of Marcel Proust was the most subtle in that he established as the starting point of his book the level of consciousness from which the exploration actually began. He presented the process as well as the results of his exploration of the unconscious memory. In the first pages of his book he described how he concentrated upon a vaguely remembered feeling of past malaise, which he experienced in waking at night and trying to establish the identity of his room. It was a particular form of the familiar feeling: "I have felt this, been here, seen this, somewhere, somehow, before." We might almost say that Marcel Proust gives us an account of his technique in penetrating such a sensation and gradually dragging up to the surface of full consciousness, forgotten but decisive experiences.

This singularity of Marcel Proust's approach—implied in the general title, *À la recherche du temps perdu*—involving as it does a perpetual reference to the present adult consciousness of the author, is important. It gives a peculiarly French sense of control to his whole endeavour, and a valuable logical (or psychological) completeness to his work, in which is unfolded the process by which first a distinct and finally a supreme importance came to be attached to these presentiments of past experience. They are the precious moments of existence; they hold the secret of life. The growth of this conviction is the vital principle of Marcel Proust's book. The conviction becomes more immediate, the sense of obligation to devote himself to penetrating these moments more urgent, so that even though the work is still unfinished, we can already see that the end will come when this necessity becomes fully conscious and in-eluctable—an end strictly and necessarily identical with the beginning. *À la recherche du temps perdu* is at once a philosophical justification of its own existence and the history of its own creation.

That internal completeness is peculiar to Marcel Proust, and it gives him the position of conscious philosopher of a literary impulse which arose, quite independently, in two other minds at the same moment. Simply because it is the most conscious, Marcel Proust's effort subsumes those of James Joyce and Dorothy Richardson, though it is not for that reason more important than they. But common to them all is an insistence upon the immediate consciousness as reality. In Miss Richardson this insistence is probably instinctive and irrational; it has a distinctively feminine tinge. In James Joyce it is certainly deliberate, but less deliberate than in Marcel Proust. But the differences in conscious intention are un-important compared with the similarity of the impulse.

To discover the origin of the impulse we should have to consider the history of the human consciousness, in its double form of sensibility and intelligence, from Rousseau through the nineteenth century. There we find the instinctive individualism of the artistic sensibility more and more exasperated by the sense that society in its new demoplutocratic form had neither room nor respect for such an unprofitable activity of the human spirit as art. This increase of instinctive individualism received a rational reinforcement from the advance of science. The anthropocentric conception of the universe was finally abandoned, and an indifferent universe lent its weight to a hostile society in thrusting back the individual upon himself.

The extreme and deliberate subjectivism of the latest developments of the novel is the culmination of Rousseauism. Rousseau's social indifference permitted him to proclaim the intoxicating but misleading gospel that all men are spiritually equal, and the social consequences of that doctrine have made his descendants outlaws. They have accepted their destiny with a certain bravado, and have come to believe that social isolation is an eternal condition of artistic eminence. The conception of the artist as a superman is now more than a century old. The examples of Chateaubriand, Byron, Hugo, Baudelaire, Nietzsche, Dostoevsky, have given it the force of tradition, even of an absolute law. And science, by its necessary insistence on a fundamental materialism, has given the law a double sanction. It is not for us to lament over this evolution; at most we may have to consider whether a reaction against it is desirable, or possible, or probable. The important thing is to know where we are.

This movement towards artistic subjectivism has affected all the arts; but it is most obvious in prose fiction. The aim of the characteristic modern novelist—we are speaking only of those who consider the novel as a medium of expression which can satisfy the highest demands of the soul—is the presentation of his immediate consciousness. This alone is true, he believes; this alone is valuable, or at any rate, this alone has the chance of being of some permanent value. But the driving impulse is the demand for truth. A complete and fearless exploration of the self reduces the chance of self-deception to a minimum. To a generation before all things fearful of self-delusion, the persuasion is of vital importance. And is he not merely carrying to its logical outcome the practice of all the great novelists of the past? They endure in so far as they have rendered their own consciousness of life. Not the stories they told but the comprehensive attitude to life embodied in their stories makes them important to us to-day. Then why not abolish the mechanism of the story completely, if the end to which it is a means can be achieved without it? And there is more than this. A story seems necessarily to involve a falsification, a distortion of the reality. Life does not shape itself into stories; much less does an individual and unique consciousness lend itself to complete expression by means of an invented plot. Let us do away with this illusory objectivity, this imposition of completeness and order upon the incomplete and chaotic. All that we can know is our own experience, and the closer we keep to the immediate quality of that experience, the nearer shall we be to truth.

Such are the arguments, conscious or unconscious, upon which the subjective movement in modern fiction depends. They are not final, but they are at least persuasive; and they are serious enough to show that the tendency which they support is more than a puerile esotericism. They remove all cause for wonder that many of the most gifted writers of the present generation have embraced it.

Nevertheless, the desire of the creative writer for objectivity cannot always be so easily suppressed. We have to take count of another movement, which may be described as an attempt, again no doubt not wholly conscious, to reconcile subjectivism with objectivity. To give it a label we may call it the Tchekhov tendency, although in fact it seems to have originated with Baudelaire's *Prose Poems*. But Baudelaire had no influence upon Tchekhov, the direction of whose genius was finally determined, I believe, by the reading of Tolstoy's *Ivan Ilyitch*. Like the subjectivists, Tchekhov was obsessed by a passion for truth; like them, he believed that the only reality was the individual consciousness; like them, he had conceived a deep mistrust of the machine of story. But in a higher degree than they, he possessed the purely creative genius of the writer, which is an instinct for objectivity and concreteness. He reconciled the two conflicting impulses in an individual creation. The short story of Tchekhov was an innovation in literature. The immediate consciousness remains the criterion, and the method is based on a selection of those glimpses of the reality which in themselves possess a peculiar vividness, and by virtue of this vividness appear to have a peculiar significance. Baudelaire, who had practised the method with brilliant success, though on a simpler scale, in some of his *Prose Poems,* defined the principle in words which are worth repeating. "Dans certains états de l'âme presque surnaturels," he said, "la profondeur de la vie toute entière se revèle dans le spectacle, si ordinaire qu'il soit, qu'on a sous les yeux. Il en devient le symbole." This certainty that a fragment of experience is symbolic of the whole is subjective and immediate. The artist can attempt to present it without any misgivings about self-delusion or distortion. It was so; therefore, it is true. Presented, the episode is objective, but its validity arises from an immediate intuition. To present such episodes with a minimum of rearrangement, as far as possible to eliminate the mechanism of invented story, was Tchekhov's aim. This is not to suggest that Tchekhov invented nothing; but his constant effort was to reduce the part of invention. He strove rather to link moments of perception, than to expand the perception by invention. And certainly the impressive originality of his work lay in the closeness of his fidelity to what we feel was his immediate experience.

It was impossible for Tchekhov, therefore, to write anything which could be reasonably given the name of a novel. Not, as some have said, because his constructive power was defective, but simply because the effort would have involved too wide a departure from the vivid moments of his own consciousness. He would have seemed to himself like the constructor of a metaphysical system, who leaves the solid ground of truth for cloudland. His feet once lifted from the firm earth, the very motive for flight would have failed him. What was the good of yet another attempt to impose finality upon the incessant?

But the method persists in modern fiction as the internal antithesis to complete subjectivism. The most finished modern example is to be found in the short stories of Katherine Mansfield. The finest stories in *Bliss* and the *Garden Party* adhere closely to the Tchekhov formula. But to speak of a formula is misleading. It is quite impossible to imitate, almost impossible to be influenced by a method so completely intuitive as Tchekhov's. It is simply that Katherine Mansfield is a similar phenomenon: her work is of the same kind as Tchekhov's, and precisely because it is of the same kind it is utterly different from his.

The two significant methods in the most modern fiction are, on the one hand, the presentation of a consciousness, on the other, the presentation of the vivid moments of a consciousness. Both are essentially subjective. They differ, however, in this important particular that, whereas the subjectivist novelists seem to be chiefly moved by a desire to express the truth alone, the story-writers aim at an *art* which is compatible with the truth. The most obvious consequence is that the second are much more easily comprehensible than the first, because they speak a universal language. A writer who presents an object perceived, interests us immediately, because there is common ground between his perceptions and our own. It is also easier for us to feel the individual quality of such a writer's consciousness than it is to disentangle it from the work of a writer who is busy in insisting upon the nature of his consciousness. In a short story by Tchekhov or Katherine Mansfield it is as though an intense beam of peculiar light were cast upon a fragment of reality. By watching the objects revealed by it, we can tell the colour of the light far more easily than we could if the colour were described to us: above all, because we are made sensible of the light at the moment when it is, or is felt by the writer, to be more illuminating than the ordinary light: "dans certains états de l'âme presque *surnaturels.*"

On the other hand, an extreme subjectivism, without the control of this intuitive selection, tends to become incomprehensible. A consciousness is a flux, it needs to be crystallised about some foreign object to have an intelligible shape. Marcel Proust's historical and philosophical preoccupations supply such a thread; but even he can be excessively tedious when his grasp on the external world is slackened. Miss Richardson can be as tiring as a twenty-four-hour cinematograph without interval or plot. And in *Ulysses,* James Joyce at times carries his effort of analysis to such lengths as to become as difficult as a message in code of which half the key has been lost. The process of consciousness has, indeed, a fatal fascination for him, and he perceptibly diminishes the significance of two such splendidly conceived (or observed) characters as Leopold and Marion Bloom by his inability to stop recording their processes of mind. Nevertheless, we must freely admit that *Ulysses* is a magnificent attempt by an extreme subjectivist to overcome the formlessness into which the method must so easily degenerate. The narrative, more or less remotely based upon the *Odyssey,* is enclosed within the limits of a day in Dublin twenty years ago. All the characters who come into contact with the hero's consciousness have a place in it, and the minds of two of them are submitted to the same exhaustive analysis as his own. But in spite of this considerable degree of objectivity, a complete and satisfying clarity is seldom attained. The objective is chiefly an excuse for another plunge into subjectivity, and we become weary of the effort to follow the processes of three different minds. For us they are exhausted long before Mr. Joyce has done with them. We long to escape from this incessant web of consciousness in which we are everywhere entangled, and to be allowed to trust to the revelation of the object. But we are forbidden. Either the consciousness of Bloom-Ulysses, or of Marion-Penelope, or of Mr. Joyce in his avatar as Stephen Dedalus-Telemachus, or in his apotheosis as the demiurge of the book itself, is ever before us to mist and complicate the thing we desire to see. Mr. Joyce is determined to give us everything, by devious and supersubtle ways: a day of human existence, with all its heritage of the past, its dreams of the future, shall be completely explored.

Ulysses is a work of genius; but in spite of its objective moments, it is also a *reductio ad absurdum* of subjectivism. It is the triumph of the desire to discover the truth over the desire to communicate that which is felt as truth. This desire to communicate is, so far as we can see, essential to literature, though not to genius; nor is it by any means necessary that a perceived truth should be communicated. But literature is, almost by definition, a communication of intuitions; and they can only be communicated in terms of a generally perceived reality. It is as though the external world were a common language which the writer speaks with new inflections and accents, giving new life to the old, and revealing a hidden significance in the familiar. The writer's duty is to make the approach to his intuitions and sentiments as simple as possible, and he does this by shaping the common reality in accordance with them, so that the reality becomes the symbol of his profoundest certainties.

In this process, Mr. Joyce is only casually interested. Rather than sacrifice one atom of his truth of detail, he is arcane and incomprehensible; and it is impossible not to feel he enjoys his own mysteriousness. . . .

Therefore we may speak, without rhetoric, of the break-up of the novel. We do not have to deplore the dissolution. Obviously we are in a period of transition, in which new elements are being gathered together for a more perfect artistic realisation in the future. New standards of truth, new standards of brilliance and directness in presentation are being introduced into fiction. When they have been absorbed, the art of the novel will obey its own internal law as an art of literature, and evolve towards a new combination of lucidity and comprehensiveness. At present the comprehensiveness is massed on one side and the lucidity upon the other of the small band of important writers of modern fiction. No single writer has been big enough to make the creative synthesis, so that the only possible synthesis at this moment is the critical one. But we do not doubt that the creative synthesis will be made. . . .

HAWKINS: *Stream-of-Consciousness Novel*

In order to enjoy the modern psychological novel, one need not be a student of modern psychology, but decidedly one must be of a certain type of mind. Between the acts, at an early performance of Werfel's *Goat Song* in New York, a male voice in the audience was heard to say plaintively, "You can't have *fun* at a show like this." One cannot have fun floating down the stream of consciousness if one feels that analysis and introspection verge on the morbid; that life, to be a fit subject for fiction, must "compose" properly, with a decent regard for values; that no one is living vividly who is not living dramatically; that such matters as the cessation of a toothache, or a sudden darkening of the atmosphere, or the surprise of a perfectly new expression on a face well known, have nothing to do with the soul on its pilgrimage. Readers of this type can have little patience with those who believe that the stream-of-consciousness method doubles and quadruples the possibility of drawing the life of the spirit; still less with those of the left wing, who believe that the psychological fiction of an earlier day did hardly more than draw the door of human consciousness ajar and peep tentatively within.

Among the English who have adopted this Continentally born, Continentally nurtured method, half analytical, half lyrical, three brilliant women writers—Dorothy Richardson, English pioneer in stream-of-consciousness fiction, Katherine Mansfield, and Virginia Woolf—are interesting for their individuality in likeness. They share the slightly grim spirit characteristic of the school, shot through with the keen pity, also characteristic, only to be found in the nature wholly pure of sentimentalism; they share, too, the passion for beauty, and the sense of the enormous part played by sunshine—not in the Pollyanna but in the literal sense—in any impressionable human consciousness. But each draws in her separate star.

Surely no reader whose acquaintance with the stream of consciousness in English fiction was made through Dorothy Richardson will forget "the cool silver shock of the plunge." The wonderfully limpid quality in her work, as of clear water, clear sunshine, is felt as instantaneously as its newness. This is particularly true of the earlier novels in the long series called *Pilgrimage,* for in the later volumes, with their supersubtlety and their tight-packed thought, there often is some loss of this cool, limpid clearness. In its enormous mass of detail, *Pilgrimage* is like Proust's *A la recherche du temps perdu;* in its single focus, unlike. For throughout the seven volumes, of which the latest brings Miriam Henderson not quite to her thirtieth year, every episode, whether she is actor or onlooker, is presented through her consciousness, and every abstract reflection, whether on the incidents narrated or on life itself, is made through the medium of her thought. The conception of Miriam's character, no less than the rendering of her experience, is typical of stream-of-consciousness fiction. She is no idealized heroine, but a humorous, independent girl, impressionable and analytical in the highest degree; "socially incompatible," incapable of light give-and-take, half envious and half contemptuous of it in others; with a somewhat masculine mentality and a very feminine outfit of delights and repulsions. Her only claim to remarkableness lies in her imperishable sense of the wonder of life and her imperishable delight in living. This vitality and resiliency of spirit is shown, with fine art, as altering in quality with the passing of years; but it is not more strongly felt in the young Miriam's rapture at the ball, in *Backwater,* than in the matured Miriam's power to suck savor from life, in *The Trap.* "Life flowed in a new way. Many of the old shadows were gone; apprehensions about the future had disappeared. Side by side with the weariness, with nothing to explain the confidence, was the apprehension of joy." "I am a greedy butterfly flitting in sunlight," Miriam reflects. "Enviable, despicable. But approval of my way of being speaks in me, a secret voice that knows no tribunals."

Whether the reader's prepossessions cause him to see the fifteen hundred or more pages of *Pilgrimage* as a wealth or as a welter of psychological chronicle, it is probable that he will not dispute the wit and the beauty in it, and certain that he will not dispute the reality. The young ecstasy of Miriam and her sisters in their preparations for the ball, in *Backwater;* Miriam's anguished vigilance over her mother's insomnia, and blackness of horror and despair at her mother's death, in *Honeycomb;* the complexity of Miriam's feelings in the masterly restaurant scene in *Deadlock,* when her dawning passion for the young Russian, Michael Shatov, fights with her recoil at his strange and terrible way of absorbing his tea; her discomfort, in *Revolving Lights,* as the guest of Alma, whose notion of the proper way to heal a hurt mind is to minister to it with infinite chirpings and gay little rushes—the art with which these states of consciousness and innumerable others are rendered makes them strike with a ringing note on the sense of recognition.

The conversations in the several volumes faithfully echo the psychology. Just as the current of thought and feeling is shown, in the manner grown increasingly familiar in English fiction of the past decade, as a drifting, easily deflected thing that makes the mental processes of Maggie Tulliver or Eustacia Vye in their moments of overmastering emotion seem as orderly as a French thesis, so the talk has the inconsecutive, ejaculatory quality less often encountered in novels of an earlier day than in real life. The gabble of Miriam's pupils, the gay nonsense of her sister Harriett, the maddening preciosity of Miss Holland, the half affectionate, half-elusive banter of "Hypo," the difficult, careful English of Michael Shatov, the bewildering sequences of Mrs. Corrie, are only a few of countless conversational styles, each extraordinarily consistent and natural.

In *Pilgrimage* the stream of consciousness is made a clear medium for memorably telling phrases, for wise bits of philosophy, and for flashes of beauty. Any volume read singly has much the same inconclusiveness that would be felt if a chance segment of one's own life were considered separately; the composite effect is of significance and unity, and leaves that rare impression of "a soul entirely known."

What the late Katherine Mansfield might have done with the stream-of-consciousness method in the novel one can only guess from the effectiveness with which she used it in the short story. The short story form naturally limits the scope of this method, but it proves its power to drive in emotion with one swift stroke, or—to change the metaphor—to reveal the recesses of a spirit by a flash. This is excellently shown in L. Borgese's *La Talpa,* in which a smug and stupid man is roused uncomfortably to his first abstract speculation by the long, shrill despairing squeal of a mole that the clumsiness of his investigating boot is killing—a squeal obviously addressed to some inattentive deity; or in *Fox-Trot,* that light laughing tragedy by the same author, in which the head of a family, prancing elated to the strains of *Si! non abbiamo banani!* raucously shouted by his new phonograph, sees suddenly in the eyes of his children and his servants that he is making a fool of himself—that middle age has treacherously crept up and taken him. So in Katherine Mansfield's work. It is hard to imagine the beautiful vitality and the bitterness of the story called "Bliss" achieved in any other way; or the light tenderness of "Her First Ball"; or the pathos of "Miss Brill," the sketch of the lonely little old spinster who pretends to herself that her life is not pinched and empty, but rich in entertainment, almost indeed a game that she and a friendly world are playing together—a gallant pretense, smashed beyond mending one day by a comment and a laugh overheard. Least of all does it seem as if any other method could have produced "The Garden Party," that masterpiece of heady sunshine and sudden dark shadow.

In conveying the sense of beauty, and the sense of the pitifulness in human life, both so characteristic of stream-of-consciousness fiction, Katherine Mansfield excelled. It is customary to compare her with Chekhov, and certainly she had much of his power to take possession of the reader's sympathy without asking for it. No one ever barred the door more firmly against sentimentality; and the result is her mastery of pathos. The reader's tears do not drizzle voluptuously upon her pages, but his heart contracts with true pity. But there was also "a deal of Ariel" in Katherine Mansfield. There was something spiritlike in her power to conjure up beauty—its exquisiteness and fugitiveness. The flash of a blue dragon fly in the sunshine is like her touch upon beauty. The most characteristic quality, however, of her use of the stream-of-consciousness method is the feeling she conveys through it of the essential isolation of every highly organized spirit.

The evolution—or, more accurately, the gradual intensification—of this method may best be traced in the three novels of Virginia Woolf— *The Voyage Out, Jacob's Room,* and *Mrs. Dalloway. The Voyage Out* is episodic, and done from a dozen points of view. Like those two beautiful tissues of Katherine Mansfield's, "At the Bay" and "Prelude," it presents not a plot but a pattern. It is true that there is a central figure, Rachel Vinrace; but the reader watches with equal interest the weaving in of the thread of Rachel's experience, of the dash of bright color that is the transit of the Dalloways, or of the sombre involutions that are the tormented introspections and indecisions of Hirst. Rachel goes on a voyage; wakens, under the influence of one man, from childish unawareness to the sense of a new heaven and a new earth, astounding and perturbing; falls in love, slowly, painfully, and entirely, with another man; and embarks on that other voyage out, beyond the horizon of life. This is the story. As for the characters, the dozen or more varied types, they are drawn with subtlety and truth; they leave, however, after the book has been read, no clear objective impression—rather they take on, for all their traits of reality, a certain dreamlike quality. This is because the reader has looked, in the main, not at them but through them. The incidents of the voyage and of the stay at Santa Marina he has been made to feel with the response now of this character, now of that. This method gives a fragmentary but not a scattered effect, and conveys sensation and emotion with sharpness and immediacy. For example, the suffocated, aching restlessness of passion undeclared and not quite certain of itself, and the suspense, the monotony, the exasperation, the numbness, and the anguish of watching the slow illness and the death of someone loved, close with a pressure almost physical on the reader's heart.

Jacob's Room has still less continuity. This novel is not strictly a narrative. Pictures flash and are gone, varying moods flash and are gone, and out of it all emerges the personality of the young Englishman, Jacob

Flanders—whole-hearted, faulty, lovable, above all so splendidly young and arrogant that at the end it is not easy to believe him dead. Jacob's psychological history begins with his entrance into the novel as a strong little boy playing by himself on the Cornish shore, suddenly breaking into sobs as a panic sense of loneliness sweeps over him, suddenly absorbed and comforted by his rich discovery of a sheep's skull among the seaweed. His last appearance is thoroughly characteristic of Mrs. Woolf's method: the reader sees him walking through London streets before his enlistment, recognized in Piccadilly, but too late for speech, by a man who had taught him and been fond of him when he was a child; recognized, from the motor that whirls her past to the opera house, by a girl who loves him and will not see him again. Equally characteristic, in its swift effectiveness and in its carrying out of the pattern conception of life, is the way in which the great impersonal fact of the war is made to cut across the small fact of Jacob's individual existence.

"Jacob," wrote Mrs. Flanders . . . "is hard at work after his delightful journey."

"The Kaiser," the far-away voice remarked in Whitehall, "received me in audience."

The pattern idea of life is again emphasized in the scene at the opera, where the first measures of the overture set each listener afloat on his own current of memories or anticipations; in the constantly shifting scene of Mrs. Durrant's party, with its perfect rendering of the interruptedness, thwartedness, and gigantic futility of social contacts in a crush; in the fireside scene, after tea, which shows Jacob's mother writing him the tiny news of her quiet life, while her heart is crying out, in the manner of the hearts of "mothers down at Scarborough," to write instead the things that are never written to sons in London: "Don't go with bad women, do be a good boy; wear your thick shirts; and come back, come back, come back to me." But what most distinguishes this novel is the richer flowering of beauty. For the style, in spite of flagrantly faulty sentence structure here and there, has very rare beauty; and the imagery seems not to reproduce beauty in skillful words but rather to call it actually into the presence of the reader. Surely sea and sun and wind have never flashed and breathed more livingly from the prose page than in the marvelous passage that shows Jacob and his friend Timothy Durrant rounding Land's End in their sailboat.

Mrs. Dalloway, the history of one day in the life of a woman, is stream of consciousness undiluted, and pure pattern. Through it run a primary and a secondary figure, sometimes drawing near, never intersecting, sometimes swerving far apart, always held in relation, as by a woven strip of gold, by the striking of Big Ben through the hours of the day. The primary figure is the heart of Clarissa Dalloway, who loves life with passion, whose only creed is that "one must pay back from the secret deposit of exquisite moments"; the secondary figure is the heart of poor young Septimus Smith, victim of deferred effects of shell shock, to whom life has become an intolerable horror. The pattern that results is a curiously living thing. As in *Jacob's Room,* sunlight seems poured across the pages; and, more than in *Jacob's Room,* the reader is made aware of a background of innumerable lives. More subtly than either of the other novels, this shows the play of one personality upon another. The method is like the flick of a wing in flight; the revelation is complete. Clarissa's loathing of her own hatred for the fanatical Miss Kilman, who would do anything for the Russians, starved herself for the Austrians, but in private inflicted positive torture, so insensitive was she; the panic and despair of poor Septimus under the robust authoritativeness of the great neurologist; the comfort felt by old Mrs. Hilbery, at Clarissa's party, in the jolly laughter of Sir Harry, "which, as she heard it across the room, seemed to reassure her on a point which sometimes bothered her if she woke early in the morning and did not like to call her maid for a cup of tea; how it is certain we must die"—countless sharp impressions such as these strike up from the smooth flow of the stream Smooth, for—though in this novel, too, the point of view constantly shifts—the transitions are made with suavity. The impersonal voice of Big Ben, falling upon different ears, is not the only device used. Clarissa in her exultant morning mood and Septimus in his agony of apprehensiveness are stopped by the same traffic block; the golden sunlight that lifts up the heart of young Elizabeth Dalloway as she rides on the top of a London bus makes patterns on the wall of Septimus's sitting-room, and gives his tormented mind one last moment of vague pleasure; and the bell of the ambulance that is carrying his shattered, unconscious body to the hospital clangs pleasantly to Peter Walsh, speaking to him of the efficiency of London. This novel throws light, as by a prism, not upon a score of lives, but upon life as felt by a score of people; its pursuit of Clarissa Dalloway through one day in London leaves an impression of a real woman, but a stronger impression of a woven fabric of life, gay and tragic and dipped in mystery.

To one reader the highly developed manner of such a novel as *Mrs. Dalloway* seems intolerably artificial; to another it seems an excellent vehicle for wit, for acute sympathy, for the sense of beauty, above all for the sense of life as a thing "absorbing, mysterious, of infinite richness." Probably the most vehement apostle of stream-of-consciousness fiction no more wishes that all novels now and hereafter should be cast in that form than he deplores that *Tom Jones* is not written in the manner of *Fräulein Else*. But he must wonder passionately—and surely it is no fanaticism to wonder—how long so potent a movement in the art of literature will continue to be regarded by a large part of the reading public as an eccentric fad.

5

MAPMAKERS AND HISTORIANS

SHIV K. KUMAR, "A Survey of the Various Theories Advanced to Explain the Nature and Scope of the Stream-of-Consciousness Technique," introduction to *Bergson and the Stream of Consciousness Novel* (New York: New York University Press, 1962), pp. 1-16.

In this survey of stream-of-consciousness novels and novelists and the various theories about them, Kumar summarizes the major critical conclusions about the stream-of-consciousness technique.

ERWIN R. STEINBERG, "The Psychological Stream of Consciousness," *The Stream of Consciousness and Beyond in ULYSSES,* (Pittsburgh: University of Pittsburgh Press, 1973): 161-77.

An analysis of the psychological stream of consciousness indicates that, since it involves more than language, it can not be presented by the stream-of-consciousness novelist, but must be simulated.

JUSTIN O'BRIEN, "Proust Confirmed by Neurosurgery," *PMLA* 85 (March 1970): 295-97.

The research of Dr. Wilder Penfield, a neurosurgeon, confirms, according to this article, the theory of involuntary memory which Proust used in *Remembrance of Things Past.*

KEITH LEOPOLD, "Some Problems of Terminology in the Analysis of the Stream-of-Consciousness Novel," *AUMLA* 13 (May 1960): 23-32.

In this essay and the one following, the authors attempt rigorous definitions of the stream-of-consciousness technique and its relation to similar forms: soliloquy, internal monologue, *erlebte Rede,* and others— terms which are unfortunately very frequently used interchangeably, to the confusion of many who seek to understand the stream-of-consciousness technique. The reader may also wish to consult Lawrence E. Bowling, "What Is the Stream of Consciousness Technique?" *PMLA* 65 (June 1950); Glebe Struve, *"Monologue intérieur:* The Origins of the Formula and the First Statement of Its Possibilities," *PMLA* 69 (December 1954). The early chapters of the books listed on page 164 will also be helpful.

ERWIN R. STEINBERG, "The Stream-of-Consciousness Technique Defined," *The Stream-of-Consciousness and Beyond in ULYSSES,* (Pittsburgh: University of Pittsburgh Press, 1973), pp. 245–56.

In his *The Rhetoric of Fiction* (1961), Wayne C. Booth is also an important mapmaker and historian.

KUMAR: *Survey of Various Theories*

The emergence of the stream-of-consciousness novel in contemporary fiction has provoked much controversy, but the basic issues involved still remain vague and unexplained. The new form of narrative has been variously defined, not infrequently from conflicting points of view; its origins are traced to sources which fail to reveal the real creative impulse behind this new mode of representing human experience. All this confusion results from a fundamental misunderstanding of the underlying intention of the new novelist, who does not conceive character as a state but as a process of ceaseless becoming in a medium which may be termed Bergson's *durée réelle.*

Before inquiring into the full implications of this approach, it may be useful here first to give a brief resume of the various theories which have so far been advanced to explain the nature and scope of the new technique.

A popular theory, put forth by many critics, presents the stream-of-consciousness method as an inevitable sequel to the disintegration of values in the first quarter of this century, and an attempt to compensate by excessive experimentation for the spiritual vacuum prevailing everywhere. The new novel, therefore, is a manifestation, says H. J. Muller, of "the blurring of objective reality and the dissolution of certainties in all fields of thought."[1] Professor Weidlé also seems to support this view when he attributes extreme cultivation of technique to the highly subjective modes of artistic apprehension, unrelated to any established code of values. Proust, Joyce, Svevo, and others, in his opinion, embody in their work an exaggerated form of *principium individuationis*.[2] The new novel, therefore, is described as a withdrawal from external phenomena into the flickering half-shades of the author's private world. It will however, be shown in the course of a detailed analysis of the work of Dorothy Richardson, Virginia Woolf, and James Joyce that the new prose-fiction does not imply a "withdrawal" from objective reality but constitutes, on the contrary, a deliberate effort to render in a literary medium a new realization of experience as a process of dynamic renewal

According to others, the new technique derives from the psychoanalytical school of Jung, Freud, and Adler. The spirit of Zürich, it is suggested, broods over Joyce's Dublin, Virginia Woolf's and Dorothy Richardson's London. The "business of producing the psychological novel has much in common," says a critic, "with the business of being psychoanalysed,"[3] and it is asserted that "the thought-stream novel usually can only be appreciated fully by people whose subconscious is in the same state as that of the author."[4] F. J. Hoffman and Pelham Edgar,[5] however, do not prescribe any such limits in their interpretation of the new technique. The former attempts to explain the purport of the stream-of-consciousness novelist as the representation of four different levels of consciousness:[6] the conscious, the preconscious, the subconscious, and the unconscious, as if the author had undertaken to solve a complex psychological problem in terms of literary symbols.

Robert Humphrey stresses another psychological aspect of the technique by defining it "as a type of fiction in which strong emphasis is placed on exploration of the pre-speech levels of consciousness for the purposes, primarily, of revealing the psychic being of the characters." This type of fiction becomes for him "essentially a technical feat."

Edward Bowling presents more or less the same view when he describes the new form of novel as "*a direct quotation of the mind*—not merely of the language area but of the whole consciousness."[9] The pre-speech area thus again forms a predominant part of the range covered by the stream-of-consciousness novelist, who attempts to externalize sensations and ideas not normally expressed by words and images. Professor J. W. Beach, on the other hand, emphasizes "exploitation of the element of

ncoherence in our conscious process" as the "defining feature" of the
new technique.[10]

The interest of all stream-of-consciousness novelists in the
contemporary psychoanalytical theories cannot be overestimated;[11]
the danger lies only in exaggerating this relationship and reading their
novels as mere "liberation of suppressions."[12] To label Dorothy Richardson's *Pilgrimage* as a document of "the Daphnean furtiveness of a woman's
mind,"[13] would be as inaccurate as to treat *Ulysses* as a text-book of
psychology and psychiatry.[14] Nor again, would the work of Virginia Woolf
yield any significant results if analysed in terms of psychoanalysis, since
the stream-of-consciousness novelists are essentially concerned with
presenting individual personality and experience in terms of artistic
sensibility.

A psychoanalytical interpretation of the stream-of-consciousness novel
would hardly illuminate its treatment and presentation of *la durée,
mémoire involontaire,* and intuition,[15] nor would it bring out the significance of the various protagonists' preoccupation with the ultimate nature
of reality. It is here that Bergsonism attempts to reach out beyond the
limits of psychoanalysis. In being more sympathetic towards aesthetic
inclinations, more attuned to the mysterious nature of creative processes,
Bergson's philosophical theories of time, memory, and consciousness
provide a more useful clue to the understanding of the new technique.
The emergence of time as a new mode of artistic perception in the
contemporary novel[16] would alone justify the Bergsonian approach as
being more aesthetic than the mechanistic treatment of psychoanalysts.

The technique has also been described by some as a mere literary
embellishment, a means of investing character, scene, and incident with
"wise bits of philosophy," or iridescent "flashes of beauty," lending to
the entire narrative a touch of ethereality, of "something spirit-like."[17]
This is how Ethel Hawkins defines it—as something synonymous with a
hypersensitive awareness of phenomena highly tinged with the observer's
own evanescent moods. This theory obviously takes a restricted view of
the technique by ignoring altogether its aesthetic and philosophical
implications.

This kind of novel has been analysed by others in terms of impressionistic painting, and referred to as "the Post-impressionistic Novel." "The
problem of the twentieth-century novelist was the same as that of the
twentieth-century painter."[18] Is the technique to be photographic or
impressionistic? asks Professor Isaacs, and proceeds to show how even the

phraseology and imagery in Virginia Woolf's famous essay "Modern Fiction" are full of echoes from such works as R. M. Stevenson's exposition of Velasquez's art.[19] These novelists, as Herbert Muller also affirms, have in various ways adapted to fiction the technique of the impressionistic painters, especially as it was supplemented by Cézanne.[20]

But a closer examination will show that beyond suggesting a certain similarity of aesthetic intention, this theory also fails to offer a satisfactory explanation of the new technique of characterization. It would be incorrect to say that Virginia Woolf, Dorothy Richardson, or James Joyce was influenced by the impressionistic school of painting, which was itself a manifestation of the new awareness of reality as "les données immédiates de la conscience."[21]

There is yet another school of criticism which relates the new technique to the symbolistic modes of expression. Speaking of the characters in *Ulysses*, Edmund Wilson remarks: "When we are admitted to the mind of any of them, we are in a world as complex and special, a world sometimes as fantastic or obscure, as that of the symbolist poet—and a world rendered by similar devices of language."[22] In his use of the interior monologue—"symbolistic monologues"—Joyce fully exploits, according to Edmund Wilson, "the methods of symbolism."[23] In their anti-mechanistic intentions, their emphasis on intimating things rather than stating them, their use of a complicated association of ideas, their insistence upon inventing a special language to express individual personality, the symbolists seem to imply a metaphysic similar to Bergsonism.[24] In fact, the work of James Joyce, Virginia Woolf, and Dorothy Richardson is, in a certain sense, a continuation of symbolism.

But again, Bergsonism appears to offer a more comprehensive explanation of the literary and philosophical implications of the new novel than symbolism. Durational flux, which constitutes the essence of this technique, is obviously more Bergsonian than symbolistic in character and the former in its wider scope seems to embrace the basic principle of the latter.

And lastly, the relation of the stream-of-consciousness narrative to such popular arts as the cinema has also been studied.[25] Harry Levin suggests a similarity between this technique and *montage* under which he analyses the various aspects of *le monologue intérieur.* "Bloom's mind," he observes, is neither a tabula rasa nor a photographic plate, but a motion picture, which has been ingeniously cut and carefully edited to emphasize the close-ups and fade-outs of flickering emotion, the angles of observation and the flashbacks of reminiscence. In its intimacy and in its continuity, *Ulysses* has more in common with the cinema than with other fiction. The movement of Joyce's style, the thought of his characters, is like unreeling film; his method of construction, the arrangement of this raw material, involves the crucial operation of *montage*.[26]

There may be some justification for each of these expositions[27] of the stream-of-consciousness novel, which has undoubtedly some elements in common with the post-impressionistic painting, the symbolist modes of expression, or even the cinema. But as mentioned earlier, none of these theories presents a comprehensive view and explains fully the precise nature and scope of the technique. The new novelist is neither exclusively an impressionistic delineator of character and scene, nor a psychoanalyst whose primary function is to render a clinical analysis of human motives and impulses.[28] Characters like Mrs. Dalloway, Miriam Henderson, and Stephen Dedalus are self-sufficient, deriving their validity from their creator's vicarious experience. They do not require the help of a psychoanalyst for any fuller understanding of them, for the "business of producing the psychological novel" is not the same as "the business of being psychoanalysed." Nor again is the stream-of-consciousness technique an esoteric jigsaw of words and sentences,[29] implying a withdrawal from objective reality into the author's own private world.[30] On the contrary, this kind of novel seems to make a positive affirmation of a view of experience which can be apprehended better in terms of Bergson's durational flux.

Before investigating this parallelism more fully, it may be profitable to say a word about *le monologue intérieur* as employed by Edouard Dujardin, whose novel *Les Lauriers sont coupés* (1888) is supposed to have influenced James Joyce.[31] Dujardin is also responsible for popularizing in literary criticism this term which, according to him, was invented by Valery Larbaud; "L'invention de l'expression, dans le sens que nous lui donnons aujourd'hui, semble être dûe à Valery Larbaud lui-même."[32]

The credit, however, of originating the term *"monologue intérieur"* and presenting a detailed analysis of its various aspects, together with a comprehensive survey of its theory and practice in literary and philosophical history, belongs to Victor Egger who published in 1881 his scholarly treatise *La Parole intérieure*. He defines it as "un des éléments les plus importants . . . de nos actes; la série des mots intérieurs forme une succession presque continué . . . le moi et la durée sont des idées équivalentes . . . c'est le moi; *je suis une pure succession.*"[33]

Later in 1930 when Edouard Dujardin, in the course of a series of literary conferences, gave an elaborate analysis of the interior monologue he had little to add to Victor Egger's definition of it. "Le monologue intérieur," says Dujardin, "est, dans l'ordre de la poésie, le discours sans auditeur et non prononcé. . . ."[34]

The important point to note, however, is that both these commentators emphasize the element of fluidity in our states of consciousness. In the words of Dujardin: "La nouveauté *essentielle* qu'a apportée le monologue intérieur consiste en ce qu'il a pour objet d'évoquer *le flux ininterrompu* des pensées qui traversent l'âme du personnage. . . ."[35]

It is precisely this inner *flux ininterrompu* that Bergson designates as *la durée*, a process of creative evolution which does not lend itself to any logical or intellectual analysis. *La durée* or psychological time thus becomes the distinguishing feature of the stream-of-consciousness novel. The new novelist accepts with full awareness inner duration against chronological time as the only true mode of apprehending aesthetic experience. Only in terms of the emergence of time as the fourth dimension can therefore, one of the most important literary movements of this century be understood. "There is a plane geometry," writes Marcel Proust in a letter to his friend Antoine Bibesco, "and a geometry of space. And so for me the novel is not only plane psychology but psychology in space and time. *That invisible substance, time, I try to isolate.*"[36] Again, towards the end of *Remembrance of Things Past,* he sums up his entire aesthetic theory: "I should endeavour to render that Time-dimension by transcribing life in a way very different from that conveyed by our lying senses. . . . Everybody feels that we are occupying an unceasingly increasing place in Time, and this universality could only rejoice me since it is the truth, a truth suspected by each one of us which it was my business to try to elucidate. . . . If, at least, time enough were allotted to me to accomplish my work, I would not fail to mark it with the seal of Time . . . and I would therein describe men, if need be, as monsters occupying a place in Time infinitely more important than the restricted one reserved for them in space. . . ."[37]

Every stream-of-consciousness novel bears this seal of time. Time, or as Bergson prefers to call it *la durée*, enters the field of creative thought as something incapable of measurement and intractable to such symbolical representations as hours, days, months, and years which are only its spatialized concepts. Edouard, André Gide's protagonist in *The Coiners*, enunciates his theory of the novel as a breadthwise and depthwise cutting of "a slice of life," in preference to "the naturalist school" that "always cuts its slice in the same direction; in time, lengthwise."[38] Gide, obviously, implies the durational as an integral mode of apprehension of reality as contrasted with the spatial rendering of life in fiction, for in the latter, time projected lengthwise is nothing but space.

The extent to which this new concept of time as an immeasurable and multidirectional process had permeated the European novel of the first quarter of this century, may be assessed from these novelists who employed this stream-of-consciousness method in representing *la durée*.

Jacques Goddard, Jules Romains's protagonist in *The Death of a Nobody*, reflects on the theme of time: "In particular he had pondered upon time. Time seemed to him something quite arbitrary and elastic. He found it difficult to believe it was a dependable entity, and clocks seemed to him fallacious mechanisms for measuring it."[39]

A similar realization of the elasticity of time dawns within the consciousness of Italo Svevo's hero in *The Nice Old Man:*

I, on the contrary, am obstinately trying to do something else in this present and if, as I hope, there is time to develop an activity in it, I shall have proved that it is longer than it appears. It is hard to measure it and the mathematician who tried to do so would come hopelessly to grief, thus showing that it is not his work.[40]

Virginia Woolf stresses this discrepancy between "time in the mind" and clock time more explicitly in *Orlando*.[41] Thomas Wolfe in *Look Homeward, Angel*[42] and Gertrude Stein in *Composition as Explanation*,[43] affirm almost the same view of duration. The work of Dorothy Richardson and James Joyce is no less an illustration of this subjective notion of time.

This "time in the mind" is symbolically represented by most of these novelists as a flowing river with memories and visions as its chief constituents.[44] The flux of human experience consists in this perpetual mixing of memory with desire, making one "live in a mixed tense, as is man's lot, the grammar of which has, however, those pure tenses which seem made for the animals."[45] This "horrible activity of the mind's eye,"[46] lies in our ceaseless response to a multiplicity of sensory impressions and recollections, the latter conditioning and therefore, in a sense, recreating each moment of experience. Time, no longer a mere extended image of space, now becomes the pure essence of reality, which may be described as "a succession of qualitative changes, which melt into and permeate one another, without precise outlines, without any tendency to externalize themselves in relation to one another,"[47] or, as a principle "of becoming which is reality itself."[48]

The key to the emergence of the stream-of-consciousness novel lies in this new awareness of experience, this marked shift from a conception of personality as built round a hard and changeless core to a realization of it as a dynamic process. This reality is to be realized in immediate experience as flux, to be grasped by intuition or intellectual sympathy.[49] *La durée* is the stuff of which this kind of novel is made.

To understand completely the durational aspect of the new novel, it will be necessary to examine in detail the philosophical significance of the work of Marcel Proust,[50] who is often associated with certain aspects of the technique as employed by Dorothy Richardson, Virginia Woolf, and James Joyce. It must, however, be admitted at the outset that Proust does not use the stream-of-consciousness method of narrative; in fact, instead of completely immersing himself in the stream of becoming, he retains the right to elucidate, analyse, comment, and judge. But in most of his observations on the art of the novel, he seems to provide the new novelist with a suitable working credo.

Proust always claimed to have presented in his work "a whole theory of memory and consciousness, although not directly projected in logical terms."[51] In denouncing intellect as a spatializing tendency,[52] in recognizing the supremacy of involuntary memories over voluntary memories[53] and the validity of fugitive impressions as significant phenomena,[54] in endeavouring to bring reality within the fold of his work with the "least possible shrinkage," in "respecting" in the matter of style "the natural progress of my thought,"[55] and lastly, in emphasizing the importance of *la durée* in a work of art, Proust supplies all the ingredients of the stream-of-consciousness technique, except, of course, its practical application.

The work of Proust has, therefore, a two-fold significance to the student of the stream-of-consciousness novel; first because many younger novelists found in him a confirmation of what was already dawning within their own minds, and secondly, because he proved to be, though quite unwittingly, a provocative introduction to Bergson's philosophy of time, memory, and consciousness. Although it is often futile to trace direct influences, the relation between a particular philosophy and a certain form of art may be so intimate that the study of one in terms of the other becomes immensely rewarding.

In the case of Proust at least it is not difficult to establish even direct relationship between him and the French philosopher. A pupil of Bergson's at the Sorbonne (1891-93), and his nephew by virtue of the philosopher's marriage with his cousin Neuburger,[56] he found himself oscillating all his life between Yea and Nay.[57] In a letter to Georges de Lauris in 1909, he wrote:

> I am glad you have read some Bergson and liked him. It is as though we had been together on a great height. I don't know *L'Evolution créatrice* . . . but I have read enough of Bergson, the parabola of his thought is already sufficiently discernible after only a single generation. . . . Besides, I think I have told you of my great respect for him . . . and of the great kindness he has always shown me. . . .[58]

On the other hand, in an interview he gave to Elsie Joseph Bois, published in *Le Temps* of November 1913, he said:

> I should not in any way feel ashamed to describe my books as "Bergsonian novels,"[59] if I thought they were, for in every period, literature has tried to attach itself after the event, naturally, to the reigning philosophy. But it would not be accurate, for my work is dominated by the distinction between the "mémoire involontaire" and "mémoire volontaire," a distinction which is not only not to be found in M. Bergson's philosophy, but is even contradicted by it.[60]

We shall have occasion to show in a subsequent chapter how this basis on which Proust always tried to deny Bergson's influence is refuted by the latter's clear distinction between "pure memory" and "voluntary memory."[61] But whatever be his relation with Bergson, Proust certainly renders a very faithful presentation of the Bergsonian theories of memory, *la durée,* and consciousness.

Among the English writers of the first quarter of this century, we may mention T. E. Hulme who, through his various critical essays on Bergson's aesthetics and translation of *Introduction à la métaphysique,* enabled many contemporary poets and novelists to realize in Bergson an articulation of their own awareness of experience as flux. In his essay entitled "Bergson's Theory of Art," he seems to justify the impulse behind the new technique:

The process of artistic creation would be better described as a process of discovery and disentanglement. To use the metaphor which one is now so familiar with—the *stream of inner life,* and the definite crystallized shapes on the surface—the big artist, the creative artist, the innovator, leaves the level where things are crystallized out into these definite shapes, and, diving down into the inner flux, comes back with a new shape which he endeavours to fix.[62]

This "new shape" is obviously a durational pattern which reveals an inner reality of things as against their crystallized surface. Therefore, although one may find oneself in this durational flux, as if one were "en présence d'une désorganisation," this is none the less reality itself.

During the last years of his life Hulme was contemplating a book on "Modern Theories of Art," a synopsis of which appears as an appendix to his *Speculations.* In the third chapter of this proposed book he planned to show how "rough analyses which artists themselves have given . . . can be interpreted in the light of new psychology—Bergson."[63] In another chapter he intended further to elaborate Bergson's theory in terms of "actual and intimate acquaintance with emotions involved—*Time and Free Will, Introduction à la métaphysique—L'Effort intellectual—Laughter."*

Many other English contemporaries of Hulme felt sympathetically interested in the new philosophy. When Bergson came to the notice of the so-called Bloomsbury Group is not clear, but it is worth noting that Desmond MacCarthy, in a dedicatory letter to Roger Fry (dated 1914), accompanying his translation of Jules Romain's novel, *The Death of a Nobody,* drew Bergson to Fry's attention:

At the end of the book there is an attempt to portray in the emotions of a young man walking down a rain-swept boulevard one late afternoon, a conception of the world not unlike that which M. Bergson's philosophy suggests. How far such experiences are engendered by reading M. Bergson, and how far they are independent, M. Romains can tell better.[64]

This is, however, not an essential question to ask Jules Romains or any other stream-of-consciousness novelist. To suggest that the new form of fiction emerged under the direct influence of Bergson would be rather misleading. In fact, Bergson was himself, like those he is supposed to have influenced, a manifestation of the *Zeitgeist*. It should, therefore, be more appropriate to say that in his philosophy one finds a more effective articulation of that intuitive sense of fluid reality of which sensitive minds were becoming aware in the early years of this century. This new realization of experience as flux manifests itself in contemporary fiction in the form of the stream-of-consciousness novel.

William James's analysis of consciousness seems to supplement Bergson's theory of the "stream of life";[65] it may, therefore, also be helpful to understand the former's presentation of thought as a continuum. The phrase "stream of consciousness," it may be noted, was first used by William James in the *Principles of Psychology* (1890), and later introduced into literary criticism by May Sinclair who, in her article on Dorothy Richardson in the *Egoist* of April 1918, wrote: "... There is no drama, no situation, no set scene. Nothing happens. It is just life going on and on. It is Miriam's stream of consciousness, going on and on."[66]

William James, like Bergson, believes that "empty our minds as we may, some form of changing process remains for us to feel, and cannot be expelled."[67] Our psychic kaleidoscope is perpetually forming itself into new patterns. Like Bergson again, he exposes the Humian doctrine that our consciousness consists of discrete fragments capable of repeating themselves. On the contrary, he observes that consciousness cannot be analysed into fragments or "chopped up in bits."

Such words as "chain" or "train" do not describe it fitly as it presents itself in the first instance. It is nothing jointed; it flows. A "river" or a "stream" are the metaphors by which it is most naturally described. In talking of it hereafter, let us call it the stream of thought, of consciousness, or of subjective life.[68]

In this "wonderful stream of consciousness" sensory images form the halting places or "substantive parts," and the thoughts of relations or "transitive parts" denote places of "flight." But it must be remembered that the former are mere terms of convenience and do not indicate or suggest any break in the continuous flow of consciousness, for even these "substantive parts" are invariably suffused with notions of "flight" or "movement."

Elsewhere, William James refers to the "halo or penumbra surrounding the image," "the overtone, halo, or fringe,"[69] suggested also by Virginia Woolf in her description of life as "a luminous halo, a semi-transparent envelope surrounding us from the beginning of consciousness to the end."[70] And when she calls upon the new writers to convey "this varying, this unknown and uncircumscribed spirit, whatever aberration or complexity it may display . . . ," and, citing the example of James Joyce, asks them to "record the atoms as they fall upon the mind in the order in which they fall . . . trace the pattern, however disconnected and incoherent in appearance,"[71] she defines the basic philosophical sanction behind the stream-of-consciousness novel.

What James calls "halo, or fringe," and Virginia Woolf "luminous halo," is nothing else than those transitional phases of our mental processes which mark the merging of the past into the present, and the fading of the present into the future, thus making experience a continuum. In James's words again, "The knowledge of some other part of the stream, past or future, near or remote, is always mixed in with our knowledge of the present thing . . . these lingerings of old objects, these incomings of new, are the germs of memory and expectation, the retrospective and the prospective sense of time. They give that continuity to consciousness without which it could not be called a stream."[72] It is this durational aspect of consciousness which defines the basis of the stream-of-consciousness novel.

We may here say a word about the present moment of experience which forms the exclusive material in the traditional novel, unless a writer chooses to introduce the past in a flashback, or what Dr. David Daiches calls "memory digression." According to the new concept of durational flux, the present loses its static nature and ceaselessly fades into the past and future. William James gives this concept a new name—"the specious present,"[73] and defines it as "a bow and a stern, as it were—a rearward—and a forward-looking end."[74] In contemporary psychological fiction this specious present is always instinctively felt and sometimes directly described by novelists who employ a highly subjective, though not necessarily the stream-of-consciousness, technique. Gertrude Stein for instance, calls it the "prolonged present:" "I wrote a negro story called *Melanctha*. In that there was a constant recurring and beginning there was a marked direction of being in the present although naturally I had been accustomed to past present and future, and why, because the composition forming around me was a prolonged present."[75]

We can easily see a certain correspondence between Gertrude Stein's and William James's conception of fluid present. Their exposition of the qualitative aspect of time, however, is not as comprehensive as that of Bergson, who remains the true embodiment of the new awareness of *durée créatrice.* In the context of these observations, it will be seen that much new light can be thrown on the stream-of-consciousness form of narrative and characterization by studying it in relation to the theory of durational flux as expounded by Bergson. Interpreted in terms of *mémoire involontaire, la durée,* and intuition, this kind of novel acquires a new meaning and coherence, and ceases to be "the offspring of a creator's negative mood."

In Bergson's philosophy one finds an attempt to correlate the new philosophical awareness with methods and ideals of literary composition, particularly prose-fiction. We shall now try to present in the next chapter, what may be called, "Bergson's theory of the novel," based on his observations on the novelist's art, scattered in his various philosophical writings.

STEINBERG: *Psychological Stream of Consciousness*

Confronted with a stream-of-consciousness passage in a novel, many readers think that the author has presented them with an actual stream of consciousness, the flow of thought and awareness as it occurs from moment to moment in the mind. An examination of what we know about consciousness, thinking, and language, however, indicates that a stream-of-consciousness novelist can at best *simulate* the psychological stream of consciousness. Such an examination also indicates some of the problems facing him when he attempts that simulation.

Unfortunately there is no single source in which to find a summary of what the psychologists know about the stream of consciousness. One must construct an understanding of it from diverse—and often divergent—sources. I shall undertake such a construction in this chapter, perhaps in more detail than some readers may wish. Such detail is necessary, however, if we are to understand what happens in the mind, how we perceive the world, and what we read on the printed page—particularly, of course, what we read in a stream-of-consciousness novel, but also in other forms of literature; for all literature seeks to present a view of the world, widely or narrowly perceived.

Critics and plain readers tend to psychologize too glibly (and superficially) about perception, thought, and the mind, and how these all relate to the world outside. The jargon and statistics of the social scientists may make reading psychology difficult, sometimes as difficult as reading literary criticism; but just as the student of psychology has much to learn from literature about the patterns of mind and behavior he seeks to understand, so the student of literature has much to learn from psychology about the patterns of mind and behavior a writer seeks to portray.

An example of how far back careful attempts to describe thinking go can be found in what is perhaps the oldest of the theories about the nature of thought, association: "Generally speaking, associationism is a mechanistic doctrine, conceiving of mental processes as the more or less automatic elaboration—combination and recombination—of materials derived from the sense organs. The development of the theory centers around the attempt to reduce the mechanism to its simplest, most concrete terms and to discover the "laws" according to which it works."[1]

We can trace the beginnings of this theory to the Greeks. Socrates says in *Phaedo:* "So much is clear—that when we perceive something, either by the help of sight, or hearing, or some other sense, from that perception we are able to obtain a notion of some other thing like or unlike, which is associated with it but has been forgotten."[2] And, too, in his *De Memoria,* Aristotle says:

Acts of recollection, as they occur in experience, are due to the fact that one movement has by nature another that succeeds it in regular order.

If this order be necessary, whenever a subject experiences the former of the two movements thus connected, it will invariably experience the latter; if, however, the order be not necessary, but customary, only in the majority of cases will the subject experience the latter of the two movements.[3]

The British associationists are largely responsible for developing the concept into a school of psychology. Thomas Hobbes, John Locke, David Hume, David Hartley, Thomas Brown, James Mill, and Alexander Bain, to name just the important ones, added considerably to the body of writing discussing the theory. "Since Bain's time, associationism has persisted in one form or another, but as an aspect of behavior rather than as its sum and substance."[4]

Contemporary psychology also owes much of its interest in the nature of thought and its understanding of it to William James. James begins with a very elementary statement: *"The first fact for us . . . is that thinking of some sort goes on."* By "thinking" James means "every form of consciousness indiscriminantly." "Continuous thought" James characterizes as "the stream of thought" or "the stream of consciousness,"[5] defined as

the conscious experience of an individual, likened to a stream in order to emphasize its continuity, in opposition to the conception of it as a series of discrete states [a term introduced by James]. . . .[6]

[It contains] sensations of our bodies and of the objects around us, memories of past experiences and thoughts of distant things, feelings of satisfaction and dissatisfaction, desires and aversions, and other emotional conditions, together with determinations of the will, in every variety of permutation and combination.[7]

According to James, thought has five characteristics:

1. Every thought tends to be part of a personal consciousness.
2. Within each personal consciousness thought is always changing.
3. Within each personal consciousness thought is sensibly continuous.
4. It always appears to deal with objects independent of itself.
5. It is interested in some parts of these objects to the exclusion of others, and welcomes or rejects—chooses from among them, in a word— all the while.[8]

Little of this material is now controversial. James argues that every person's world is split into the "me" and the "not-me," and thought is an irrevocable part of the "me." Thought, therefore, is personal. And it is never the same. Inasmuch as it is directly connected with our sensations and feelings, which are always undergoing change, and since it is the function of a brain content which is ever being modified, which is never the same, which can never return to a previous state, thought must always change, not only from year to year, but from hour to hour. That thought is continuous to James means two things:

1. That even where there is a time-gap the consciousness after it feels as if it belonged together with the consciousness before it, as another part of the same self;
2. That the changes from one moment to another in the quality of the consciousness are never absolutely abrupt.[9]

Thus thoughts color one another. We do not think thought *a*, then thought *b*, and then thought *c;* but rather thought *(x) a (b)*, then thought *(a) b (c)*, then thought *(b) c (d)*. Even after sleep we "mentally . . . [reach] back and . . . [make] connection with . . . the . . . [stream] of thought which . . . [was] broken by the sleeping hours."[10] Point four needs little expansion; in these days of the semanticist's insistence on the separation of the symbol from the object, there should be little disagreement, philosophical or psychological, about the distinction of the thought from the object. And point five has to do with the individual differences of perception and abstraction that have been dwelt on at great length by the psychologists who followed James.

That "consciousness, from our natal day, is of a teeming multiplicity of objects and relations"[11] is borne out by a contemporary psychiatrist, the late Harry Stack Sullivan, in his discussion during a lecture of a single moment of consciousness:

I shall remember this moment as it exists, with all its implications past, present, and future—most of these implications having been present as tensional elements, and not as formulated statements. Let me illustrate: there is the spatial orientation—this beautiful and acoustically excellent auditorium; the rostrum, the microphone and its related system which tonight seems to be unmonitored, the audience as a certain amazingly large number of people, a friend who is deaf in the ear nearest me, the stenotype reporter, and many and many another detail of the geometric and local geographic situation—coupled with the most significant first experience of the related spatial orientation at the start of the first lecture in this series. There is the temporal orientation along several significant lines; the night after our unusually timed Thanksgiving, the "place" of the moment in a prehended durability of the lumped attention of the audience and their tolerance for my presentation; the "place" in the attention-tolerance of certain more personally significant members of the audience; and various other details. There is the orientation in terms of my personal career-line; the lucidity of my formulation, the adequacy of its verbal expression—or rather, verbal indication, for one has no time to be exact and precise, if one is to cover these topics without exhausting the auditors—the effect on this moment of gaps in the early presentations, the "coming" ideas that should grow out of this, its organization of all these statements and indications in terms of changes in the general audience, and new insights in the more personally significant auditors—including, very significantly, myself. I have mentioned these orientations without reference to the zones of interaction that are involved. I have omitted reference to the patterns of kinesthetic and related data that exist in me, in connection with them. I can but invite your attention to the complex pattern of vocal—sound productive and sound receptive—past and future verbal and other voice-communicative processes concerned, and the effective or partially ineffectual and unfortunate function of these patterns in terms of what makes up this moment in each of you. I will only mention as yet other coordinates of the present moment, states of my visceral and skeletal musculature as terms in relative satisfaction or dissatisfaction with the momentary situation and with the accomplished and the potential performances of the whole lecture, the series of lectures, and with events before and to follow on the lecture. These are some of the items that may be abstracted from the momentary state of the organism—of a vast series of which one's memory is composed.[12]

If an instant of consciousness is so complex, how much more so, then, is the stream of consciousness from which such an instant has been arbitrarily torn in order to hold it up, threads trailing, for examination?

According to Sullivan, consciousness, and therefore the stream of consciousness, contains: language; spatial, temporal, and purposive orientation; kinesthetic elements and related data; vocal patterns; states of visceral and skeletal musculature; and many other items. Further, all of these items are interacting, so that even in such a suspended moment of consciousness as that described by Sullivan, to list them separately is to distort the picture.[13]

This emphasis on "the teeming multiplicity of objects and relations" in the stream of consciousness raises many problems. For example, if all of these elements appear in the consciousness, how do they appear, how are they embodied; or, to put it another way, in what guise do they appear, how are they presented? At the risk of distorting, we must organize these components somehow in order to talk about them. The method involving the least risk would seem to be to describe them just as various schools of psychology claim to have found them.

The structuralists, led by Wundt and Titchener, attempted to determine the elements of consciousness by introspection:

Analysis of mental contents by this method seemed to reveal that all mental processes are composed of simple, irreducible elements, namely, sensations, affections, and images, each with characteristic dimensions, or "attributes." Sensations, the basic data arriving in the sense organs, and classified accordingly, are marked by specifiable quality, *e.g.,* cold, blue, salt, by intensity of a given amount, by variations in clearness, and by a given duration. They are compounded into perceptions, following the laws of such a mixture. Similarly, affections, with their describable attributes, lacking the dimension of clearness, are compounded into feelings, or simple emotions. Images . . . are derived from sensations. They constitute the elements of which ideas are composed and thus form the basic content of thought. The differences between sensations and images grow out of their relationship, for an image has less distinctive quality, less intensity, and shorter duration than the corresponding sensation.

The structuralists explained all thinking as the occurrence of images, combining and recombining, according to requirements.[14]

Since we shall be concerned with some of these elements later, they warrant a more careful definition here:

sensation
(1) *(psychol.)* an experience aroused from outside the nervous system, which is not further analyzable by introspection; i.e., an element of consciousness; (2) *(physiol.)* an afferent neural process which commences in a receptor and extends to the cerebrum.

perception
(1) the awareness of external objects, qualities or relations, which ensues directly upon sensory processes, as distg. fr. memory or other central processes; (2) a mental complex or integration which has sensory experience as its core; (3) awareness of present data, whether external or intraorganic

image
(1) an element of experience which is centrally aroused and which possesses all the attributes of sensation; (2) an experience which reproduces or copies in part and with some degree of sensory realism a previous perceptual experience in the absence of the original sensory stimulation.[15]

The so-called Würzburg school, insisting that there could be imageless thought, approached the problem in a somewhat different way:

They contributed   the concepts of task, set, and determining tendency. According to the usual formulation, the *task* gives the subject a particular *set,* and this set influences his associative sequence by means of unconscious *determining tendencies* that guide the process to its proper completion. . . . These concepts bear a very close resemblance to what we have called, in preceding chapters, contextual constraints or associative connections. Determining tendencies must operate in the extemporaneous patching together of words in ordinary speech.[16]

The early years of the twentieth century saw two new schools of psychology: in the United States, behaviorism; in Germany, Gestalt psychology.

The two movements were contemporaneous and each protested against the same orthodoxy. . . . Orthodox psychology in 1910 was (1) experimental, (2) introspective, (3) elementalistic, and (4) associationistic. Behaviorism and Gestalt psychology were agreed only on the first: both schools thought psychology should and could be experimental.[17]

The behaviorists claimed that thinking is the action of language mechanisms. J. B. Watson put it very concisely: "Thinking is then largely a verbal process; occasionally expressive movements substitutable for word movements (gestures, attitudes, etc.) enter in as part of the general stream of implicit activity."[18] The Gestaltists, in their rejection of "elementalistic psychology," announced the principle of isomorphism, "the essence of [which] is that phenomenologically ascertained forms actually correspond to psychophysical forms. Psychophysical forms in the brain are viewed as not essentially different from the physical forms of inorganic nature."[19] Perceptions and thoughts, then, may not be embodied in or composed of anything, but may simply be neural excitations or chemical changes; perhaps "the forms of experience correspond to recognizable physical forms in the nervous system."[20]

Neither school had much use for images. In the United States particularly, under the influence of behaviorism, "imagery, attention, states of consciousness, and other such central concepts of the old era were anathematized as 'mentalistic' and cast into outer darkness."[21]

It took almost fifty years to recall the image from outer darkness and reinstall it as an appropriate—and for some a significant—concern for psychology. In 1962 Robert R. Holt gave as his presidential address to Division Twelve of the American Psychological Association a paper entitled "Imagery: The Return of the Ostracized."[22] Published studies by Jerome L. Singer indicated that, for some people, at least, visual imagery is "the most pervasive underlying feature of the ongoing thought stream" and "the predominant modality for fantasy."[23] And in 1969 Alan Richardson published a book entitled *Mental Imagery*, the purpose of which was "to bring together in one place a representative sample of facts and hypotheses concerning the phenomena of mental imagery."[24]

The studies reported by Richardson show that people differ in their use of imagination imagery. Some people are primarily visualizers, and others primarily verbalizers; and still others use a mixture of both. A study of tonal memory shows that some people have more dominant auditory imagery than others.[25] Still other studies report kinesthetic images, tactile (including thermal) images, and olfactory images.[26] There is also the suggestion that image dominance may be related to personality type: visualizers tending to be active, independent, and hypersensitive; verbalizers—passive, dependent, submissive, slow, calm, and even-tempered; and those who are both impatient, aggressive, and intolerant.[27]

I have offered this brief history to demonstrate that the psychological stream of consciousness is not merely a string of words and that therefore what the stream-of-consciousness writer writes is not a presentation but can at best be only a simulation of what occurs in the mind. The discussion serves at the same time to point out what it is that the stream-of-consciousness writer must simulate if he is to be convincing.

We must now look at the problem of simulating the "teeming multiplicity of objects and relations" in the stream of consciousness by means of only one of the components of that stream—language. Semanticists have been insisting for some time now that there is a fundamental difference between the world we live in and the language we use to describe it. For example, Alfred Korzybski makes the statement that "the common A[ristotelian]-system and language which we have inherited from our primitive ancestors *differ entirely in structure* from the well-known and established 1933 structure of the world, ourselves and our nervous systems included." The world, our perception of it, and often our thinking about it are "structural," "multi-dimensional," whereas language is linear and additive.[28] Perhaps an example will make the point more clearly. We are always highly amused at the episode in *Alice in Wonderland* in which Alice, talking to the grinning Cheshire cat, sees the cat slowly disappear while the grin remains. How could the grin be separated from the cat? That would be preposterous. And yet that is exactly what our language does. In the sentence "The cat grins," we have done precisely the same thing—separated the cat from the grin. We were forced to do so because of the subject-predicate pattern of our language. As Lessing puts it, "The coexistence of the body comes into collision with the consecutiveness of language."[29]

Benjamin Lee Whorf wrote in considerable detail about this problem:

Segmentation of nature is an aspect of grammar—one as yet little studied by grammarians. We cut up largely because, through our mother tongue, we are parties to an agreement to do so, not because nature itself is segmented in exactly that way for all to see. . . . Thus English and similar tongues lead us to think of the universe as a collection of rather distinct objects and events corresponding to words. Indeed this is the implicit picture of classical physics and astronomy—that the universe is essentially a collection of detached objects of different sizes.

This is a problem that arises particularly with the Indo-European languages:

Some languages have means of expression—chemical combination, as I called it—in which the separate terms are not as separate as in English but flow together into plastic synthetic creations. Hence such languages, which do not paint the separate-object picture of the universe to the same degree as do English and its sister tongues, point toward possible new types of logic and possible new cosmical pictures.

. . . .

Our Indian languages show that with a suitable grammar we may have intelligent sentences that cannot be broken up into subjects and predicates. Any attempted breakup is a breakup of some English translation or paraphrase of the sentence, not of the Indian sentence itself.[30]

Perhaps some of the languages of the American Indians that Whorf writes about would be better adapted than are the Indo-European languages to the work of the physicist—and to the problems of the stream-of-consciousness novelist! At any rate, Whorf's analyses underline further the fact that reproducing reality in an Indo-European language is beset with difficulties.

Actually, what is being propounded here is in one way quite similar to Lessing's argument in *Laokoon* about the proper subjects for painting and poetry:

I reason thus: if it is true that painting and poetry in their imitations make use of entirely different means or symbols—the first, namely, of form and colour in space, the second of articulated sounds in time—if these symbols indisputably require a suitable relation to the thing symbolized, then it is clear that symbols arranged in juxtaposition can only express subjects of which the wholes or parts exist in juxtaposition; while consecutive symbols can only express subjects of which the wholes or parts are themselves consecutive.

Subjects whose wholes or parts exist in juxtaposition are called bodies. Consequently, bodies with their visible properties are the peculiar subjects of painting.

Subjects whose wholes or parts are consecutive are called actions. Consequently, actions are the peculiar subject of poetry.[31]

Lessing is saying here what the semanticists say in a more technical way — that visual perception or imagining is structural, relational, multidimensional. The stream-of-consciousness writer must deal with this multidimensionality, however, because unlike Lessing's poet he is not merely concerned with action but also with people and things in action. Thus a stream-of-consciousness novelist tries to depict a multidimensional consciousness in the process of flow.

It could be argued here that all novelists have always attempted to depict reality. But the problem is peculiarly acute for the stream-of-consciousness writer, for he is trying to simulate the effect of reality impinging upon the consciousness. We have heard Virginia Woolf, herself a stream-of-consciousness novelist, speaking of Joyce: "Let us record the atoms as they fall upon the mind in the order in which they fall, let us trace the pattern, however disconnected and incoherent in appearance, which each sight or incident scores upon the consciousness."[32] Thus, as A. A. Mendilow says, the stream-of-consciousness novelist tries to "plumb the deeper levels of human nature, the foreconscious, the subconscious, the depths where experience and awareness proceed not entirely or even mainly in a verbal medium, but are tactile and motile and visual and aural too."[33] Other novelists attempt rather to summarize the flow of consciousness than to simulate it and thus operate on a much higher level of abstraction.

In order to reproduce reality, an author would have to have at his command a medium like the "feelies" in *Brave New World,* in which the audience feel the sensation on their lips; and when "a little love [is] made" on a bearskin, the audience feel "every hair . . . separately and distinctly."[34] But since the novelist has only language at his command, he cannot reproduce reality. The stream-of-consciousness writer, however, tries to simulate reality, to give the impression to the reader that he is receiving the raw data of consciousness as they arrive in the mind of the character.

The problem of the stream-of-consciousness novelist thus begins to take shape: how can he simulate multidimensional reality in a linear, additive medium? A few examples of how the nature of language similarly complicates undertakings in other fields may help to underline the problem. As Herbert J. Muller puts it, the physicist runs into this difficulty: "Another way of describing the revolution in physics is to say that key nouns have changed into verbs—to move, to act, to happen. What moves and acts, physicists do not care; 'matter' to them means 'to matter,' to make a difference. But our language is still geared to express 'states of being' rather than processes."[35] James encounters a similar difficulty at the beginning of his chapter on the stream of thought: "If we could say in English 'it thinks,' as we say 'it rains' or 'it blows,' we should be stating the fact most simply and with the minimum of assumption. As we cannot, we must simply say that *thought goes on*."[36] John Livingston Lowes recognizes that difficulty several times in *The Road to Xanadu*. At the beginning of the book, as he prepares to plumb the "deep well" of Coleridge's imagination, he warns: "Above all . . . , it may not be forgotten that we are disengaging the strands of an extremely complex web. . . . It is not a gratuitous precaution, therefore, to repeat that in the paragraphs which follow the whole story is not being told at once." When he examines the components of the dream that led to "Kubla Khan," he says:

That Coleridge was conscious of constituent elements in the entrancing spectacle that rose before him . . . I do not for a moment believe. . . . The cluster of images so caught together had coalesced like light, and neither the links which we have been at such pains to discover nor the several images which we have sedulously disengaged were present as such (we may be sure) to consciousness at all.

And, analyzing one of his own associations, he discusses separately its several strands, but then adds in parentheses: "although in reality the strands of recollections were simultaneously interweaving like a nest of startled snakes."[37] Physicists, psychologists, literary critics—their difficulties with language because of its very nature help us to understand the almost insurmountable problem facing the novelist who tries to simulate the stream of consciousness.

While we are discussing the nature of language, we should take notice of one more point made by Korzybski. He outlines the levels of abstraction leading to speech as follows: "(1) the event, or scientific object, or the submicroscopic physico-chemical processes, (2) the ordinary object manufactured from the event by our lower nervous centres, (3) the psychological centers, and (4) the verbal definition of the term."[38] If this is the process by which atoms of experience, falling upon the mind, come finally to find expression in words, it is actually impossible to "record the atoms as they fall" or to "trace the pattern," since language is the fourth step in a process the first three steps of which are preverbal.

A. A. Mendilow summarizes all these problems very neatly: "Language cannot convey non-verbal experience; being successive and linear, it cannot reveal the unbroken flow of the process of living. Reality cannot be expressed or conveyed—only the illusion of it."[39]

To return to consciousness, its focus and the direction of its flow are a function of a bipolar regulatory system: on the one hand is the environment with all its demands; on the other, individual needs. Gardner Murphy's discussion of perception in bipolar terms is applicable to all of consciousness: "an organized process which is both outer and inner, which is organized in terms of saliences both of the world without and of the world within. Organization is not molded exclusively by the need pattern or by the stimulus pattern."[40] Now the outer world dominates, now the inner.

This bipolar regulating system results, as might be expected, in a consciousness which operates on a bipolar continuum: when the needs of the outer world dominate, consciousness is focused on problem solving; when inner needs dominate, consciousness yields to imagination and various forms of autistic thinking. "Creative thought . . . seems to be intermediate between problem solving and imagination, occurring in special situations involving nearly indistinguishable problem-solving behavior and imagination."[41] Very seldom, of course, is the state of consciousness a result of just one of the two sets of stimuli, external or internal. Although at various times one or the other dominates, any particular moment of consciousness is generally the result of a resolution of forces.

Since stream-of-consciousness writers concern themselves very little with problem solving and much with imagination, we shall focus on the latter.

Summarizing Vinacke's statements about the bipolarity of consciousness would seem to give the following continuum:

problem solving—creative thinking—imagination

Imagination, which aims at fulfilling "inner need-states," Vinacke breaks down into: (1) imaginative thinking, which "refers to mental processes in which the free activities of imagination are evoked primarily by external stimuli; typical situations of this kind are *play* and *projective tests*" and (2) autistic thinking, which "refers to mental processes in which the free activities of imagination are evoked or influenced primarily by internal stimuli, namely, *fantasy, dreams,* and *wishful thinking.*" The term *fantasy* distinguishes "the wish-fulfilling mental activity of waking life from that which occurs during sleep, i.e., dreams." In *wishful thinking,* "the wish [that is, the need, impulse, feeling] may be unconscious and the manifest content of the response [may] disguise the latent content."[42]

Recent research reported by Singer supports this model of the "general pattern of self-awareness or introspective behavior. At one end of this dimension of inner experience one finds the person given to extremely fantastic, fanciful daydreams, while at the other end the pattern suggests a considerably controlled, orderly, and objective type of daydreaming." Singer reports further that

both extremes represent responsiveness to internally produced cognitive experiences quite different from the extrovert's push for direct perceptual and physical contact with the environment. It is of particular interest that both poles of this dimension of daydreaming are also associated with a measure of curiosity differing chiefly in the relative interpersonal-impersonality of reported interests. Persons emphasizing control of their thought processes tend also to be curious about natural events or the physical world; by contrast, the more fanciful daydreamers appear more curious about people and their motives or characteristics.[43]

Psychologists also differentiate other states of consciousness or use other terms to characterize or to identify particular states of consciousness. For example, Murphy uses and defines:

1. thought—"all those processes by which the answer to a problem is found."
2. imageless thought—"the result of taking account of the nature of an object without the use of images."
3. memory—"function whereby past experience is revived or relived with a more or less definite realization that the present experience is a revival."
4. daydream—"a reverie or waking fantasy, particularly one in which the dreamer is represented as playing an enjoyable role."
5. reverie—"the result of dwelling upon a train of images without much attempt to control their direction."

6. hallucination—"extremely vivid image in any sensory field. Usually the term is used only when there is acceptance of the image by the subject, as a present fact of the environment."[44]

The difficulty with all these terms and discussions of the states of consciousness they seek to identify is that in the first place they continue to be used differently by different psychologists and that secondly they have additional meanings for the layman, sometimes entirely different from the meanings of the psychologists. Vinacke thus avoids the use of the term *consciousness,* which we have used here frequently, because of its "numerous, ill-defined meanings" and resultant ambiguity.[45] It should be noted that we are not concerned here with defending any particular description of consciousness. We are attempting merely to establish an understanding and a vocabulary that will be useful later in examining Joyce's stream-of-consciousness writing.

We have said nothing yet of the differences of individual consciousnesses. Because of the differences of environment in which individuals find themselves and the differences in their personal needs, psychologists have long agreed that no two consciousnesses are alike. Thus, for example, individuals associate differently. Jung found in his experiments that "the associations vary, within the range of the normal, chiefly under the influence of: (1) Attention. (2) Education. (3) The individual peculiarity of the subject."[46] As we will see later, an individual's associations are organized into idiosyncratic structures or constellations which are released to consciousness by internal or external stimuli, or which are sometimes repressed if they are painful.[47] Perception, too, "usually occurs in association with congruent personality characteristics," so that environment and an individual's needs play determining roles in how and what he sees, literally and figuratively.[48] We have already noted above that some people think largely in images and others do not, a fact which has caused considerable controversy in psychological circles. And we have also noted that a person's inner needs and the accidents of the environment control the focus and flow of consciousness, a fact which again points to myriad individual differences, since the environment and personal needs exist and interact entirely differently for each individual.

The nature of the psychological stream of consciousness and the problems facing the writer who would simulate it should now be clear enough that we can examine Joyce's simulation and his introduction of the stream-of-consciousness technique into the early chapters of *Ulysses.*

In Part Two from time to time we shall return briefly to a continued examination of the psychological stream of consciousness to see what the linguists, psycholinguists, and psychiatrists know about the language components of the stream and what tools of linguistic analysis they have developed to examine it and to characterize cognitive styles.

O'BRIEN: *Proust Confirmed by Neurosurgery*

Marcel Proust stated clearly and repeatedly in his vast *A la recherche du temps perdu* his determining theory of the involuntary memory, without which his many volumes would have lacked the essential composition on which he so justly insisted. Probably his clearest statement occurs in III, 870, of the Pléiade edition in three volumes:

Oui, si le souvenir, grâce à l'oubli, n'a pu contracter aucun lien, jeter aucun chaînon entre lui et la minute présente, s'il est resté à sa place, à sa date, s'il a gardé ses distances, son isolement dans le creux d'une vallée ou à la pointe d'un sommet, il nous fait tout à coup respirer un air nouveau, précisément parce que c'est un air qu'on a respiré autrefois, cet air plus pur que les poètes ont vainement essayer de faire régner dans le Paradis et qui ne pourrait donner cette sensation profonde de renouvellement que s'il avait été respiré déjà, car les vrais paradis sont les paradis qu'on a perdus. (III, 870)

On the following page Proust attempts to explain the strange joy he always feels on such occasions:

Or, cette cause je la devinais en comparant ces diverses impressions bienheureuses et qui avaient entre elles ceci de commun que je les éprouvais à la fois dans le moment, actuel et dans un moment éloigné, jusqu'à faire empiéter le passé sur le présent, à me faire hesiter à savoir dans lequel des deux je me trouvais; au vrais, l'être qui alors goûtait en moi cette impression la goûtait en ce qu'elle avait de commun dans un jour ancien et maintenant, dans ce qu'elle avait d'extra-temporel, un être qui n'apparaissait que quand, par une de ces identités entre le présent et le passé, il pouvait se trouver dans le seul milieu où il pût vivre, jouir de l'essence des choses, c'est-à-dire en dehors du temps. (III, 871)

Marcel Proust's entire work was based on that discovery within himself— whether or not he knew, at the time of his writing, *La Psychologie des sentiments* (1896) of Théodule Ribot or *La Fonction de la mémoire et le souvenir affectif* (1904) of Frédéric Paulhan.[1] In any event, Proust had experienced such a total recall—as had other writers before him; among them Rousseau, Gérard de Nerval, and Baudelaire.[2]

As so often happens among the greatest, men of science eventually catch up with the creative artist and confirm his observations. André Gide, daring to call Freud an "imbécile de génie," justly said: "Nous avons découvert son Amérique sans lui."[3]

Now, long after Proust's death in 1922, science has eventually caught up with him and gone far beyond such earlier experimenters as Ribot and Paulhan. Dr. Wilder Penfield of the Montreal Neurological Institute delivered before the National Academy of Sciences on 18 November 1957 a stimulating paper entitled "Some Mechanisms of Consciousness Discovered during Electrical Stimulation of the Brain,"[4] which has unfortunately not received the attention it deserves from students of Proust.

As a neurosurgeon, Dr. Penfield has carried on "experiments which only disease and injury can carry out upon the brains of unfortunate men and women." This inevitably makes the reader of Proust recall his remark that "un peu d'insomnie n'est pas inutile pour apprécier le sommeil, projeter quelque lumière dans cette nuit. Une mémoire sans défaillance n'est pas un très puissant excitateur à étudier les phénomènes de mémoire" (II, 651-52:SG).

From Sir Charles Sherrington, Dr. Penfield learned as a graduate student that "brain function is made possible by transient electrical potentials traveling the fibers of the nervous system." Accordingly, operating by osteoplastic craniotomy, he applied gentle electric stimuli on the cortex itself. For instance, he tells this case history:

Twenty-six years ago I was operating upon a woman under local anesthesia in the Royal Victoria Hospital and was applying to different points on the temporal lobe of her brain a stimulating electrode. She (E. W.) told me suddenly that she seemed to be living over again a previous experience. She seemed to see herself giving birth to her baby girl. That had happened years before, and meanwhile the girl had grown up. The mother was now lying on the operating table in my operating room, hoping that I could cure her attacks of focal epilepsy.

This, I thought, was a strange moment for her to talk of that previous experience, but then, I reflected, women were unpredictable, and it was never intended that men should understand them completely. Nevertheless, I noted the fact that it was while my stimulating electrode was applied to the left temporal lobe that this woman had had this unrelated and vivid recollection. (p. 53)

Years later a similar case recalled music from the past as in some of Proust's experiences:

When the electrode was applied in gray matter on the cut face of the temporal lobe at point 23, the patient observed: "I hear music." Fifteen minutes later, the electrode was applied to the same spot again without her knowledge, "I hear music again," she said. "It is like radio." Again and again, then, the electrode tip was applied to this point. Each time, she heard an orchestra playing the same piece of music. It apparently began at the same point and went on from verse to chorus. Seeing the electrical stimulator box, from where she lay under the surgical coverings, she thought it was a gramophone that someone was turning on from time to time.

She was asked to describe the music. When the electrode was applied again, she began to hum a tune, and all in the operating room listened in astonished silence. She was obviously humming along with the orchestra at about the tempo that would be expected.

Other points were stimulated with no result, except at three points, quite close to 23, where the same song was reproduced. (p. 57)

Dr. Penfield concludes the results of many operations by stating:

One must conclude that there is, hidden away in the brain, a record of the stream of consciousness. It seems to hold the detail of that stream as laid down during each man's waking conscious hours. Contained in this record are all those things of which the individual was once aware—such detail as a man might hope to remember for a few seconds or minutes afterward but which are largely lost to voluntary recall after that time. The things that he ignored are absent from the record. (p. 58)

As early as 1910, William James described the "stream of consciousness" as a river forever flowing, but Dr. Penfield would prefer to compare it to "the sequence on a wire recorder or to a continuous filmstrip with sound track" (p. 58).

The experiences reproduced are usually unimportant ones. They had often been "forgotten," although the subject never seemed to doubt that they were his own experiences. . . .

The experience that appears as the first experiential response when stimulation is begun in any case seems to depend on chance. It may be recent or it may come from childhood many years before. When a response has been produced, however, it seems to have an immediately facilitating effect on the result of subsequent stimulations. A second stimulus at approximately the same point, if not too long delayed, is apt to reproduce the same experience, beginning at the same moment of time. (pp. 58–59)

A certain number of passages well known to every Proustian deserve to be juxtaposed here to the findings of the neurosurgeon:

Ce qui nous rappelle le mieux un être, c'est justement ce que nous avions oublié (parce que c'était insignifiant et que nous lui avions laissé toute sa force). (I, 643:JF)

Les images choisies par le souvenir sont aussi arbitraires, aussie étroites, aussi insaisissables, que celles que l'imagination avait formées et la réalité détruites. Il n'y a pas de raison pour qu'en dehors de nous un lieu réel possède plutôt les tableaux de la mémoire que ceux du rêve. (II, 752:SG)

La mémoire, au lieu d'un exemplaire en double toujours présent à nos yeux des divers faits de notre vie, est plutôt un néant d'où par instant une similitude nous permet de tirer, ressuscités, des souvenirs morts. (III, 146:P)

Most certainly Dr. Penfield would agree with these statements by Proust. Continuing his "Special Report" Dr. Penfield says:

Curiously enough, two experiences or strips of time are never activated concurrently. Consequently, there is no confusion. There seems to be an all-or-nothing organization which inhibits other records from being activated.

This is not a memory, as we usually use the word, although it may have some relation to it. No man can recall by voluntary effort such a wealth of detail. A man may learn a song so that he can sing it perfectly, but he probably cannot recall in detail any one of the many times he heard it. Most things that a man is able to recall to memory are generalizations and summaries. If it were not so, we might find ourselves confused, perhaps, by too great a richness of detail.

Many a patient has told me that the experience brought back by the electrode is much more real than remembering. And yet he is still aware of the present situation. There is a doubling of consciousness, and yet he knows which is the present. (p. 59)

Surely this is not remote from Proust's seminal remark:

Comme il y a une géométrie dans l'escape, il y a une psychologie dans le temps, où les calculs d'une psychologie plane ne seraient plus exacts parce qu'on n'y tiendrait pas compte du temps et d'une des formes qu'il revêt, l'oubli. (III, 557:F)

Examining "The Ganglionic Record," Dr. Penfield asks:

How is this record of the past stored in the brain? and where? One may assume that at the time of the original experience electrical potentials passed through the nerve cells and nerve connections of a recording mechanism in a specific patterned sequence and that some form of permanent facilitation preserves that sequence so that the record can be replayed at a later time, in a manner analogous to the replaying of a wire recorder or tape recorder. But this remains a supposition. (p. 60)

Despite his vast experience with artificial stimulation, he can say:

When these interpretations of the present are produced by the electrode, we call them illusions, since they are false interpretations. But in normal life and under normal conditions these feelings are not illusions. They are true. They are reliable signals that can rise into consciousness only after a comparison is made between past records and the present experience. How else could the sudden awareness that this has happened before come to us with true meaning? Or how else could we know that this or that brings danger before we have had "time to think"?
Cortex for Comparative Interpretation.—Thus it is evident that the temporal cortex, on stimulation, yields two types of response which are psychical rather than sensory or motor. The two forms are (1) a flash-back of past experience and (2) a signaling of interpretation of the present experience. The two types of response would seem to form parts of one subconscious process, the process of comparing present experience with past similar experiences. (p. 63)

Is this not precisely young Marcel's experience of the three beckoning trees seen on the horizon near Balbec from Mme de Villeparisis' carriage that vaguely recall the three towers of Martinville and Vieuxvicq as they changed relation to Dr. Percepied's carriage near Combray? (I, 179–82 and I, 717–18).
In summary Dr. Wilder Penfield seems to summarize the whole of Proust's theory:

There is a permanent record of the stream of consciousness within the brain. It is preserved in amazing detail. No man can, by voluntary effort, call this detail back to memory. But, hidden in the interpretive areas of the temporal lobes, there is a key to a mechanism that unlocks the past and seems to scan it for the purpose of automatic interpretation of the present. It seems probable also, that this mechanism serves us as we make conscious comparison of present experience with similar past experiences. (p. 65)

Optimistically the neurosurgeon can speak of opening "a new chapter in the physiology of the brain" (page 65). But he was not forced, as Marcel Proust was, to be both the experimenter and the subject experimented upon, both the subtle handler of the electrode and the bare lobe of the brain.

"Grave incertitude," says Proust, "toutes les fois que l'esprit se sent dépassé par lui-même; quand lui, le chercheur, est tout ensemble le pays obscur où ʾil doit chercher et où tout son bagage ne lui sera de rien. Chercher? Pas seulement; créer. Il est en face de quelque chose qui n'est pas encore et que seul il peut réaliser puis faire entrer dans sa lumière" (I, 45:S).

LEOPOLD: *Some Problems of Terminology*

In the literature that has grown up round the technique of the novels of Dorothy Richardson, James Joyce, Virignia Woolf, and other authors to whose work the term "stream of consciousness" is usually applied, there is a remarkable lack of uniformity in terminology. Scholars frequently use different terms to describe the same device, or, worse still, use the same term to describe different devices.

In the four major American studies of the last ten years, a number of disparities emerge. L. E. Bowling[1] talks of "the stream-of-consciousness technique" and sees as its two main devices "interior monologue" and "internal analysis." Robert Humphrey[2] rejects "the stream-of-consciousness technique" but admits "the stream-of-consciousness novel" and sees as its two main devices "direct interior monologue" and "indirect interior monologue," to which he adds the additional devices of "omniscient description" and "soliloquy." M. J. Friedman[3] simply takes over the terminology of Bowling and Humphrey but claims that "internal analysis" (Bowling) is different from "indirect interior monologue" (Humphrey).[4]

As Friedman gives no examples to illustrate his terms, the difference remains obscure. Leon Edel,[5] who seldom comes to grips with basic problems of technique, uses the term "internal monologue," equates it with "stream of consciousness" and applies it on page 84 to a monologue in the first person and on page 108 to monologues in the third person. In German the confusion is at least as great as in English. A recent study by K. R. Meyer bears the title *Zur erlebten Rede (The Interior Monologue) im englischen Roman des 20. Jahrhunderts,*[6] thus clearly equating "erlebte Rede" and "interior monologue." It is then rather puzzling to find in the body of the work a statement to the effect that it is absolutely necessary to distinguish between "Bewusstseinsstrom" or "innerer Monolog" on the one hand and "erlebte Rede" on the other.[7] So eminent a scholar as Gerhard Storz[8] equates "erlebte Rede" and "le monologue intérieur," while the equally eminent Wolfgang Kayser[9] points out that the stream of consciousness may be represented by *either* "innerer Monolog" or "erlebte Rede."

Even in French, in which language the term "interior monologue" first appeared, some confusion exists. For example, the famous study by Dujardin[10] distinguishes between "le monologue intérieur" and "le monologue intérieur indirect" but does not take account of "le style indirect libre," which term had already been coined to describe the device that Dujardin calls "le monologue intérieur indirect."

Those who have sought to bring together the English, German, and French terms have not added greatly to the clarity of the picture. Warren and Wellek[11] call "stream of consciousness" the "loose, indirect correspondent" for "erlebte Rede," "le style indirect libre" and "le monologue intérieur." M. J. Friedman says that critics in English prefer the term "stream of consciousness" and in French the term "interior monologue" whilst the Germans use "erlebte Rede," which term is much closer to "monologue intérieur" than to "stream of consciousness."[12]

In practice most of this confusion has arisen from loose use of the general term "stream of consciousness" and from uncertainty about the exact nature of, and the differences between, two of the main techniques of the stream-of-consciousness novel. In what follows I shall first examine the term "stream of consciousness" and then list the six methods of representation that may be employed in the stream-of-consciousness novel, at the same time showing that four of the six methods give rise to no grave terminological problems but that the remaining two—"erlebte Rede" and "interior monologue"—have given rise to endless confusion.

The term "stream of consciousness" is in many ways a misnomer, since Joyce and some of the other stream-of-consciousness novelists are obviously more concerned with "the stream of pre-consciousness" than with the stream of consciousness, which suggests something rational, shaped, and ordered. However, the term is too well established to be displaced or altered now. It was unfortunate that "stream of consciousness," although coined by William James about the turn of the century, became fashionable in English and American criticism at about the same time as the term "le monologue intérieur" emerged in French.[13] i.e., in the early 1920s. Both terms seem to have been used more or less indiscriminately. At first Dorothy Richardson, for example, objected strongly to the term "stream of consciousness" but claimed that its "transatlantic equivalent," the term "interior monologue," was not quite as objectionable.[14] (If "stream of consciousness" ever was an English term and "interior monologue" an American term, the distinction has long since disappeared.) Some scholars, such as Leon Edel, still equate the two terms, but it seems fairly generally accepted nowadays that "stream of consciousness" refers to the subject-matter of a certain type of novel, while "interior monologue" is *one* of the methods of presenting this subject matter. In the classification of novels according to subject-matter, "the stream-of-consciousness novel" has become an accepted category. On the other hand, the term "the interior monologue novel," although a quite legitimate category in a classification based on methods of representation, is of very rare occurrence, simply because there are extraordinarily few novels that are entirely in interior monologue.

The procedure of Robert Humphrey in this connection has a great deal to recommend it. He uses "stream of consciousness" as a general term to describe ". . . novels which have as their essential subject-matter the consciousness of one or more characters; that is, the depicted consciousness serves as a screen on which the material in these novels is presented."[15] Consequently he admits "the stream-of-consciousness novel" but rejects "the stream-of-consciousness technique," since a number of techniques are involved. It may be assumed that Humphrey also admits "stream of consciousness" in reference to subject-matter use such as: "In this novel the stream of consciousness of the principal character is represented."

In German no generally accepted equivalent of "stream-of-consciousness novel" has emerged. "Stream of consciousness" in reference to subject matter is expressed quite normally by "Strom des Bewusstseins" or

"Bewusstseinsstrom." ("Der Strom des Bewusstseins in einer erdichten Gestalt wird darstellbar durch den inneren Monolog. . . .[16]) However, neither term lends itself to attributive use and one does not say "ein Roman des Bewusstseinsstroms," though such a term would be comprehensible. Some attempts have been made to express the idea in a slightly different way: thus K. R. Meyer uses "Bewusstseinskunst" as a general term for "the stream-of-consciousness novel"; which still leaves the problem of "*a* stream-of-consciousness novel." The explanation of this lack of German terms may well be that, although there are German novels that represent the stream of consciousness and use the techniques of the English novelists, there is no group of novelists that correspond to, or go as far as Dorothy Richardson, James Joyce, and Virginia Woolf, all of whom followed obviously related aims and techniques. The stream-of-consciousness novel in Germany is a much more isolated phenomenon and no need has been felt to express an idea such as "the German stream-of-consciousness novel." When German scholars use the English term, as they frequently do, they are usually referring to the English or American novel.

In French the situation is much the same as in German and probably for much the same reason. "Stream of consciousness" in relation to subject matter is expressed by "le courant de la conscience," but the term does not lend itself to attributive use. "A stream-of-consciousness novel" may be rendered by a paraphrase such as "un roman du type courant de la conscience," but there seems to be no standard phrase.

When we come to consider the terminology relating to the techniques of the stream-of-consciousness novel, it is helpful to begin by listing the possible methods of representation available to the author who seeks to represent the stream of consciousness. Merely the listing of them will, of course, introduce problems of terminology.

1. Direct speech
2. Indirect speech
3. Unspoken direct speech ("fingierte direkte Rede")
4. Authorial report
5. "Erlebte Rede"
6. Interior monologue

One and 2 are well established concepts and need no explanation. They can never be a major part of the representation of the stream of consciousness, since the author of this type of novel must necessarily go deeper than articulate speech.

In 3 the term "fingierte direkte Rede" seems to have been coined by O. Funke[17] to describe the technique of presenting as direct speech words that are not actually spoken. For example: "At intervals a misgiving shot like a thin flying needle through the solid satisfaction of his sensations: *She is a strange and incalculable woman—why am I doing this?*" Shot, and was gone, almost before perceived!"[18]

Sustained examples of unspoken direct speech appear to be what Humphrey means by "soliloquy." They are in the first person like interior monologue but are much more articulate and coherent than interior monologue.

In 4 some problems of terminology may arise. Humphrey, for example, uses the term "omniscient description," and other designations occur. However, these problems are rarely grave, since it is almost always clear that the critic is talking of the report in the third person by the omniscient author: the author who describes from his vantage-point what happens around, to, and inside his characters. It is the oldest and most widely used method of representation in all narrative.

The real confusion of terminology in the analysis of the techniques of the stream-of-consciousness novel has arisen in connection with 5 and 6. Neither of these devices is invented by the stream-of-consciousness novelists, but both are used far more frequently and extensively by them than by any previous novelists. They warrant detailed consideration.

Erlebte Rede. The phenomenon consists in reporting speech or thought in a form intermediate between direct and indirect discourse. It lacks the basic characteristics of direct discourse in that the first person is not used and no quotation marks are employed: it lacks the basic characteristics of indirect discourse in that it is not prefaced by "he said," "he thought," "he felt," etc., may not follow the tense sequence of indirect discourse, and—in German—uses the indicative instead of the subjunctive. From another point of view, the narrator is, as Wolfgang Kayser puts it both there and not there: everything in "erlebte Rede" is seen from the perspective of the character, but the use of the third person suggests a report by the omniscient author. Examples are legion in the modern novel and short story. The following example is from Dorothy Richardson

The first four sentences (down to "originality") are authorial report The remainder is "erlebte Rede." Moving between authorial report "erlebte Rede," and sometimes unspoken direct speech and interior monologue is characteristic of the stream-of-consciousness novel.

Sitting there dully listening she began to have a sort of insight into the way these jests were made. It was a thing that could be cultivated. Her tired brain experimented. Certain things she heard she knew she would remember; she felt she would repeat them with an air of originality. They would seem very brilliant in any of her circles—though the girls did that sort of thing rather well; but in a less "refined" way; that was true! This was the sort of thing the girls did; only their way was not half so clever . . . if she did, every one would wonder what was the matter with her; and she would not be able to keep it up, without a great deal of practice; and it would keep out something else . . . but perhaps for some people there was something in it; it was their way. It had always been Alma's way, a little. Only now she did it better. . . .[19]

This device is found frequently from the period of Naturalism on, but examples can also be found from the much more remote past. Fehr quotes examples in English from as far back as Scott's *Guy Mannering,* and Wilpert claims that there are examples even in Latin literature. The device is analysed and classified by French and German scholars in the decade after 1912, following the publication of an article by Charles Bally, who coined the term "le style indirect libre." There was a considerable controversy about a suitable German designation, but eventually, in 1921, E. Lorck coined the term "erlebte Rede," which, though often attacked as inadequate and misleading, has maintained itself.[20]

In English the earliest analysis and classification of "erlebte Rede" with which I am familiar was by G. O. Curme,[21] who used the unwieldy designation "independent form of indirect discourse." After Curme there seems to have been very little discussion of "erlebte Rede" in English, and certainly no term emerged for it. Lubbock, in his chapter on Flaubert in *The Craft of Fiction,* seems constantly to be talking about "erlebte Rede" but without defining it closely or designating it. Jespersen[22] was one who did describe the phenomenon and invent a term for it. He called it "represented speech," a translation of his own suggested German designation "vorgestellte Rede." Neither Jespersen's English nor his German term has achieved any currency, though A. A. Mendilow has revived "represented speech."[23]

In view of this lack of adequate analysis and classification of "erlebte Rede" in English, it was no wonder that its designation should have been a major source of confusion in studies of the stream-of-consciousness novel. As was mentioned at the beginning, Edel appears to subsume both "erlebte Rede" and "interior monologue" under the term "internal monologue"; Bowling calls "erlebte Rede" "internal analysis," Humphrey "indirect interior monologue" and Friedman both "internal analysis" and "indirect interior monologue."

In German it is surprising to find that some confusion of terminology exists despite the fact that "erlebte Rede" is a meaningful and generally understood concept. As was shown above, "erlebte Rede" is equated by some scholars with "interior monologue" or "le monologue intérieur." However, the problem is not as grave in practice as the titles of the works by Meyer and Storz might suggest. Of recent scholars only Gerhard Storz perpetuates the identification of "erlebte Rede" with "innerer Monolog." Despite the confusing title of his book, Meyer makes it quite clear that he differentiates between the two. Wolfgang Kayser is quite emphatic that "erlebte Rede" and "innerer Monolog" are two different things. Wilpert's entry under "innerer Monolog"[24] defines clearly the difference between the two. There can, then, be no doubt that most German scholars consistently use "erlebte Rede" for the device described above and "innerer Monolog" for what is described in the next section.

In French "le style indirect libre" is the established and accepted equivalent of "erlebte Rede." The only complication that occurs is that Dujardin's term "le monologue intérieur indirect" exists alongside "le style indirect libre" and designates the same thing. However, no real confusion arises. As was said above of Humphrey's "indirect interior monologue," Dujardin's term is a literary one, applicable to sustained passages and consequently particularly applicable to the stream-of-consciousness novel. "Le style indirect libre," on the other hand, is a general term applicable to "erlebte Rede" in all its forms.

Interior monologue. As good a definition as any of interior monologue is still the one given by Dujardin[25] in 1931:

Le monologue intérieur, comme tout monologue, est un discours du personnage mis en scène et a pour objet de nous introduire directement dans la vie intérieure de ce personnage, sans que l'auteur intervienne par des explications ou des commentaires, et, comme tout monologue, est un discours sans auditeur et un discours non prononcé;

· ·

mais il se différencie du monologue traditionnel en ce que:
quant à sa matière, il est une expression de la pensée la plus intime, la plus proche de l'inconscient;
quant à son esprit, il est un discours antérieur à toute organisation logique, reproduisant cette pensée en son état naissant et d'aspect tout venant;

quant à sa forme, il se réalise en phrases directes réduites au minimum syntaxial;
et ainsi réspond-il essentiellement à la conception que nous nous faisons aujourd'hui de la poésie.

It also emerges quite clearly from Dujardin's analysis that interior monologue is always in the first person.

The standard example of interior monologue is Molly Bloom's monologue in *Ulysses*. The following is a brief extract from it.

Yes because he never did a thing like that before as ask to get his breakfast in bed with a couple of eggs since the *City Arms* hotel when he used to be pretending to be laid up with a sick voice doing his highness to make himself interesting to that old faggot Mrs. Riordan that he thought he had a great leg of and she never left us a farthing all for masses for herself and her soul greatest miser ever was actually afraid to lay out 4d for her methylated spirit telling me all her ailments. . . .[26]

Most other exponents of interior monologue have not gone as far as Joyce in the matter of punctuation, but the method is otherwise basically the same.

If one compares this passage of interior monologue with the example of "erlebte Rede" from Dorothy Richardson, one is immediately struck by the difference in person. There are other differences –quite apart from the difference in punctuation: differences in the level of consciousness represented, in syntactical coherence, in situational relevance, in the degree of mediation by the author. But the unmistakable difference is that the "erlebte Rede" is in the third person and the interior monologue in the first person. This basic characteristic of "erlebte Rede" and "interior monologue" is never stressed sufficiently by writers on the subject, all of whom seem to assume or ignore the difference in person.

If one is clear that "interior monologue" means this direct representation of the innermost thoughts of a character in the first person, then little confusion is possible. The term "interior monologue" is accepted and used in the above sense, at least by Bowling, Humphrey, and Friedman, though Humphrey does add the unnecessary attribute "direct." Confusion arose in the past through the equation of "interior monologue" with "stream of consciousness" and failure to distinguish clearly between "interior monologue" and "erlebte Rede." The term "internal monologue" is sometimes used but "interior monologue" seems to have achieved much greater currency.

The confusion that existed in German between "erlebte Rede" and "innerer Monolog" was discussed above under "erlebte Rede." "Innerer Monolog" seems now to be a generally accepted equivalent of "interior monologue" as described above. Franz Stanzel[27] uses "der stille Monolog," but he appears to be alone in this.

In French "le monologue intérieur" has been used since about 1921 to designate the device described above and seems to have maintained its position without competitors.

It is clear that most problems of terminology in the analysis of the stream-of-consciousness novels have been connected with the term "stream of consciousness" and with the devices of "erlebte Rede" and "interior monologue." It may well be asked whether it matters very much at this stage whether there are terminological problems or not in connection with the stream-of-consciousness novel. After all, the first novels of Dorothy Richardson appeared over forty years ago. *Ulysses* belongs to 1922 and even Faulkner's stream-of-consciousness novels are some thirty years old. The stream-of-consciousness novel as a separate and special novel-type belongs to the past, and the total volume of critical literature about it is small compared with that about some individual novelists and other aspects of the novel. Yet it must not be forgotten that the innovations of the few become the stock-in-trade of the many. Every novelist today, even though his works may have little in common with those of James Joyce and Virginia Woolf, has at his disposal the devices in which the stream-of-consciousness novelists specialized. Consequently greater clarity about the techniques of the stream-of-consciousness novel means greater clarity about the techniques of the modern novel in general.

STEINBERG: *Stream-of-Consciousness Defined*

In discussing James Joyce's *Ulysses,* critics frequently use interchangeably a whole series of terms: "stream of consciousness, stream of thought, *monologue intérieur,* internal monologue, interior monologue, soliloquy, silent soliloquy." Are they all appropriate? Certainly "monologue" and "soliloquy," even when qualified by such adjectives as "interior" and "silent," are odd terms to apply to thought and consciousness, which, while they may contain words, have many other components.

Jacques Souvage raises the problem again in his careful survey of what the critics have said about the dramatized novel in his *Introduction to the Study of the Novel:*

> Mr. Edel makes an attempt at clearing up the confusion which has arisen round the terms "stream of consciousness" and "internal monologue." He finally draws the following tentative distinction between the two terms: "The term 'internal monologue' becomes merely a useful designation for certain works of fiction of sustained subjectivity, written from a single point of view, in which the writer narrows down the stream of consciousness and places us largely at the centre of the character's thoughts—that centre where thought often uses words rather than images." May I, by way of qualifying Mr. Edel's statement, propose that the terms "internal (or interior) monologue" and "stream of consciousness" be reserved for, respectively, the cases where the inner flux is being released and those where sensory experience is superimposed upon the inner flux in process of releasement.[1]

We must go on from Edel's definition, however, as, in fact, he himself does, because, as I shall show below, the problem is not only one of "where thought often uses words rather than images," but also where consciousness often uses images rather than—or in addition to—words.

What is needed to distinguish usefully among these terms so that they themselves will distinguish what various authors are attempting is a valid psychological or semantic framework. Such a framework would help differentiate not only the levels of speech involved but also the pre-speech levels of consciousness. One could then meaningfully sort out the various terms and assign them according to their literal meaning (rather than the meaning arbitrarily assigned to them by a critic) and the level of speech or pre-speech which they can most adequately define. An adequate framework for such a purpose is, in fact, available.

At this point it will be useful to examine again what the stream-of-consciousness novelists and some other critics claim the stream-of-consciousness technique to be. Placing Joyce's stream-of-consciousness technique in such a context will help to show more clearly what it is and may help to sharpen the term "stream-of-consciousness technique" and other terms associated with it.

Dujardin, regarded by many as the innovator of the technique, writes:

> Le monologue intérieur est, dans l'ordre de la poésie, le discours sans auditeur et non prononcé, par lequel un personnage exprime sa pensée la

plus intime, la plus proche de l'inconscient, antérieurement à toute organisation logique, c'est-à-dire en son état naissant, par le moyen de phrases directes réduites au minimum syntaxial, de façon à donner l'impression "tout venant."[2]

And Dujardin quotes Valéry Larbaud, an early enthusiast of the stream-of-consciousness technique, as saying that the *monologue intérieur* is the expression "des pensées les plus intimes, les plus spontanées, celles qui paraissent se former à l'insu de la conscience et qui semblent antérieures au discours organisé."[3] Budgen says that Joyce told him, "I try to give the unspoken, unacted thoughts of people in the way they occur"; and Djuna Barnes notes that Joyce said, "I have recorded, simultaneously, what a man says, sees, thinks, and what such seeing, thinking, saying does, to what you Freudians call the subconscious."[4] Virginia Woolf, herself acclaimed a successful stream-of-consciousness novelist by the critics, discusses at some length what modern novelists should try to do:

Examine for a moment an ordinary mind on an ordinary day. The mind receives a myriad impressions—trivial, fantastic, evanescent, or engraved with the sharpness of steel. From all sides they come, an incessant shower of innumerable atoms; and as they fall, as they shape themselves into the life of Monday or Tuesday, the accent falls differently from of old.

The task of the novelist, then, as she sees it, is "to convey this varying, this unknown and uncircumscribed spirit, whatever aberration or complexity it may display with as little mixture of the alien and external as possible." She gives what well may be a credo for stream-of-consciousness writers: "Let us record the atoms as they fall upon the mind in the order in which they fall, let us trace the pattern, however disconnected and incoherent in appearance, which each sight or incident scores upon the consciousness." Of *Ulysses*, she says:

Mr. Joyce . . . is concerned at all costs to reveal the flickerings of that innermost flame which flashes its messages through the brain, and in order to preserve it he disregards with complete courage whatever seems to him adventitious, whether it be probability, or coherence, or any other of these signposts which for generations have served to support the imagination of a reader when called upon to imagine what he can neither touch nor see.[5]

She made this analysis on the basis of chapters of *Ulysses* which were then (April 1919) appearing in the *Little Review.*

More recent critics have also attempted definitions. Lawrence E. Bowling writes:

> The stream-of-consciousness technique may be defined as that narrative method by which the author attempts to give *a direct quotation of the mind*—not merely of the language area but of the whole consciousness. . . . The only criterion is that it introduce us directly into the interior life of the character, without any intervention by way of comment or explanation on the part of the author.[6]

And Robert Humphrey finds that "we may define stream-of-consciousness fiction as a type of fiction in which the basic emphasis is placed on exploration of the pre-speech levels of consciousness for the purpose, primarily, of revealing the psychic being of the characters."[7]

These statements agree on several important points. First, they suggest that the stream-of-consciousness writer must not intervene "by way of comment or explanation"; he must provide "as little mixture of the external and alien as possible." Other statements by some of the authors quoted above support this contention. For example, Dujardin says that the *monologue intérieur* "est un discours du personnage mis en scène et a pour objet de nous introduire directement dans la vie intérieure de ce personnage, sans que l'auteur intervienne par des explications ou des commentaires."[8] An oft-quoted statement of Joyce holds that "the artist, like the God of creation, remains within or behind or beyond or above his handiwork, invisible, refined out of existence, indifferent, paring his fingernails."[9] The intrusive author of old, then, must disappear.

Second, the statements agree that the stream-of-consciousness technique is not soliloquy, either spoken or unspoken; and third, they agree that the stream-of-consciousness technique expresses, or explores, or simulates, or is concerned with a pre-speech level of consciousness: "sa pensée . . . la plus proche de l'inconscient, antérieurement à toute organisation logique"; "des pensées . . . qui paraissent se former à l'insu de la conscience et qui semblent antérieures au discours organisé"; "unspoken, unacted thoughts"; "the atoms as they fall upon the mind"; "a direct quotation of the mind—not merely of the language area but of the whole consciousness"; "the pre-speech levels of consciousness."

Before we can decide, therefore, just exactly what we mean by the stream-of-consciousness technique, we must first decide what the pre-speech levels of consciousness are. Alfred Korzybski has included them in his outline of the four basic levels of abstraction: "(1) the event, or scientific object, or the submicroscopic physico-chemical processes, (2) the ordinary object manufactured from the event by our lower nervous centres, (3) the psychological centres, and (4) the verbal defini-tion of the term."[10] According to the stream-of-consciousness novelists and to the critics quoted, the stream-of-consciousness technique deals with the levels below, or at least before, Korzybski's fourth or verbal level. Furthermore, it cannot possibly be concerned with Korzybski's first level, the physico-chemical level; for as Phyllis Bentley says, "James Joyce records the swift succession of thought association, but even he does not detail the physical nerve processes of which they are a result."[11]

Miss Bentley might have said that a novelist cannot (rather than does not) detail the physical nerve processes, for contemporary science is still not sure of what they are and how they operate. And even if the pro-cesses were thoroughly understood, they would be so far removed from our organization of them into what we know as reality and so numerous that the author could not possibly present them in such a way that the reader could collect them into meaningful patterns of any sort. Instead of being confronted by a simulation of the stream of consciousness, the reader would be confronted by William James's "booming, buzzing confusion." It might be further argued that, psychologically at least, Korzybski's first level is not a level of consciousness.

The stream-of-consciousness technique, therefore, is concerned with the second and third levels of abstraction set up by Korzybski. It is at these levels that one finds psychological images, sensations, and perceptions. And, as we have already seen, it is precisely these two levels of consciousness that Joyce simulates in "Proteus" and "Lestrygonians." We have already seen that all the examples of Joyce's presentation of sensations, images, and perceptions used in the discussion of simulating the psychological stream of consciousness came from "Proteus" and "Lestrygonians." There are no such examples in "Penelope," for in that chapter Joyce was doing something else. I would prefer, therefore, to use the term "stream-of-consciousness technique" for what Joyce attempts in "Proteus" and "Lestrygonians" and to apply another term to "Penelope."

"Penelope," Molly's monologue, represents Korzybski's fourth, or verbal level. At this next higher level, an author presents the ruminations of a character who has organized his thoughts into language, translating the matters of paramount importance in his stream of consciousness into language patterns. At this level, the character is speaking silently to himself. Interior monologue or silent soliloquy would therefore be a very apt characterization of what the author is attempting. As Edel points out, the term "monologue" (or "soliloquy") "because of its associations with the theatre, has distinct literary and dramatic connotations that do not convey the idea of flux." They indicate a character speaking in some coherent, organized way, even if silently. Thus interior monologue and silent soliloquy are more adequately suited to the characterization of a level of abstraction higher than the stream of consciousness.[12] "Penelope," then, would be a good example of silent soliloquy. As Humphrey says, soliloquy in the stream-of-consciousness novel "tacitly" assumes an audience, and "respects the audience's expectation of mental wandering."[13]

We can continue to employ Korzybski's concept of abstraction to describe still higher levels of abstraction in writing. The next level would be the spoken monologue or soliloquy, which is seldom used in the novel. Edel says: "In the traditional monologue—in its original Greek sense it was a 'speaking alone'—the character gives the audience logical and reasoned thoughts. These are 'structured' even while they represent inner reflection or reverie, and are rendered without relation to external stimuli." The great soliloquies of Shakespeare, Edel points out, "are structured monologues in which the mind presents reasoned and ordered thought, the 'end-product' of the stream of consciousness, not the disordered stream itself."[14]

Much of the "Cyclops" episode in *Ulysses* is a variety of spoken monologue:

I was just passing the time of day with old Troy of the D.M.P. at the corner of Arbour hill there and be damned but a bloody sweep came along and he near drove his gear into my eye. I turned around to let him have the weight of my tongue when who should I see dodging along Stony Batter only Joe Hynes.—Lo, Joe, says I. How are you blowing? Did you see that bloody chimneysweep near shove my eye out with his brush? (287:1/292:1)

Gilbert characterizes the chapter nicely: "The story, here, is told by a simple and bibulous Dubliner, a nondescript, in the highly coloured idiom of the profane vulgar, and his simple periods are punctuated by Our Lady's adjective."[15]

At the next level we have *erlebte Rede,* or narrated monologue, a term not used in discussions of *Ulysses.* Dorrit Cohn defines *erlebte Rede* as

the renderings of a character's thoughts in his own idiom, while maintaining the third-person form of narration. Its transposition into present tense and first person ... yields an interior monologue. It would appear ... that these two techniques for rendering a character's psyche differ only by simple grammatical details. But when we see *erlebte Rede* in a surrounding epic context, its distinctiveness becomes clear: by maintaining the person and tense of authorial narration, it enables the author to recount the character's silent thoughts without a break in the narrative thread.

She offers the following example from Kate Leslie's thoughts in D. H. Lawrence's *The Plumed Serpent:*

Yet she could not be purely this, this thing of sheer reciprocity. Surely, though her woman's nature was reciprocal to his male, surely it was more than that! Surely he and she were not two potent and reciprocal currents between which the Morning Star flashed like a spark out of nowhere. Surely this was not it? Surely she had one tiny Morning Star inside her, which was herself, her very own soul and star-self![16]

Mrs. Cohn finds a version of *erlebte Rede* in *A Portrait:*

The slide was shot suddenly. The penitent came out. He was next. He stood up in terror and walked blindly to the box.

At last it had come. He knelt in the silent gloom and raised his eyes to the white crucifix suspended above him. *God would see that he was sorry. He would tell all his sins. His confession would be long, long. Everybody in the chapel would know then what a sinner he had been. Let them know. It was true. But God had promised to forgive him if he was sorry. He was sorry.* He clasped his hands and raised them toward the white form, praying with his darkened eyes, praying with all his trembling body, swaying his head to and fro like a lost creature, praying with whimpering lips.[17]

About this passage she makes the comment: "Unlike Kate's thoughts, Stephen's—which are not italicized in the original—are presented in alternation with outer happenings, including his own actions. He waits, stands up, kneels, raises his eyes, clasps and raises his hands, and so forth. At the same time he thinks his thoughts of fervent penitence in *erlebte Rede* (past tense and third person)."[18]

At the next level, the author summarizes in omniscient author's sentences what his characters think, feel, and do. A passage from Dorothy Richardson's *Pilgrimage* quoted by Edel exemplifies this level very well:

She glanced through the pages of its opening chapter, the chapter that was now part of her own experience; set down at last alive, so that the few pages stood in her mind, growing as a single day will grow, in memory, deep and wide, wider than the year to which it belongs. She was surprised to find, coming back after the interval of disturbed days, how little she had read.[19]

As we have seen, Joyce uses omniscient author's sentences in "Proteus" and "Lestrygonians."

The highest level of abstraction would be the one in which the author quite obviously intrudes, as does Trollope in the following passage:

But let the gentle-hearted reader be under no apprehension whatsoever. It is not destined that Eleanor shall marry Mr. Slope or Bertie Stanhope. And here, perhaps, it may be allowed to the novelist to explain his views on a very important point in the art of telling tales. He ventures to re-probate that system which goes so far to violate all proper confidence between the author and his readers. . . . Our doctrine is, that the author and the reader should move along together in full confidence with each other.[20]

Joyce gives a satiric sample of such writing in *Ulysses* in "Oxen of the Sun": "Did heart leap to heart? Nay, fair reader. In a breath 'twas done but—hold! Back! It must not be! In terror the poor girl flees away through the murk. She is the bride of darkness, a daughter of night. She dare not bear the sunnygolden babe of day." (406:37/413:36)

The six levels described above should be thought of as points on a vertical continuum rather than as steps on a ladder. Similar continua can be made of points which fall between those specified above. For example, Dickens characterizes a waterman at the beginning of chapter 2 of *The Pickwick Papers* as "a strange specimen of the human race, in a sackcloth coat, and apron of the same, who with a brass label and number round his neck, looked as if he were catalogued in some collection of rarities." Because Dickens says that the man is "a strange specimen of the human race" instead of supplying the reader with the necessary details by which he can form the same conclusion for himself, the statement is a higher level of abstraction than the quotation from ·Dorothy Richardson cited above. It is not as high a level of abstraction as the quotation cited from Trollope, however, because it does present some detail; thus Dickens is less intrusive than Trollope in the passages quoted.

Similarly the omniscient author's sentences in *Ulysses* are not quite as high a level of abstraction as the passage quoted from Dorothy Richardson, for Joyce would never say that one of his characters "was surprised to find . . . how little she had read."[21] Yet they are certainly higher than the example from the "Penelope" chapter of *Ulysses* which was labeled above as silent soliloquy. For example:

Stephen, an elbow rested on the jagged granite, leaned his palm against his brow and gazed at the fraying edge of his shiny black coatsleeve. Pain, that was not yet the pain of love, fretted his heart. Silently, in a dream she had come to him after her death, her wasted body within its loose brown graveclothes giving off an odour of wax and rosewood, her breath, that had bent upon him, mute, reproachful, a faint odour of wetted ashes. (7:25/5:29)

The omniscient author is apparent here, much more so than in soliloquy.

Any single paragraph or passage may draw from several levels of abstraction, as does this passage from *Ulysses,* which includes an omniscient author's sentence and silent soliloquy: "Stephen bent forward and peered at the mirror held out to him, cleft by a crooked crack, hair on end. As he and others see me. Who chose this face for me? This dogsbody to rid of vermin. It asks me too" (8:21/6:27). Or this one, which contains stream of consciousness, silent soliloquy, and omniscient author's statement: "He passed, dallying, the windows of Brown Thomas, silk mercers. Cascades of ribbons. Flimsy China silks. A tilted urn poured from its mouth a flood of bloodhued poplin: lustrous blood. The huguenots brought that here. *La causa è santa!* Tara, tara. Great chorus that. Tara. Must be washed in rainwater. Meyerbeer. Tara: bom bom bom" (165:41/168:17).

Finally, we must recognize that none of the sections from *Ulysses* are what could be called pure stream of consciousness. "Proteus" and

"Lestrygonians" contain silent soliloquy and omniscient author's sentences. And, as I have already indicated, "Penelope" is interior monologue or silent soliloquy; so, it cannot be pure stream of consciousness either. Indeed, pure stream of consciousness would be difficult, if not impossible, to read; for it would be a mass of psychological images, sensations, and perceptions which would provide little or no orientation or method of organization for the reader. Furthermore, it would be much too inefficient. As Phyllis Bentley points out, summary is particularly useful and efficient in dispatching unimportant matters on which the author does not wish to dwell.[22] Attempts to locate a character in time and space by means of a device of a lower level of abstraction than omniscient author's statements also lead to the same sort of self-conscious writing so typical of Dujardin's *Les Lauriers sont coupés*. Here is a typical passage from the opening pages:

The hour is striking, six, the hour I waited for. Here is the house I have to enter, where I shall meet someone; the house; the hall; let's go in. Evening has come; good the air is now; something cheerful in the air. The stairs; the first steps. Supposing he has left early; he sometimes does; but I have got to tell him the story of my day. The first landing; wide, bright staircase; windows.[23]

Dujardin might have done better if his opening sentence in the paragraph above stated simply, "Prince entered the house, walked through the hall, and began to mount the first set of steps." His character oriented, he could then have focused on Prince's thoughts, pausing only now and then to maintain the orientation with a phrase or two. As the passage stands, most of it is taken up with really unimportant matters. Joyce regularly locates or moves his characters in both "Proteus" and "Lestrygonians" by means of omniscient author's sentences, which, as summaries, take less time to inform the reader than do the simulated raw data on the stream of consciousness. Frequently, however, because he presents these sentences in the idiom and style of the character's stream of consciousness, they are not as obtrusive as they otherwise would be.

We have thus characterized "Proteus," "Lestrygonians," and "Penelope" by means of the vertical continuum which we have built up:

statement by an obviously intrusive author
summary statement by an omniscient author
narrated monologue *(erlebte Rede)*

spoken soliloquy or monologue

silent, internal, or interior soliloquy or monologue *(monologue intérieur)*

(simulated) stream of consciousness[24]

The lowest level of abstraction is the one to which I would limit the term "stream of consciousness." "Proteus" and "Lestrygonians" would thus be stream-of-consciousness chapters. Again according to my definition, silent, internal, or interior soliloquy or monologue occurs when a character speaks silently to himself, in his own mind; the character can hear himself in his mind's ear, but no one else can hear him or need even be aware that he is thinking. "Penelope" would thus be classified as internal monologue or silent soliloquy. Simple summary statements appear in "Proteus" and "Lestrygonians" as the omniscient author's sentences which help to orient the reader.

Neither spoken soliloquy nor statement by an obviously intrusive author appears in "Proteus," "Lestrygonians," or "Penelope." The characters in those three chapters sometimes speak to themselves (for example, "Here. Am I going to Aunt Sara's or not?"—at 39:28/38:38), but there is nothing to suggest that they do so aloud. The obviously intrusive author, of course, would have no place in either passages of stream of consciousness or of silent monologue. In the light of Joyce's statement about the desirability of the author's being "invisible," one would not expect him to intrude in his works. (Critics generally agree that the "Oxen of the Sun" chapter, from which an example of the intrusive author was given above, is a series of parodies. Joyce does intrude, however, particularly in the second half of *Ulysses*. We shall examine this intrusion and the possible reasons for it in chapter 14.)

Discrimination between the different levels of abstraction is useful for several reasons. First, the technique Joyce used in "Proteus" and "Lestrygonians" is different from the one he used in "Penelope." It should not, therefore, be given the same label. Second, the series of terms that the critics tend to use indiscriminately ("stream of consciousness, stream of thought, *monologue intérieur,* internal monologue, soliloquy, silent soliloquy, *erlebte Rede*") have different connotations, which causes critical confusion. I have, therefore, attempted to assign them to the different levels of abstraction according to the meanings of the words which make up those terms so that the terms would be meaningful critically and psychologically.

What, then, may finally be said about Joyce's stream-of-consciousness technique? First of all, it certainly does not provide an "exact reproduction" of thought or "the total contents of thought" as some critics have claimed; it simulates the psychological stream of consciousness. From the evidence provided by the analyses in this study and from the evidence of the extensive revisions that Joyce made in the various manuscripts during the various stages of *Ulysses*, it is also apparent that any charges that his stream-of-consciousness technique was simply automatic writing or that it presented gibberish or confusion must be discarded. Careful planning and extensive revising on the one hand and automatic writing on the other are mutually exclusive. And the fact that from the streams of consciousness of Stephen and Bloom and from the internal monologue of Molly the reader sees three distinctly different personalities is ample evidence that while Joyce's technique may give the appearance of confusion (an appearance carefully cultivated by the author, it should be noted), it is actually highly selective and very carefully organized.

The analyses indicate, finally, that the stream-of-consciousness technique provides the novelist with an additional means of projecting the personality of his characters beyond what is available to the traditional author. A novelist generally develops the personality of a character by having him do and say certain things, by having other characters say certain things about him, and by omniscient author's descriptions and comments. These devices are all available to the modern novelist; as we have seen, even Joyce, who thought that an author should be "invisible, like God," did not forgo entirely the use of omniscient author's sentences in "Proteus" and "Lestrygonians," the two chapters in *Ulysses* in which the stream-of-consciousness technique is used most consistently and extensively. In addition to the traditional devices, however, the novelist now has available the stream-of-consciousness technique. The technique is thus not only a method of dramatizing the mind, to use Bowling's phrase; it is also a device which the novelist may use to aid him in one of his important problems, character projection and development.

6

SOME EARLY STREAMS
ANALYZED AND CHARTED

LIISA DAHL, "The Stream-of-Consciousness Techniques of Joyce, Woolf, and O'Neill," conclusion to *Linguistic Features of the Stream-of-Consciousness Techniques of James Joyce, Virginia Woolf, and Eugene O'Neill* (Turku, Finland: University of Turku, 1970), pp. 66-69.

There have been several books which examine the early use of the stream-of-consciousness technique by various writers. Liisa Dahl's is one. Others are Robert Humphrey, *Stream of Consciousness in the Modern Novel* (1954); Leon Edel, *The Psychological Novel, 1900-1950* (1955); Melvin J. Friedman, *Stream of Consciousness: A Study in Literary Method* (1955); and Erwin R. Steinberg, *The Stream of Consciousness and Beyond in ULYSSES* (1973). Humphrey focuses on James Joyce, Virginia Woolf, and William Faulkner; Edel on Henry James, Dorothy Richardson, Marcel Proust, Joyce, Woolf, and Faulkner; Friedman on Edouard Dujardin, Valéry Larbaud, Richardson, Woolf, and Joyce. Steinberg's book deals only with Joyce and, as the title indicates, largely with *Ulysses*.

DAHL: *Stream-of-Consciousness Techniques of Joyce, Woolf, O'Neill*

Aspects of vocabulary. The vocabulary used in the reproduction of stream of consciousness in the different techniques—the direct interior monologue and sometimes the sensory impression of James Joyce, the indirect interior monologue of Virginia Woolf, and the thought asides of Eugene O'Neill—has no common distinguishing feature.

James Joyce is distinguished from the others as a linguistic explorer and innovator. The vocabulary of his interior monologues, and in particular of his sensory impressions, is characterized by the frequent use of onomatopoeia. Besides imitating natural sounds, such words convey an impression of the monotonous persistence of some idea in a character's mind. Polyglottism and word-play reveal Joyce's interest in linguistic matters. The cutting of words into "stumps" is used to present a pre-speech level of consciousness at which associations flow rapidly through a character's mind. The combination of several words into a long series, or the repetition of one word, marks the prolonged duration of a predominant idea in the mind.

Virginia Woolf and Eugene O'Neill never cut or combined words to reproduce the effect of an accelerated or prolonged flow in the stream of consciousness. This is because these writers were not attempting to reach and project a pre-speech level of consciousness through vocabulary, as was James Joyce.

In Virginia Woolf, abstract nouns ending in *-ity, -y,* and *-ness* abound throughout her stream-of-consciousness novels and are particularly characteristic of *Mrs. Dalloway.* Joyce limited the frequent use of the ending *-ness* to a few passages in *Ulysses.* In Virginia Woolf the abstract nouns reproduce vivid impressions; in Joyce they do not represent a genuine stream of consciousness but are used in imitation of a bookish style.

Clusters of adjectives ending in *-ed* and of adverbs ending in *-ly* are particularly typical of Virginia Woolf and emphasize the flowing character of her indirect interior monologue.

As regards word-meanings, only Joyce's interior monologue shows deviations from normal usage. His use of words in their older meanings and his free conversions suggest "Elizabethan" spontaneity, which lends Joyce's interior monologue a touch of freshness and spontaneity not present in the vocabulary of Virginia Woolf and O'Neill.

The novelist, as here Virginia Woolf and Joyce, has greater freedom in making the vocabulary of the stream-of-consciousness presentation different from that of the straightforward narrative. The playwright is limited by the demands of realism and plausibility on the stage. Largely because of this, O'Neill's vocabulary in thought asides does not differ from the normal language used in the actual dialogue.

Aspects of syntax. The most conspicuous similarities between the stream-of-consciousness techniques of James Joyce, Virginia Woolf, and Eugene O'Neill are found in the syntax.

Some similarities in the word-order are evident in Joyce and Virginia Woolf. Both writers favoured the front-position of those parts of the sentence carrying the predominant idea in a character's mind. This is allowed exceptionally in normal English, but Virginia Woolf used it as a stylistic device in giving several coordinate modifiers front-position. She never exaggerated the use of front-position and limited it to the presentation of strong impressions flashing through the mind. Joyce, influenced to some extent by the word-order of Anglo-Irish, used the front-position of the object, the predicate complement, and adverbial modifiers throughout the interior monologue of *Ulysses.* O'Neill's thought asides rarely differ in this respect from normal English word-order.

The linking of sentences or units in stream-of-consciousness presentation is to some extent similar in O'Neill and Joyce. In both writers these independent sentences, often nominal in character, could be combined into longer passages by eliminating the punctuation, anyway an arbitrary device. O'Neill, however, often joined the different units with conjunctions, whereas Joyce did not use any connective links, thus achieving a more nearly natural effect.

Joyce's long sentence type, to be found in Molly Bloom's monologue, has no equivalent in the syntax of the other two writers. An analysis of the eight sections of this chapter shows that though they seem at first sight quite incoherent the sections are divisible into shorter independent units. The absence of punctuation is a trick to reproduce the impression of an unorganized rambling of ideas in Molly's mind before she falls asleep.

Virginia Woolf's use of anaphora as a linking device makes her sentences more rhetorical than those of Joyce and O'Neill and gives an impression of deliberate artistry. This contributes to the indirect character of Virginia Woolf's interior monologue, in which the intervention of the author is clear. The repetition of key-words as a device to link long sentences together produces the impression of an even flow of associations. In O'Neill's short sentences repetition has the opposite effect, that of indicating a staccato-like progression of ideas.

The frequency of the conjunction *when* in Virginia Woolf contributes to the slightly rhetorical effect. In O'Neill the frequent use of the conjunctions "but," "and," "if," "when," etc., opening individual sentence units gives them an unnatural emphasis, as if a character were repeating them under stress.

In the use of nominal sentences the three writers have much in common. They are most frequently found in Joyce, less often in Virginia

Woolf. In Joyce's interior monologue the short pure nominal sentences predominate, serving the expressionistic purpose of emphasizing the essential, characterizing the unformulated linguistic stage of the pre-speech level of consciousness, and suggesting colloquial speech habits.

The descriptive aspect of nominal sentences is occasionally to be found in Joyce, but is predominant in Virginia Woolf's impressionistic writing. Her long nominal sentences reproduce reminiscences of the past, paint landscapes, or recreate the atmosphere of a character's mind. The few short nominal expressions to be found in Virginia Woolf's monologue resemble colloquial utterances. Her nominal sentences never represent an incomplete linguistic stage of consciousness because this was a region she did not aim to present. O'Neill's expressionistic use of pure nominal sentences is comparable with that of Joyce. Like Joyce, O'Neill tried to reproduce the effect of tension in the language of a character. Strong emotions cause such an acceleration of the flow of associations in a character's mind that formulation is not complete. Another feature shared by O'Neill and Joyce, and even Virginia Woolf, is colloquialism; many nominal utterances used in stream-of-consciousness presentation resemble those to be found in conversation where the missing finite verb is completed from the previous sentence, the situation, the tone of the voice, or gesture.

The presentation of a dispute in a character's mind, often achieved through nominal sentences, is a further point of comparison between the three writers. The device of question and answer, typical of some Shakespearean soliloquies, is well suited to the reproduction of this inner dialogue. In Virginia Woolf and O'Neill it occurs at moments of acute stress but only in Virginia Woolf's characters does any distancing from the situation take place. In Joyce disputation is to be found even when a character is not overwrought. It is close to colloquialism and only presents what goes on in the mind if it is analyzed. The subject-matter and the linguistic expressions used to reproduce it are realistic. In most passages of inner dialogue in *Strange Interlude* the inner conflicts and uncertainties of the characters are reproduced by the excessive use of interrogative and exclamatory sentences. This contributes to the strained atmosphere of the thought asides. In Virginia Woolf the questions and exclamations intensify the expression of emotion. In Joyce exclamatory sentences are not used in the reproduction of interior monologue. His interrogative sentences are often colloquial in character.

Both Joyce and O'Neill omit personal pronouns (the first and the third person singular) as the subject. This serves a double purpose, characterizing the incompleteness of the linguistic formulation in the speaker's mind, and revealing the economy of language in situations in which the speaker ("I") and the third person referred to are obvious from the context. O'Neill sometimes omits not only the subject but also the auxiliary of the main verb. In their economical character Joyce's interior monologue and O'Neill's thought aside are comparable to colloquial speech, in which unnecessary words are left unsaid.

Joyce's syntax has several features typical of his writing alone. His nonintroduced indirect questions and the absence of the relative pronoun as the subject reveal the influence of Anglo-Irish. By multiple negation Joyce attempted to reproduce some patterns of spontaneous uneducated speech and perhaps also to revive old forms of expression.

In his use of broken phrases or sentences Joyce was a highly original stylistic inventor. Like Joyce, O'Neill occasionally used the figure of *aposiopesis* by giving the article but omitting the noun. The broken sentences in Joyce and O'Neill serve the same purpose: to illustrate a staccato-like progression of associations through the speaker's mind. This similarity suggests Joyce's influence on O'Neill, though the latter's use of broken utterances was more limited, largely because he was less concerned with the pre-speech level of consciousness. As a dramatist, moreover, O'Neill was more restricted than Joyce by the demands of instant comprehensibility.

Virginia Woolf never used broken sentences in her indirect interior monologue, which deals mainly with the language area of consciousness.

Other aspects. Musicality is typical of Joyce's interior monologue, and is evident in his choice of words and also in his use of leitmotifs to carry the main themes throughout the novel. A rhythmic repetition of the motifs creates a coherence and unity in seemingly disconnected chaos. In Virginia Woolf a rhythmic repetition works inside some passages of indirect interior monologue but not throughout the novel as a whole. The harmony of her technique is emphasized by her prose rhythm, which in its lyric tone at times approaches poetry. In O'Neill's *Strange Interlude* leitmotifs contribute to a rhythmic effect. Some of them only affect individual thought asides, others, such as the Gordon theme for Nina and the brothel scene for Marsden, run through the whole play.

Joyce stands apart from the other two writers in his experimentation with extreme forms of language. In his interior monologue he often explored consciousness at its pre-speech level, sometimes using the technique of sensory impression. The language used at this level is fresh and "raw" as if it had not yet undergone any exact formulation. In Virginia Woolf's language the length of the sentences illustrates the tempo with which associations proceed from a character's consciousness, but the utterances are never incomplete. In O'Neill only a few features resemble the "raw-material" description of Joyce.

Besides the differences stemming from the impressionistic technique of Virginia Woolf and the expressionistic techniques of Joyce and O'Neill there are the basically different demands of the two literary genres, the novel and the play. In addition, the area of consciousness traversed and the directness of the quotation from a character's mind are also decisive factors. Since Joyce's interior monologue is a direct reproduction of the mind of his characters and covers the entire area of consciousness, including the "pre-speech" level, he requires the widest variety of linguistic devices. Virginia Woolf's indirect interior monologue, which never quotes directly from the character's mind but is filtered through the author's personality, mainly covers the language area of consciousness. The language used does not therefore differ essentially from normal English. O'Neill's thought aside is a direct quotation but, partly because of the dramatic structure, it does not penetrate very deep levels of consciousness. O'Neill stands half-way between Joyce and Virginia Woolf so far as the area of consciousness reproduced and the linguistic means used are concerned. There are a few points of similarity between these three writers. They each, however, possess many individual features which mark their specific techniques in the presentation of stream of consciousness.

7

INTO THE MAIN STREAM

ROBERT HUMPHREY, "The Results," *Stream of Consciousness in the Modern Novel* (Berkeley: University of California Press, 1954), pp. 113-21.
Humphrey examines briefly the way in which the stream-of-consciousness technique has entered the main stream of fiction.

HUMPHREY: *The Results*

> *Once reality has been disclosed to us in this particular way, we continue to see it in this shape.*
>
> Ernst Cassirer

It has become apparent that there is a pattern of development within the stream-of-consciousness genre. From the earliest experiments with impressionistic rendering of the inner world, illustrated at its best in Virginia Woolf's *Mrs. Dalloway* and at its most extensive in Dorothy Richardson's *Pilgrimage,* through the extremely forceful presentation of psychic life in Joyce's *Ulysses,* to the culmination of experiment in *The Waves* and *Finnegans Wake*—which led to stream of consciousness *en fleur,* and obscurity—we have come to a subtle retrenchment in Faulkner's novels. Faulkner's work represents a return to the fundamental basis of fiction, the prominent use of significant external action, which he combines with stream of consciousness.

Into the main stream. The stream-of-consciousness novel has entered the main stream of fiction. To look back on the era of experimentation with a sigh of relief and a reluctant admission that the experimenting produced some of the major literature of the century is not to appreciate the entire significance of the movement. The tremendous result is this: stream-of-consciousness methods are, now, conventional methods; the vagaries of pre-speech mental life are established twentieth-century forms; the devices for conveying private consciousness are ones which writers use confidently and readers accept without a murmur. Stream of consciousness as a method of character depiction is a newly admitted reality. Art has always attempted to express, to objectify the dynamic processes of our inner life. Now that "inner life" is a reality which we recognize as available to any consciousness, and now that techniques, devices, and forms have been established for conveying this reality, fictional art has come closer than ever before to achieving its purpose.

But the acceptance of the reality of inner life, of the pre-speech levels of consciousness, as a proper subject of fiction is the significant thing for us to notice. If we look at random, at the work of some of the most important mid-century writers, this acceptance becomes obvious. One might notice it (and accept it as a standard convention) in the fiction of Elizabeth Bowen, Graham Greene, Katherine Anne Porter, Robert Penn Warren, Delmore Schwartz, and Eudora Welty—to mention but a few, and to overlook entirely the vast amount of more ephemeral work in which unuttered consciousness is not only casually accepted as a legitimate subject, but is even *automatically* formed in the image of the great experimental stream-of-consciousness novels.

We shall need but a few examples from the work of the authors listed above to amplify these observations. Mr. Warren's *All the King's Men,* a superb novel and a relatively popular one, was published in 1946. This novel, to get to the heart of the matter and to overlook a great deal of its power, is fundamentally a study of moral development and ethical awakening in the central character, Jack Burden. Burden's story, of course, is contingent on parallel and contrasting moral changes in the other main characters. For these—Willie Stark and Ann Stanton, principally— the development is almost entirely realized through action. For Burden, it is realized chiefly as *psychic drama.* Much of the writing in the novel is focused on depicting this inner drama of consciousness. Warren's method here is naturalistic (that is, he uses symbols and concrete images) rather than impressionistic. Like Faulkner, he takes the dense and chaotic materials of the mind and through symbols and motifs objectifies them. It is through rhetoric that he maintains the texture of density and chaos.

Warren's method of projecting Burden's unspoken mental activities is, however, not an imitation of Faulkner; the suggestion of stream of consciousness in *All the King's Men* is disarmingly conventional. It is usually presented in the first person, and sometimes in the more objective second person. ("Going to bed in the late spring afternoon or just at the beginning of twilight, with those sounds in your ears, gives you a wonderful sense of peace" [p. 325].) Warren avoids mechanical devices, syntactical aberrations, fragments, and logical obscurity. This avoidance reflects his dislike of the purely mechanical (the psychoanalytical and theoretical) aspects of mental functioning. Warren's interest is in spiritual struggle (growth or decay), which manifests itself dramatically in the unuttered confusion of the mind. He depends on rhetoric, symbols, and free association to represent this confusion. It is significant that both the ignoring of psychological theories of consciousness and the accepting of the basic description which these theories have given Warren's generation are present in his depiction of his character. A brief example from the novel will suggest Warren's method. The first-person point of view and the third-person narrative indicate the dual function of the passage. That is, the narrative is carried forward, but more important, the mental state of Burden, the narrator, is clearly given also.

She had been there since Adam's funeral. She had gone down with the body, trailing the sun-glittering, expensive hearse in an undertaker's limousine. . . . I didn't see her as she sat in the rented limousine which moved at its decorous torturer's pace the near-hundred miles, lifting the miles slowly off the concrete slab, slowly and fastidiously as though you were peeling an endless strip of skin off the live flesh. I didn't see her, but I know how she had been: erect, white in the face, the beautiful bones of her face showing under the taut flesh, her hands clenched in her lap. For that was the way she was when I saw her standing under the moss-garlanded oaks, looking absolutely alone despite the nurse and Katy Maynard and all the people—friends of the family, curiosity-seekers come to gloat and nudge, newspapermen, big-shot doctors from town and from Baltimore and Philadelphia—who stood there while shovels did their work.[1]

The first sentence of this quotation is narrative. The rest is the imaginative association Burden makes. The images indicate the obsessive state of his mind, the insistent lingering on an object (the picture of Ann). At the same time, the associations with other events, themes, and motifs in the novel are skillfully (and realistically) recalled.

A more obvious echo from stream of consciousness can be found throughout Warren's later novel, *World Enough and Time* (1950). It is interesting to observe that in this novel the impressionistic method of Virginia Woolf is reflected. Again, there are no signs of direct imitation or even of direct influence. The stream-of-consciousness texture of Warren's work appears as spontaneous and it is smoothly worked in with the basic method of his novel, the journal combined with the omniscient third-person narrative of external events. The following example comes immediately after a description of the character Jeremiah as he is peering in the window of a friend's house. From the description of external events, the narration flows into a description of Jeremiah's consciousness. The italics are Warren's.

So that was Fort's wife, he thought. He had known that she existed, but he had never seen her, she had not been real. But now she was real, and for an instant he felt some shift in the center of his intention, . . . and he strained to make out the words she was speaking but could hear nothing. Then he thought: *She doesn't love him, I can see from her face that she does not.* And thought with a sickening fear: *but if she did, if she did love him, could I . . . ?* And could not finish the notion, even in his mind, and with a leap of release, and sudden certainty, thought: *but she does not.* She could not, not with that face and that dead gaze upon him.[2]

This combination of omniscient description with internal monologue will recall to the reader the method used in *Mrs. Dalloway* and *To the Lighthouse.*

As a final example of the pervading influence of the stream-of-consciousness genre on recent fiction, notice of Katherine Anne Porter's *Pale Horse, Pale Rider* (1939) is illuminating. The particular interest here is the reflection, in a very lucid and otherwise conventionally managed story, of James Joyce's most radical technical innovations in *Ulysses.*

I refer to the use of elaborate symbolism to express the dream qualities of consciousness. In Miss Porter's novelette the reader is introduced, with an extremely effective montage of symbols, to the dream life of the character, Miranda. Later, in the story, the dream-fantasy, with all of its incoherency and disjointedness, is used in the representation of Miranda's fevered battle with death.

These more recent novels, influenced as their authors were by Woolf, Joyce, and Faulkner, are not stream-of-consciousness novels. The genre has been absorbed for the most part into the greater body of fictional method. The depiction of mental life in Mr. Warren's and Miss Porter's fiction (and in that of many other novelists as well) is similar to the psychological probing to be found in such pre-stream-of-consciousness novels as those by Henry James and Marcel Proust. But there is an important difference: James's and Proust's fiction was either obscure, or esoteric, or shockingly new, but the more recent novels are immediately available to a fairly wide reading public without the barriers of obscurity or strangeness present. Stream of consciousness had come between Henry James and Robert Penn Warren.

The intellectual interests and social forces which engendered and encouraged the stream-of-consciousness writers had intervened also. Consequently, when, in 1932, Professor Beach saw stream of consciousness as limited in its future by its invariable application to "neurotics," he was dismissing it altogether too soon. But when Professor Hoffman, twenty years later, regards the subject of stream-of-consciousness fiction as a "historically interesting" phase of novelistic method, corollary to popular interest in Freudian approaches to sex life, he is ignoring the results (and to some degree the achievements) of this phase. Both Professor Beach's and Professor Hoffman's errors are those of misplaced emphasis.[3] The aspects of stream-of-consciousness literature which emphasize the neurotic and Freudian sex life are not what distinguish it. One might argue, for example, that the characters in *Ulysses* and *To the Lighthouse* are no more—possibly much less—"neurotic" than are those in *An American Tragedy, Point Counter Point,* and *The Sun Also Rises,* to say nothing of those in *Antic Hay* and *Sanctuary.* Nor is the historical reflection of popular Freudianism more apparent in *Mrs. Dalloway* and *Pilgrimage* than it is in *Sons and Lovers* and *The Great Gatsby.* What has happened is this: when personality is examined as closely and candidly as it has been in the twentieth-century novel—in and out of stream of consciousness—it appears as an individual and not as a "norm." And if we have not been convinced in this century that everyone is abnormal, that the so-called neurotic condition is the general condition, we have learned nothing essential about ourselves at all. The stream-of-consciousness novel has given us empirical evidence for this truth. It has given us evidence of the metempirical also. We have learned from the explorers of man's psyche that the individual attempts, and sometimes achieves, a transcendency of what Balzac depicted as the *condition humaine*. The empirical world produces the neurotic personality; but that personality is able to yearn for contact with what is stable, for knowledge of the center of meaning. It is, then, with the overwhelming trend in fiction of our time to investigate meaning in human personality rather than in social action and reaction that stream of consciousness is allied. Representing an extreme concentration on unuttered consciousness, it produced its landmarks, towering ones, but it was subsumed by something basic in the nature of fiction: the need for surface action and external reality to make whole reality as man knows it, for man, as Joyce has illustrated, is only half-aspiring.

Summary. The new dimension in literature which the major stream-of-consciousness writers have created has been attempted before; it was attempted by the stream-of-consciousness writers themselves in non–stream-of-consciousness works. The special sense of immanent vision in *Mrs. Dalloway* and *To the Lighthouse* was suggested by Virginia Woolf in the earlier *Jacob's Room* and in the later *The Years,* but only when she used the basic techniques of stream of consciousness could she communicate it. Likewise, Joyce's satiric-pathetic comedy of existence was asserted in the stories in *Dubliners,* but it was wholly communicated only in the stream of consciousness of *Ulysses.* And Faulkner's sense of ironic tragedy, though powerful often in such novels as *Sanctuary* and *The Hamlet,* reaches the credibility necessary for the sharpest effectiveness only in his stream-of-consciousness works in which psychic drama prevails over grandiose rhetoric.

The basic techniques for presenting consciousness in literature are not inventions of the twentieth century. Both direct and indirect interior monologue can be found in works from previous centuries, and omniscient description and soliloquy were primary features of fiction even in its embryonic stages. The unique employment of these which produced stream of consciousness came with the twentieth-century novelists' awareness of the significance of the drama which takes place within the confines of the individual's consciousness.

There are two aspects of this drama of consciousness which posed particularly difficult problems for the writers who wanted to represent it. Among the philosopher-psychologists, William James and Henri Bergson convinced the following generations that consciousness flows like a stream and that the mind has its own time and space values apart from the arbitrary and set ones of the external world. Thus, flux and *durée* are aspects of psychic life for which new methods of narration had to be developed if writers were to depict them. The other aspect was more obvious: the mind is a private thing. The problem this posed was simply how could what is private be made public and still seem to have the qualities of privacy?

The chief device the writers hit upon for depicting and controlling both the movement and the privacy of consciousness was the utilization of the principles of mental free association. These provided a workable basis for imposing a special logic on the erratic meanderings of consciousness; thereby giving the writer a system to follow and the reader a system to hold on to. The process of free association further proved to be applicable to any particular consciousness in such a way as to show a pattern of association that depended on the individual's past experiences and his present obsessions. In this manner, the privacy problem was more than half solved.

But additional devices were needed to convey the unconventional movement and the enigma of privacy on the pre-speech levels of consciousness. The ingenious minds of the writers we have been considering, like their contemporaries in the sister arts, especially in the cinema, found techniques which were devised to project the duality and the flux of mental life. Montage, with its function of presenting either more than one object or more than one time simultaneously, was especially adaptable to fiction. The corollary devices of "flash-back," "fade-out," and "slow-up" proved useful adjuncts to montage and free association. Literary tradition itself was rummaged for devices and yielded such ready-made materials as classical rhetoric and poetry could offer, including the particularly useful ones of metaphor and symbol. Even the conventions of punctuation were reshaped to produce the qualities of pre-speech consciousness in words. The difficult job was finally accomplished, but where was the form of art in this?

Consciousness is in its pre-speech levels unpatterned; a consciousness by its nature exists independent of action. In short, plot had to go by the wayside. Yet some kind of pattern had to be superimposed on the chaotic materials of consciousness. In lieu of a well-made plot, the writers devised all sorts of unities. They managed the closest adherence to the classical unities that the novel had ever produced; they patterned their work after literary models, historical cycles, and musical structure; they used complex symbolic structure, and finally they even managed to fuse external plot with stream of consciousness!

The Sound and the Fury and *As I Lay Dying,* latecomers in the stream-of-consciousness genre, are not pure examples of it. They contain an important element of plot, and they represent the point in the development of the twentieth-century novel at which stream of consciousness entered the main stream of fiction. It is still there, and the sacred waters of that stream are more potent than they were.

NOTES

FOREWORD

1.   Leon Edel, *The Psychological Novel, 1900-1950* (New York: J. B. Lippincott, 1955), p. 7.
2.   Erwin R. Steinberg, *The Stream of Consciousness and Beyond in* Ulysses (Pittsburgh: University of Pittsburgh Press, 1973).
3.   Maurice Beebe, "Editor's Introduction," *Journal of Modern Literature* 1 (1971): 644-45. Although they vary in the date they think should be put on the tombstone, many others agree on the demise of Modernism. See, for example: Randall Jarrell, "The End of the Line," *Nation* 154 (February 21, 1942): 222-28; Richard Ellman and Charles Feidelson, Jr., eds., preface to *The Modern Tradition: Backgrounds of Modern Literature* (New York: Oxford University Press, 1965), p. vi; Leslie Fiedler, "Bloom on Joyce; or, Jokey for Jacob," *Journal of Modern Literature* 1 (1970): 21.

Souvage, NARRATIVE TECHNIQUE

1.   See, e.g., Bertil Romberg, *Studies in the Narrative Technique of the First-Person Novel* (Stockholm: Almqvist & Wiksell, 1962), p. 5: "Not only *is* he [i.e., Thackeray] omniscient in everything concerning the people in the novel—as of course all authors are—but he is also frequently anxious to appear omniscient to the reader."
2.   Martin Steinmann, Jr., "The Old Novel and the New," *From Jane Austen to Joseph Conrad,* ed. Robert C. Rathburn and Martin Steinmann, Jr. (Minneapolis: University of Minnesota Press, 1958), p. 290.
3.   *The Novels of Jane Austen* . . . 5, ed. R. W. Chapman (3rd ed.; London: Oxford University Press, 1933): 248.
4.   "Everyman's Library," no. 134 (London: J. M. Dent, 1956), p. 540.
5.   "Everyman's Library," no. 298 (London, 1908), p. 699.
6.   "Everyman's Library," no. 288 (London, 1955), p. 1.
7.   "Everyman's Library," no. 27 (London, 1960), p. 473.
8.   Quoted in Martin Steinmann, Jr., op. cit., p. 297.
9.   See, e.g., Karl Beckson and Arthur Ganz, *A Reader's Guide to Literary Terms*

(London: Thames & Hudson, 1961), p. 92: "The novelist who stops his story to address the reader in his own person . . . sacrifices illusion to gain some other end." However, as Herman Meyer writes, "Es gibt . . . Grade der Einmischung, Grade vielleicht auch von deren Schicklichkeit. Ist das Epische ein Strom, so soll der Dichter mindestens mit einem Fusse im Wasser stehen. Und dies ist nun wieder dort am schwierigsten, wo ausdrücklich theorisiert und Weltanschauung verhandelt wird" ("Zum Problem der epischen Integration," *Zarte Empirie. Studien zur Literaturgeschichte* [Stuttgart: J. B. Metzlersche Verlagsbuchhandlung, 1963], p. 17). See also Käte Hamburger *Die Logik der Dichtung* (Stuttgart: E. Klett, 1957), pp. 86–87.

10. Percy Lubbock, *The Craft of Fiction* (first published 1921; London: Jonathan Cape, 1954), p. 62.

11. Quoted in Wolfgang Kayser, *Entstehung und Krise des modernen Romans* (Stuttgart: J. B. Metzlersche Verlagsbuchhandlung, 1954), p. 17. See also Herman Meyer, "Zum Problem der epischen Integration," *Trivium* 8 (1950): 299–318; reprinted in Herman Meyer, *Zarte Empirie. Studien zur Literaturgeschichte* (Stuttgart: J. B. Metzlersche Verlagsbuchhandlung, 1963), pp. 12–32, 391.

12. Alan Dugald McKillop, *The Early Masters of English Fiction* (Lawrence: University of Kansas Press, 1956), pp. 109–10.

13. Ibid., p. 127.

14. Quoted in Albert Thibaudet, *Réflexions sur le roman* (Paris: Gallimard, 1938), p. 24.

15. Wolfgang Kayser, op. cit., p. 26.

16. Bernard DeVoto, *The World of Fiction* (Boston: The Writer, Inc., 1950), p. 250.

17. See, e.g., Wayne C. Booth, *The Rhetoric of Fiction* (Chicago: University of Chicago Press, 1961), part 3, "Impersonal Narration," which contains the following chapters: (10) The Uses of Authorial Silence; (11) The Price of Impersonal Narration, 1: Confusion of Distance; (12) The Price of Impersonal Narration, 2: Henry James and the Unreliable Narrator; (13) The Morality of Impersonal Narration.

18. See, e.g., Edwin Muir, "The Decline of the Novel," *Essays on Literature and Society* (London: The Hogarth Press, 1949), pp. 144–45, 148; "The characteristic modern novel is a story without an ending. . . . This is another way of saying that the contemporary novelist has an imaginative grasp of origins but not of ends. . . . And the novel describing the life we live is a symptom of the order in which we live; its incompleteness is a reflection of the incompleteness of a whole region of thought and belief." "The contemporary novel is a story of time against a background of time. The traditional novel is a story of time against a permanent pattern."

19. See, e.g., Robert Liddell, *Some Principles of Fiction* (London: Jonathan Cape, 1953), p. 110: "People are not [at the present time] necessarily less moral, but there is no universal standard of Moral Taste—even among Principled persons—to which a writer can appeal." See also Alex Comfort, whom Wayne C. Booth, on page 393 of his *The Rhetoric of Fiction*, quotes to the effect that the modern novel "can make no assumptions about [the reader's] beliefs or activities comparable with those which the early nineteenth-century novel, addressed to a section of society, could make. . . . An entire world has to be created and peopled separately in each book which is written." "For the first time in recent history we have a totally fragmented society" (*The Novel and Our Time* [London: Phoenix House, 1948], pp. 13, 11).

20. Quoted in Miriam Allott, *Novelists on the Novel* (London: Routledge & Kegan Paul, 1959), p. 271.

21. Percy Lubbock, *The Craft of Fiction*, p. 147.

22. In this connexion see also the following passage from James's preface to the New York edition of *Roderick Hudson:* "The centre of interest throughout 'Roderick' is in Rowland Mallet's consciousness, and the drama is the very drama of that consciousness—which I had of course to make sufficiently acute in order to enable it, like a set and lighted scene, to hold the play" (*The Art of the Novel: Critical Prefaces.*

With an introduction by Richard P. Blackmur [New York: Charles Scribner's Sons, 1934], p. 16).
23.   Henry James, *The Art of the Novel: Critical Prefaces*, pp. 110-11.
24.   Leon Edel, *The Psychological Novel, 1900-1950* (London: Rupert Hart-Davis, 1955), p. ix. The phrase "stream of consciousness" was coined by William James in his *The Principles of Psychology* (New York: Henry Holt, 1890) 1:239: ". . . Consciousness, then, does not appear to itself chopped up in bits. Such words as 'chain' or 'train' do not describe it fitly as it presents itself in the first instance. It is nothing jointed; it flows. A 'river' or a 'stream' are the metaphors by which it is most naturally described. *In talking of it hereafter, let us call it the stream of thought, of consciousness, or of subjective life.*"
      In his book *Stream of Consciousness in the Modern Novel* (4th printing, 1st paper-bound ed.; Berkeley and Los Angeles: University of California Press, 1959), Robert Humphrey defines stream-of-consciousness fiction as "a type of fiction in which the basic emphasis is placed on exploration of the pre-speech levels of consciousness for the purpose, primarily, of revealing the psychic being of the characteis" (p. 4). He distinguishes between four basic techniques used in presenting stream of consciousness, viz., "direct interior monologue, indirect interior monologue, omniscient description, and soliloquy" (p. 23).
25.   See, e.g., Mary Burchard Orvis's definition, in her *The Art of Writing Fiction* (New York: Prentice-Hall, 1948, p. 135), of stream of consciousness: "That angle which goes directly into the mind of a character and represents *without benefit of author* is the most realistic for the description of thought processes." (Italics mine.)
26.   Quoted in Leon Edel, op. cit., p. 24.
27.   In his critical study *The Psychological Novel, 1900-1950*, pp. 30, 53-58, Leon Edel points out that Joyce singled out Edouard Dujardin as the originator [in his novel *Les Lauriers sont coupés*] of the internal (or interior) monologue. Later, in a lecture delivered in 1930 and published under the title *Le Monologue intérieur: son apparition, ses origines, sa place dans l'oeuvre de James Joyce et dans le roman contemporain* (Paris, 1931), Dujardin gave the following definition of the term "internal monologue":

The internal monologue, in its nature of the order of poetry, is that unheard and unspoken speech by which a character expresses his inmost thoughts, those lying nearest the unconscious, without regard to logical organization—that is, in their original state—by means of direct sentences reduced to syntactic minimum, and in such a way as to give the impression of reproducing the thoughts just as they come into the mind.

After having pointed out a few contradictions inherent in Dujardin's definition, Mr. Edel makes an attempt at clearing up the confusion which has arisen round the terms "stream of consciousness" and "internal monologue." He finally draws the following tentative distinction between the two terms: "The term 'internal monologue' becomes merely a useful designation for certain works of fiction of sustained subjectivity, written from a single point of view, in which the writer narrows down the stream of consciousness and places us largely at the 'centré' of the character's thoughts—that centre where thought often uses words rather than images." May I, by way of qualifying Mr. Edel's statement, propose that the terms "internal (or interior) monologue" and "stream of consciousness" be reserved for, respectively, the cases where the inner flux is being released and those where sensory experience is superimposed upon the inner flux in process of releasement. In this context it may also be of interest to give Mr. Edel's statement that "while it is interesting to think of [Paul] Bourget [to whom Dujardin attributed the first use of the term 'internal monologue'] . . . as the originator of the term, the credit of its application to the subjective or stream-of-consciousness novel really belongs to [Valéry] Larbaud." See also Gleb Struve, "Monologue Intérieur: The Origins of the Formula and the First Statement of its Possibilities," *PMLA* 69 (1954): 1101-11.

28.   (First published 1922; London: The Bodley Head, 1937), p. 742.
29.   See, e.g., his "Qu'est-ce que la littérature?" *Situations 2* (Paris: Gallimard, 1948): 256:

Ils [i.e., nos prédécesseurs] pensaient donner à la folle entreprise de conter une justification au moins apparente en rappelant sans cesse dans leurs récits, explicitement ou allusivement, l'existence d'un auteur; nous souhaitions que nos livres se tinssent tout seuls en l'air et que les mots, au lieu de pointer en arrière vers celui qui les a tracés, oubliés, solitaires, inapercus, fussent des toboggans déversant les lecteurs au milieu d'un univers sans témoins, bref que nos livres existassent à la facon des choses, des plantes, des événements et non d'abord comme des produits de l'homme; nous voulions chasser la Providence de nos ouvrages comme nous l'avions chassée de notre monde.

30.   Jean-Paul Sartre, "Qu'est-ce que la littérature?" *Situations 2: 327*. For a critical estimate of the works and techniques of Sartre and of such "nouvelle vague" novelists as Michel Butor, Alain Robbe-Grillet, and Nathalie Sarraute, see Gerda Zeltner-Neukomm, *Das Wagnis des französischen Gegenwartsromans* (Reinbek bei Hamburg: Rowohlt, 1960).
31.   Joseph Warren Beach, *The Twentieth-Century Novel: Studies in Technique* (New York: Appleton-Century-Crofts, 1932), p. 14.
32.   Quoted in Wayne C. Booth, *The Rhetoric of Fiction*, p. 25.
33.   On this subject see also Norman Friedman, "Point of View in Fiction: The Development of A Critical Concept," *PMLA* 70, no. 5 (December, 1955): 1168. "That the telling-showing distinction is established as a commonplace of the criticism of fiction is evidenced by its latest reiteration in the work of Bernard De Voto in 1950, as well as in the current handbooks—not only of fiction writing and reading but also of freshman composition." Mr. Friedman then goes on to substantiate his statement by listing an impressive number of books and critical articles in which the telling-showing distinction is respected. See also the list printed on page 1167 under note 14.
34.   Wolfgang Kayser, *Entstehung und Krise des modernen Romans*, p. 34.
35.   W. J. Harvey, *The Art of George Eliot* (London: Chatto & Windus, 1961). See especially chaps. 1 to 3.
36.   See, e.g., René Wellek and Austin Warren, *Theory of Literature* (London: Jonathan Cape, 1949), p. 223: "But the chief pattern of narrative is its inclusiveness: it intersperses scenes in dialogue (which might be acted) with summary accounts of what is happening." See especially Herman Meyer, "Von der Freiheit des Erzählers," *Festgabe für L. L. Hammerich* (Kopenhagen: Naturmetodens Sproginst., 1962), pp. 181–90; reprinted in Herman Meyer *Zarte Empirie*, pp. 1–11, 390.
37.   Kathleen Tillotson, *The Tale and the Teller* (London: Rupert Hart-Davis, 1959), p. 32. As one of the illustrations of the importance of the role of the "teller" in the novel, Mrs. Tillotson here gives the following passage from the end of chapter 29 of Henry James's *The Portrait of a Lady*, viz., the chapter in which Osmond declares himself to Isabel:

The working of this young lady's spirit was strange, and I can only give it to you as I see it, not hoping to make it seem altogether natural. Her imagination stopped, as I say; there was a last vague space it could not cross—a dusky, uncertain tract which looked ambiguous, and even slightly treacherous, like a moorland seen in the winter twilight. But she was to cross it yet.

In commenting upon this passage, Mrs. Tillotson has this to say: "James wrote nothing more powerful than that last brief menacing sentence in an early novel, which his later method would not have permitted" (p. 18). See also Karl Beckson and Arthur Ganz, *A Reader's Guide to Literary Terms*, p. 146: "Though the novel as a genre is of comparatively recent development, it has its roots in a number of forms which may be traced back to the Classical epics, for the *essence of the novel is narrative*." (Italics mine.)

38. It may here be helpful to give the following passage from Dorothy Van Ghent's study of *Clarissa Harlowe,* in which she considers the narrative implications of "point of view":

The technical problem with which we are confronted here is that of the "point of view" (or "focus of narration"), a problem which may be phrased thus: given a certain kind of subject matter, how can it be brought into focus for the reader? From what "angle," what point of observation, can the drama best be seen? From the author's own? or from that of the chief character in the novel? or from that of one of the minor characters? or from the points of view of several characters? or from some presumably automatic and mechanical point of view (like that of a camera)?

The English Novel: Form and Function (New York: Rinehart, 1953), pp. 45–46.

39. See Richard Stang, *The Theory of the Novel in England, 1850–1870* (London: Routledge & Kegan Paul, 1959), p. 107.

40. In his essay "Point of View in Fiction: The Development of a Critical Concept," from which I have already quoted, Norman Friedman lists a number of books and critical articles in which the concept of "point of view" as developed in Henry James's Prefaces was already adumbrated. According to Mr. Friedman, Selden L. Whitcomb's *The Study of a Novel* (1905) was the first critical study to devote a formal section to the rubric "The Narrator: His Point of View."

41. Henry James, *The Art of the Novel: Critical Prefaces,* pp. 37–38. Quoted in Norman Friedman, op. cit., p. 1163.

42. Ibid., p. 300. Quoted in Norman Friedman, op. cit., pp. 1163–64.

43. Ibid., p. 46.

44. 2nd ed., Philadelphia, 1954.

45. Percy Lubbock, *The Craft of Fiction,* p. 251.

46. Ibid., p. 62.

47. See my discussion of the difference between the "old" novel and the "dramatized" novel.

48. A second important criterion with Mr. Friedman is the distance at which the author places the reader from the story.

49. Mr. Friedman's classification allows also for an intermediary, minor category between types (3) and (4). This category is characterized by the fact that, "although the protagonist tells his own story, he tells it not to the reader but rather to someone of his acquaintance who thereupon relays it to the reader in his own person. Something of a combination 'I' as Witness and 'I' as Protagonist frame" (p. 1175).

50. Bertil Romberg, *Studies in the Narrative Technique of the First-Person Novel,* p. 27.

51. For a refutation of Käte Hamburger's thesis (see, e.g., her essay "Das epische Präteritum," *Deutsche Vierteljahrsschrift für Literaturwissenschaft und Geistesgeschichte,* 1953, pp. 354 ff.) that the first-person novel cannot be classified as fiction at all and that, in contrast to the preterite form's present-tense function in the third-person novel, the preterite form in the first-person novel has a preterite-tense function, see Romberg's *Studies . . . ,* pp. 30–32.

Steinberg, SOURCES OF THE STREAM

1. Wassily Kandinsky, *Concerning the Spiritual in Art,* trans. Hilla Rebay (New York: George Wittenborn, 1947), p. 52; published originally in German in 1912.

2. Mary Colum, *Life and Dream* (London: Macmillan & Co., 1947), pp. 121, 129; Richard Ellmann, *James Joyce* (New York: Oxford University Press, 1959), p. 79; William York Tindall, *Forces in Modern British Literature* (New York: Alfred A. Knopf, 1947), p. 277. See also C. P. Curran, *James Joyce Remembered* (New York: Oxford University Press, 1968): Symons's book "introduced most of us

to the movement abroad. It was ardently read. . . . Whether thanks to Symons or not, Joyce had acquaintance with Baudelaire, Verlaine, and the Symbolists in his earliest college years" (p. 31). Curran was a schoolfellow of Joyce.

3.	Arthur Symons, *The Symbolist Movement in Literature* (2d ed. rev.; New York: E. P. Dutton, 1908), pp. 9, 10, 131.

4.	Stéphane Mallarmé, *Oeuvres complètes,* 2 vols. (Paris: Gallimard, 1945), p. 366; quoted by David Hayman, *Joyce et Mallarmé* (Paris: Lettres Modernes, 1965), p. 61.

5.	Flaubert to Louise Colet, 8 March 1857, *The Selected Letters of Gustave Flaubert,* trans. and ed. Francis Steegmuller (London: Hamish Hamilton, 1954), p. 186.

6.	Oscar Wilde, *The Picture of Dorian Gray* (New York: Modern Library, 1926), p. vii. Painters were saying the same sorts of things. In 1913 Guillaume Apollinaire wrote in *The Cubist Painters* (New York: Wittenborn, Schultz, 1949), "Each god creates in his own image, and so do painters. Only photographers manufacture duplicates of nature" (p. 11).

7.	James Joyce, *A Portrait of the Artist as a Young Man* (New York: Viking Press, 1968), pp. 171, 172, 215, 221.

8.	Symons, *The Symbolist Movement,* pp. 8–9, 85, 141, 143.

9.	Djuna Barnes, "James Joyce," *Vanity Fair* 18, no. 2 (April 1922): 65 and 104; Virginia Woolf, "Modern Fiction," *The Common Reader* (1925; reprint ed., New York: Harvest-Harcourt, Brace, 1953), p. 155.

10.	Herschel B. Chipp, *Theories of Modern Art* (Berkeley: University of California Press, 1968), pp. 48–51.

11.	The quotation is from Ellmann, *James Joyce,* p. 128.

12.	George Heard Hamilton, *Manet and His Critics* (New Haven: Yale University Press, 1954), p. 193.

13.	Chipp, *Theories of Modern Art,* p. 58n. and pp. 58–59 (italics in the original). See also William Innes Homer, *Seurat and the Science of Painting* (Cambridge, Mass.: M.I.T. Press, 1964), p. 44.

14.	Homer, *Seurat,* p. 280.

15.	Ibid., pp. 139ff., 172; Hamilton, *Manet,* p. 170. See also Seurat's letter to Maurice Beaubourgh, 28 August 1890, quoted in John Rewald, *Georges Seurat* (2d rev. ed.; New York: George Wittenborn, 1946), p. 62.

16.	Albert Gleizes and Jean Metzinger, *Du "Cubisme"* (Paris: Eugène Figuère, 1912), pp. 18, 30.

17.	Joseph Prescott, *Exploring James Joyce* (Carbondale: Southern Illinois University Press, 1964), pp. 26–27.

18.	Gleizes and Metzinger, *Du "Cubisme,"* p. 30.

19.	Joyce, *A Portrait,* pp. 214–15.

20.	Flaubert to Louise Colet, 16 January 1852, in Steegmuller, *Selected Letters,* p. 131.

21.	Gauguin to Emile Schuffenecker, 8 October 1888, in John Rewald, *Post Impressionism—from van Gogh to Gauguin* (2d ed.; New York: Museum of Modern Art, 1962), p. 196.

22.	"Futurist Painting: Technical Manifesto," 11 April 1910, in Joshua C. Taylor, *Futurism* (New York: Museum of Modern Art, 1961), p. 127. The futurists made one exception: "But this truism, unimpeachable and absolute fifty years ago, is no longer so today with regard to the nude, since artists obsessed with the desire to expose the bodies of their mistresses have transformed the Salons into arrays of unwholesome flesh!" (p. 127; the exclamation point is in the original).

23.	Richard Ellmann in his introduction to Stanislaus Joyce's *My Brother's Keeper* (New York: Viking Press, 1958), p. 23.

24.   Hamilton, *Manet*, traces this development. See especially p. 26, which records a critical opinion of an early (1861) painting: "But what a scourge to society is a realist painter! To him nothing is sacred! Manet tramples under foot even the most sacred ties." Grant Richards's printer evidently felt the same way about Dubliners; see Ellmann, *James Joyce*, pp. 227–31.

25.   Symons, *The Symbolist Movement*, p. 137.

26.   William Seitz, *Claude Monet* (New York: Harry N. Abrams, 1960), p. 44.

27.   Denis Rouart, *Claude Monet* (New York: Skira Art Books, 1958), pp. 107–8.

28.   Kenneth Clark, *Civilisation* (New York: Harper & Row, 1969), p. 290.

29.   James Joyce, *Stephen Hero*, (New York: New Directions, 1944), p. 211.

30.   Ellmann, *James Joyce*, pp. 87–89. See also James Joyce, *Epiphanies*, ed. O. A. Silverman (Buffalo: Lockwood Memorial Library of the State University of New York at Buffalo, 1956).

31.   A. Walton Litz, *The Art of James Joyce* (New York: Galaxy–Oxford, 1964) pp. 132–39.

32.   William C. Seitz, *Claude Monet: Seasons and Moments* (New York: Museum of Modern Art, 1960), p. 25. Many of the impressionists and the people who wrote about them made such statements. For example, Gustave Goetschy wrote in *La Vie moderne* for 17 April 1880: Manet "is concerned above all else with rendering in the most exact and direct way the object just as it was at the moment when he set himself to reproduce it. He tries to preserve faithfully and vividly the impression which he has felt and he believes he has done enough when he sincerely expressed it" (Hamilton, *Manet*, p. 228).

33.   Daniel Wildenstein, *Monet: Impressions* (New York: French & European Publications, 1967), pp. 56–57.

34.   Quoted in Seitz, *Claude Monet: Seasons and Moments*, p. 20.

35.   Virginia Woolf, *"Modern Fiction,"* p. 154. Note also Oscar Wilde's statement in *"The Decay of Living"* (1889): "Where, if not from the Impressionists, do we get those wonderful brown fogs that come creeping down our streets, blurring the gas-lamps and changing the houses into monstrous shadows? To whom, if not to them and their master, do we owe the lovely silver mists that brood over our river, and turn to faint forms of fading grace curved bridge and swaying barge?" (*The First Collected Edition of the Works of Oscar Wilde*, ed. Robert Ross, 15 vols. London: Dawsons, 1969, 8:41).

Virginia Woolf not only repeats Monet's use of "envelope," but her word "luminous" was also a favorite word of the painters. For example, Fénéon wrote about neoimpressionist paintings in 1887, "Take a few steps back and all the multi-colored specks melt into undulant, luminous masses" (Homer, *Seurat*, p. 159); and the neoimpressionists developed a concept of chromo-luminarism (ibid., p. 160). In 1910 the futurists declared: "Your eyes, accustomed to semi-darkness, will soon open to more radiant visions of light. The shadows which we shall paint shall be more luminous than the highlights of our predecessors, and our pictures, next to those of the museums, will shine like blinding daylight compared with deepest night" (Taylor, *Futurism*, p. 126). And in 1913 Guillaume Apollinaire wrote, "These luminous signs fare around us, but only a handful of painters have grasped their plastic significance" (*The Cubist Painters*, p. 25). ("Ces signes lumineux brillent autour de nous...," Guillaume Apollinaire, *Les Peintres cubistes* [1913; reprint ed., Paris, Hermann, 1965], p. 69). It also echoes, of course, the idea behind de Maupassant's phrases "a glittering shower of light" and "a flood of yellow tones." See also "The esthetic image is first luminously apprehended as selfbound and self-contained upon the immeasurable background of space of time which is not it" (Joyce, *A Portrait*, p. 212).

36.   Cecily Mackworth, *Guillaume Apollinaire and the Cubist Life* (New York: Horizon Press, 1963), p. 17.

37.   S. L. Goldberg, *The Classical Temper* (London: Chatto & Windus, 1961), pp. 252–53.

38. The English translation is from Chipp, *Theories of Modern Art*, p. 215; for the French, see Gleizes and Metzinger, *Du "Cubisme,"* p. 34. For an early discussion of this matter, see Joseph Frank, "Spatial Form in Modern Literature," *Sewanee Review* 53 (1945): 221–40, 443–56, 643–53; reprinted in *Critiques and Essays in Criticism,* ed. R. W. Stallman (New York: Ronald Press, 1949).

39. For the story of Joyce's debt to Dujardin, see Ellmann, *James Joyce,* pp. 534–35. See also Edouard Dujardin, *Le Monologue intérieur* (Paris: Albert Messein, 1931). David Hayman has written two volumes on Joyce's debt to Mallarmé: *Joyce et Mallarmé.*

40. Francis Steegmuller, *Apollinaire: Poet among Painters* (New York: Farrar, Straus, 1963), p. 151.

41. First published in Guillaume Apollinaire, *Calligrammes* (Paris: Gallimard, 1918); reprinted in *The Cubist Painters,* p. 6.

42. First published in *Poetry* 1 (1913). Republished in Ezra Pound, *Pavannes and Divisions* (New York: Alfred A. Knopf, 1918), p. 96. See "The 'Image'" in Litz, *The Art of James Joyce,* pp. 53–61.

43. Chipp, *Theories of Modern Art,* p. 61.

44. Joyce, *A Portrait,* p. 212.

45. Symons, *The Symbolist Movement,* p. 30.

46. Quoted in Chipp, *Theories of Modern Art,* p. 210.

47. Quoted ibid., p. 211.

48. Apollinaire, *The Cubist Painters,* p. 11; *Les Peintres cubistes,* p. 48.

49. Apollinaire, *The Cubist Painters,* p. 25; *Les Peintres cubistes,* p. 69.

50. David Sutter, "Les Phénomènes de la vision," *L'Art* 20 (1880): 216; quoted by Homer, *Seurat,* p. 44. Seurat and the neoimpressionists made much of Sutter's theories and tried to put them into practice. Joyce assigned colors to eight of the chapters in *Ulysses:* "Telemachus," white and gold; "Nestor," brown; "Proteus," green; "Calypso," orange; "Hades," white and black; "Aeolus," red; "Nausicaa," gray and blue; "Oxen of the Sun," white (Stuart Gilbert, James Joyce's *"Ulysses"* [New York: Alfred A. Knopf, 1952], p. 41).

In *Ulysses* Stephen thinks of words in a poem: "He saw them three by three, approaching girls, in green, in rose, in russet, entwining, *per l'aer perso* in mauve, in purple, *quella pacifica oriafiamma,* in gold or oriflamme, *di rimirar fe piu ardenti"* (137:4/138:26).

The artists (and Joyce) were continuing an idea set out by Baudelaire in "Correspondances" in 1857 and reinforced by Rimbaud in "Voyelles" in the early 1870s:

Correspondances

La Nature est un temple où de vivants piliers
Laissent parfois sortir de confuses paroles;
L'homme y passe à travers des forêts de symboles
Qui l'observent avec des regards familiers.
Comme de longs échos qui de loin se confondent
Dans une ténébreuse et profonde unité,
Vaste comme la nuit et comme la clarté,
Les parfums, les couleurs et les sons se répondent.
Il est des parfums frais comme des chairs d'enfants,
Doux comme les hautbois, verts comme les prairies,
—Et d'autres, corrompus, riches et triomphants,
Ayant l'expansion des choses infinies,
Comme l'ambre, le musc, le benjoin et l'encens,
Qui chantent les transports de l'espirit et des sens.

Voyelles

A noir, E blanc, I rouge, U vert, O bleu, voyelles,
Je dirai quelque jour vos naissances latentes.
A, noir corset velu des mouches éclatantes
Qui bombillent autour des puanteurs cruelles . . .

I have given just the first stanza of "Voyelles." Joyce could have read all four stanzas of the poem in Symons, however, and a discussion of it (*The Symbolist Movement,* pp. 68–69).

51.   Quoted in Chipp, *Theories of Modern Art,* p. 320. I have chosen quotations from the beginning and end of a period of almost forty years, a period starting at about Joyce's birth and running to the time of the writing of *Ulysses.* Similar quotations are available – in abundance – from other writers, artists, and critics throughout those years.

52.   Percy Lubbock, *The Craft of Fiction* (New York: Charles Scribner's Sons, 1921); Melvin J. Friedman, *Stream of Consciousness: A Study in Literary Method* (New Haven: Yale University Press, 1955); Leon Edel, *The Psychological Novel, 1900-1950* (Philadelphia: J. B. Lippincott, 1955); Wayne C. Booth, *The Rhetoric of Fiction* (Chicago: University of Chicago Press, 1961). See also Jacques Souvage, *An Introduction to the Study of the Novel* (Ghent, Belgium: Story, 1965).

53.   Georges Lemaitre, *From Cubism to Surrealism* (Cambridge: Harvard University Press, 1947), p. 55.

54.   Hilla Rebay, *In Memory of Wassily Kandinsky* (New York: Solomon R. Guggenheim Foundation, 1945), p. 49.

55.   George Bernard Shaw, *Too True to Be Good; Village Wooing;* and *On the Rocks: Three Plays* (New York: Dodd, Mead, 1934), p. 105.

56.   Armand Siegel, "Operational Aspects of Hidden-Variable Quantum Theories with a Postscript on the Impact of Recent Scientific Trends on Art," *Boston Studies in Philosophy of Science,* ed. Marx W. Wartofsky (Dordrecht, Holland: D. Reidel, 1963), p. 171.

57.   Wyndham Lewis, *Time and Western Man* (New York: Harcourt, Brace, 1928); Shiv K. Kumar, *Bergson and the Stream of Consciousness Novel* (London: Blackie, 1962).

58.   Quoted by Richard Ellmann in "Two Faces of Edward," *Edwardians and Late Victorians,* ed. Richard Ellmann (New York: Columbia University Press, 1960), pp. 205–6.

59.   Sigmund Freud, *Collected Papers,* 5 vols. (London: Hogarth, 1953), 5:101–4.

60.   Quoted ibid., p. 103.

61.   William Blisset, "James Joyce in the Smithy of his Soul," *James Joyce Today,* ed. Thomas F. Staley (Bloomington: Indiana University Press, 1966), p. 115. See also "The Condition of Music" in Litz, *The Art of James Joyce,* pp. 62–74.

62.   Clive Bell, "Plus de Jazz," *New Republic* 28 (21 September 1921); 94–95.

63.   Sergei M. Eisenstein, *The Film Sense* (New York: Harcourt, Brace, 1942), pp. 95–97.

64.   See Ellmann, *James Joyce,* pp. 310–13.

65.   Eisenstein, *The Film Sense,* pp. 4, 7, 17, 30-31. Italics in the original.

66.   T. S. Eliot, "Hamlet and His Problems," *Selected Essays* (New York: Harcourt Brace, 1950), pp. 124–25.

67.   Robert Scholes and Richard M. Kain, *The Workshop of Daedalus: James Joyce and the Raw Materials for "A Portrait of the Artist as a Young Man"* (Evanston: Northwestern University Press, 1965), pp. 78–79. See also two passages in Stanislaus Joyce, *The Dublin Diary of Stanislaus Joyce,* ed. George Harris Healey (Ithaca, N.Y.: Cornell University Press, 1962):

The emotions Henry James chooses to deal with are slight, but in them his psychology is extraordinarily acute and full. He does not put you into the mind of his characters; you always feel you are reading about them, nor does he ever abandon his character of artist to disert upon what he has said—that habit of Meredith's which suggests the psychological essayist (Meredith's psychology always carries its own explanation with it)—but remains patiently impersonal. The Lord be thenkit! (Pp. 86–87)

Another passage of interior monologue at the top of p. 110.
68.   Phillip F. Herring, "The Bedsteadfastness of Molly Bloom," *Modern Fiction Studies* 15 © 1969 Purdue Research Foundation, Lafayette, Ind., 51n. The letter is dated 11 July 1912 and can be found in *The Letters of James Joyce,* vol. 2, ed. Richard Ellmann (New York: Viking Press, 1966), p. 296.

Freud, FREE ASSOCIATION

1.   [Several examples are given in section A of chap. 12 of *The Psychopathology of Everyday Life* (1901b), (Norton, 1965), where the whole topic is discussed at length.]
2.   [Paris, who eloped with Helen, was at one time a shepherd on Mount Ida, where he delivered his judgment between three competing goddesses.]

Freud, PREHISTORY OF ANALYSIS

1.   ["Zur Vorgeschichte der analytischen Technik." First published anonymously, over the signature "F," *Int. Z. Psychoanal.* 6 (1920): 79; reprinted *Ges. Schr.* 6:148, and *Ges. W.* 12:309. Translation by James Strachey.]
2.   Pointed out by Otto Rank and quoted in my *Interpretation of Dreams* (1900) [English translation, revised ed. (1932), pp. 111–12].

Bergson, DURATION

1.   *Matière et mémoire* (Paris, 1896), chaps. 2 and 3.

Woolf, ON RICHARDSON AND "ULYSSES"

1.   Probably *Jacob's Room.*
2.   T. S. Eliot.

Kumar, SURVEY OF THEORIES

1.   H. J. Muller, *Modern Fiction* (N. Y., 1937), p. 314.
2.   Wladimir Weidlé, *The Dilemma of the Arts,* trans. Martin Jarrett-Kerr (London, 1948), pp. 98–99.
3.   Oswell Blakeston, "Sang-Freud" or "The Thought-Stream Novel," *Bookman,* 87, no. 517 (October 1934): 36. Another contemporary critic remarks, "Indeed we should not look for a clearer justification for the modern novel than in Jung's writing" (Melvin Friedman, "Freud and Jung: The Problem of Consciousness," *Stream of Consciousness: A Study in Literary Method* [New Haven, 1955], p. 120).

4.   Oswell Blakeston, ibid., p. 36. Or it may be the reader who is the psychiatrist "to whom the unfortunate writer is telling everything he knows, in the hope that the welter will mean something to the listening specialist. The author is apparently the patient" (Katherine F. Gerould, "Stream of Consciousness," *Saturday Review of Literature* 4, no. 13 [October 22, 1927] : 233).

5.   Pelham Edgar, "The Stream of Consciousness," *The Art of the Novel* (N. Y., 1933), pp. 320–37.

6.   F. J. Hoffman, *Freudianism and the Literary Mind* (Louisiana, 1945), pp. 127–239. See also Edward Wagenknecht, "Stream-of-Consciousness," *Cavalcade of the Novel* (N. Y., 1949), pp. 505–32, where he discusses Dorothy Richardson "On the Stream," James Joyce "Below the Stream," and Virginia Woolf "The Stream and the World."

7.   Robert Humphrey, "Stream of Consciousness: Technique or Genre?" *Philological Quarterly* 30 (October 1951): 437.

8.   Robert Humphrey, *Stream of Consciousness in the Modern Novel* (Berkeley and Los Angeles, 1955), p. 21.

9.   Lawrence E. Bowling, "What is the Stream of Consciousness Technique?" *PMLA* 65, no. 4 (June 1950): 345.

10.   J. W. Beach, "Stream of Consciousness," *The Twentieth Century Novel* (N. Y., 1932), p. 517.

11.   Obvious from a plethora of psycho-analytical terminology in the works of these novelists. See also D. N. Morgan, "Psychology and Art Today," *Journal of Aesthetics and Art Criticism* 9 (December 1950): 81–96.

12.   Extract from J. M. Murry's review of *Ulysses* quoted by H. Gorman in *James Joyce* (London, 1949), p. 290.

13.   J. W. Beach, *The Twentieth Century Novel*, p. 388.

14.   Says Dr. Joseph Collins in his review of *Ulysses:* "I have learned more psychology and psychiatry from it than I did in ten years at the Neurological Institute" (quoted in Herbert Gorman's *James Joyce* [London, 1949] , p. 299).

15.   Intuition, it may be remembered, has hardly any place in the Freudian system of thought.

16.   See, for instance, A. A. Mendilow's *Time and the Novel* (London, 1952); particularly chap. 7, "The Time-Values of Fiction."

17.   E. W. Hawkins, "The Stream of Consciousness Novel," *Atlantic Monthly* 138 (September 1926): 356–60.

18.   J. Isaacs, "The Stream of Consciousness," *An Assessment of Twentieth-Century Literature* (London, 1951), p. 78.

19.   Ibid., p. 87. Isaacs shows how Virginia Woolf's phrases "luminous halo," "semi-transparent envelope," are suggested in Stevenson's "soft iridescence of the luminous envelope" or "the aerial envelope."

20.   Herbert Muller, "Impressionism in Fiction," *American Scholar* 7, no. 3 (Summer 1938): 357.

21.   Translated by F. L. Pogson as *Time and Free Will,* (London, 1910). Some critics of contemporary art have also attempted to relate the basic impulse of post-impressionism to Bergson's philosophy. See, for instance, Henri Seroúya's book *Initiation a la peinture d'aujourd' hui:* "Certains côtés de l'Impressionisme . . . la facon de saisir l'impression spontanée, se rattachent au Bergsonisme" ([Paris, 1931] , p. 70).

22.   Edmund Wilson, *Axel's Castle* (N. Y., 1947), p. 205.

23.   Ibid., p. 204.

24.   It would be futile to establish the influence of Bergsonism on Symbolism or vice versa, both movements being almost simultaneous manifestations of the *Zeitgeist.* See also Edouard Dujardin, *Le Monologue intérieur* (Paris, 1931), p. 95.

25.   S. M. Eisenstein, "An American Tragedy," *Close Up* 10, no. 2 (June 1933): 120–21. Mr. Eisenstein observes how the *monologue intérieur* has exercised "a profound influence on the purely technical methods" (cinematic), and after referring

to Joyce's new technique in *Ulysses,* cites an interview with him on its use in his production of "An American Tragedy."

26. Harry Levin, *James Joyce* (Connecticut, 1941), p. 88; also pp. 87–112. See a more detailed discussion of "Time-and-Space-Montage" in terms of "multiple-view," "slow-ups," "fadeouts," "cutting," "close-ups," etc., in Robert Humphrey's *Stream of Consciousness in the Modern Novel* (Berkeley and Los Angeles, 1955), pp. 49ff.

27. Another popular exposition of the new technique is in terms of music. See Friedman, "The Analogy with Music," *Stream of Consciousness: A Study in Literary Method* (New Haven, 1955), pp. 121–38. See also Vernon Hall, "Joyce's Use of Da Ponte and Mozart's *Don Giovanni,*" *PMLA* 66 (1951): 78–84.

28. Joseph Collins, *The Doctor Looks at Literature* (N. Y., 1923).

29. P. Lambert, "L'Exile: Satire on Current Literary Freaks," *Sewanee Review* 40 (October 1932): 415–24.

30. Louis Hasley, "The Stream of Consciousness Method," *Catholic World* 146 (November 1937): 210–13.

31. "In *Les Lauriers sont coupés,* Joyce told me, the reader finds himself, from the very first line, posted within the mind of the protagonist, and it is the continuous unfolding of his thoughts which, replacing normal objective narration, depicts to us his acts and experiences. I advise you to read *Les Lauriers sont coupés.*" Stuart Gilbert, *James Joyce's* "Ulysses" (London, 1930), p. 24.

32. Edouard Dujardin, *Le Monologue intérieur* (Paris, 1931), p. 33.

33. Victor Egger, *La Parole intérieure* (Paris, 1904; first published 1881), pp. 1, 71, 113. For distinction between "la parole intérieure," and "la parole extérieure," see also G. Ballet, *Le Langage intérieur* (Paris, 1886), p. 23.

34. Edouard Dujardin, *Le Monologue intérieur,* p. 59.

35. Ibid., p. 68. (Italics mine).

36. *Letters of Proust,* trans. Mina Curtiss (London, 1950), p. 188. (Italics mine).

37. Proust, *Time Regained,* trans. Stephen Hudson (London, 1951), pp. 429, 430, 433.

38. André Gide, *The Coiners,* trans. D. Bussy (London, 1950), p. 206.

39. Jules Romains, *The Death of a Nobody,* trans. Desmond MacCarthy (London, 1914), p. 5.

40. Italo Svevo, *The Nice Old Man and Other Stories,* trans. L. Collison-Morley (London, 1930), p. 153. It should be interesting to compare this with Bergson's statement in *Durée et simultanéité* (Paris, 1922), p. 60: "Le mathématicien, il est vrai, n'aura pas à s'occuper d'elle, puisqu'il s'intéresse à la mesure des choses et non pas à leur nature. Mais s'il se demandait ce qu'il mesure, s'il fixait son attention sur le temps lui-même, nécessairement il se représenterait de la succession. . . ."

41. Virginia Woolf, *Orlando* (London, 1949), p. 91.

42. Thomas Wolf, *Look Homeward Angel* (N. Y., 1929).

43. Gertrude Stein, *Composition as Explanation* (London, 1926), p. 17.

44. Even the title of Thomas Wolfe's novel *Of Time and the River* (N. Y., 1935) suggests this new realization of experience as flux.

45. Italo Svevo, *The Nice Old Man* (London, 1930), p. 152.

46. Virginia Woolf, *The Waves* (London, 1950), p. 187.

47. Bergson, *Time and Free Will,* trans. F. L. Pogson (London, 1950), p. 104 (first English translation 1910).

48. Bergson, *Matter and Memory,* trans. N. M. Paul & W. S. Palmer (London, 1913), p. 178.

49. *Time and Free Will,* p. x.

50. Stanley Jones, *The Metaphysical Basis of the Work of Marcel Proust,* Ph.D. dissertation, 1949, Cambridge University Library.

51. *Letters of Proust,* pp. 203–4.

52. "My novel is not a work of ratiocination: its least elements have been supplied by my sensibility . . ." (ibid., p. 189).

53.   Proust, *Swann's Way,* trans. S. Moncrieff, pt. 1 (London, 1922), p. 57.
54.   Proust, *The Guermantes Way,* trans. S. Moncrieff, pt. 1 (London, 1925), pp. 117-18.
55.   *Letters of Proust,* p. 332.
56.   *Henri Bergson: Essais et témoignages recueillis,* ed. Béguin and Thévanaz (Neuchatel, 1943), p. 125.
57.   Fernand Vial, "Le Symbolisme bergsonien du temps dans l'oeuvre de Proust," *PMLA* 55 (December 1940): p. 1191.
58.   *Letters of Proust,* p. 165.
59.   It may here be noted that Proust himself was the first to use the term "romans bergsoniens," which seems to be only another name for the stream-of-consciousness novel.
60.   Quoted by Martin Turnell in his book *The Novel in France* (London, 1950), p. 189.
61.   *Matter and Memory,* pp. 217-25.
62.   T. E. Hulme, *Speculations* (London, 1924), p. 149. (Italics mine).
63.   Ibid., p. 263.
64.   Jules Romains, *The Death of a Nobody,* trans. Desmond MacCarthy (London, 1914), p. vi.
65.   Bergson, *Creative Evolution,* trans. Arthur Mitchell (London, 1913), p. 188. It is not our intention here to suggest that James was in any sense influenced by Bergson or vice versa. These two "frères pensées," working independently arrived at similar conclusions. At a later stage they came to recognize in each other the same philosophic impulses. The extent to which William James later on came to corroborate Bergson's view of mobile reality may be seen from his marginal notes in the text of a copy of *L'Évolution créatrice* which the latter presented "à M. le Prof. William James, son devoué admirateur—Henri Bergson." From the markings in ink and pencil, one is surprised to observe how closely the curves and lines of their respective philosophies synchronize with each other. For instance, on p. 369 of this copy James underlines: "Le temps est invention ou il n'est rien du tout"—and adds on p. 100: "Vision is to the eye what movement is to a path."
      This copy of Bergson's *L'Évolution créatrice* (Paris, 1907) is one of the James manuscripts in the Houghton Library, Harvard University, Cambridge, Massachusetts.
66.   May Sinclair, "The Novels of Dorothy Richardson," *The Egoist* 5 (April 1918): 58.
67.   William James, *The Principles of Psychology* 1 (London, 1907): 620 (first published 1890).
68.   Ibid., 239.
69.   Ibid., 281.
70.   Virginia Woolf, "Modern Fiction," *The Common Reader* (First Series; London, 1948), p. 189 (first published 1925).
71.   Ibid., pp. 189-90.
72.   *The Principles of Psychology* 1: 606-7.
73.   William James, however, borrows this term from E. R. Clay's book *The Alternative* (London, 1882), p. 167, where he says: "The relation of experience to time has not been profoundly studied . . . . The present to which the datum refers is really a part of the past—a recent past—delusively given as being a time that intervenes between the past and the future. Let it be named the specious present."
74.   *The Principles of Psychology* 1: 609.
75.   Gertrude Stein, *Composition as Explanation* (London, 1926), pp. 16-17 (italics mine). Cf. also Bergson's definition of the "live present" in *Matter and Memory* (London, 1913), pp. 176-77.

Steinberg, PSYCHOLOGICAL STREAM OF CONSCIOUSNESS

1.   W. Edgar Vinacke, *The Psychology of Thinking* (New York: McGraw-Hill, 1952), p. 44.
2.   Benjamin Jowett, trans., *The Dialogues of Plato,* 2 vols. (New York: Random House, 1947), 1:460.
3.   Aristotle, "On Memory and Reminiscence," trans. J. I. Beaver, 451[b] (10), *Great Books of the Western World,* 54 vols. (Chicago: Encyclopedia Britannica, 1952), 8:693.
4.   Vinacke, *Psychology of Thinking,* p. 14.
5.   William James, *The Principles of Psychology* (1890; reprint ed., New York: Dover Publications, 1950), pp. 224–90 (James's italics). Although James is generally given credit for the introduction of this term, the metaphor is not new. For example, Samuel Taylor Coleridge wrote of "the streamy nature of association, which thinking curbs and rudders," of "streamy associations," and of the "streamy nature of the associative faculty" (*Animae Poetae* [London: Heinemann, 1895], pp. 55, 56, 65–66). He suspected that it was the source of "moral evil" and that "they labour under this defect [the streamy nature of the associative faculty] who are most reverie-ish and streamy—Hartley, for instance, and myself. This seems to me no common corroboration of my former thought or [on, of?] the origin of moral evil in general."
6.   Howard C. Warren, *Dictionary of Psychology* (Boston: Houghton Mifflin, 1934), p. 263.
7.   William James, *Talks to Teachers on Psychology; and to Students on Some of Life's Ideals* (New York: Henry Holt, 1921), p. 17.
8.   James, *Principles,* p. 225.
9.   Ibid., p. 237.
10.   Ibid., p. 238.
11.   Ibid., p. 224.
12.   Harry Stack Sullivan, *Conceptions of Modern Psychiatry* (New York: W. W. Norton, 1953), pp. 105–7.
13.   The reader will begin to notice here a difficulty in expressing many of the psychological concepts, and perhaps even some contradictions. For example, the items mentioned above are not really discrete items but more exactly overlapping and interrelated events and elements in a highly complex space-time continuum. The problem here is really twofold. In the first place, this sort of itemizing would seem to be necessary in order to introduce some of the basic concepts in relatively simple form so that ultimately more involved concepts may be discussed. However, whatever distortion inheres in this early presentation because of the necessity of breaking into the pattern somewhere in order to describe it will be corrected by the end of the chapter. A second difficulty is more fundamental and more serious. The physicists have much the same problem:

The fundamental difficulty of determining the place of an electron moving at a certain   velocity is expressed in a general manner by the uncertain relation originally formulated by Werner Heisenberg. This relation is characteristic of quantum physics and states among other things that the measurement of an electron's velocity is inaccurate in proportion as the measurement of its position in space is accurate, and vice versa. It is not hard to discover the reason. We can determine the position of a moving electron only if we can see it and in order to see it we must illuminate it, i.e., we must allow light to fall on it. The rays falling on it impinge upon the electron and thus alter its velocity in a way which it is impossible to calculate. The more accurately we desire to determine the position of the electron, the shorter must be the light waves employed to illuminate it, the stronger will be the impact, and the greater the inaccuracy with which the velocity is determined. (Max Planck, *The Philosophy of Physics* [New York: W. W. Norton, 1936], pp. 62–63.

So too, throwing light on the psychological stream of consciousness creates inaccuracies: to discuss a moment of consciousness as Sullivan does is to halt the flow and thus give an erroneous picture; to analyze the moment of consciousness forces itemizing, which fails to show the complex interrelationships of the components of consciousness; but to describe merely the flow on the grounds that to halt it distorts the picture is equally bad because it results in only a partial picture.

C. S. Lewis, in his diatribe against stream-of-consciousness writers, raises precisely this problem. First he inveighs against introspection:

The disorganized consciousness which it regards as specially real is in fact highly artificial. It is discovered by introspection—that is, by artifically suspending all the normal and outgoing activities of the mind and then attending to what is left. In that residuum it discovers no concentrated will, no logical thought, no morals, no stable sentiments, and (in a word) no mental hierarchy. Of course not; for we have deliberately stopped all these things in order to introspect.

And then he denies the possibility of putting it into words:

For the very nature of such unfocused consciousness is that it is not attended to. Inattention makes it what it is. The moment you put it into words you falsify it. It is like trying to see what a thing looks like when you are not looking at it. (C. S. Lewis, *A Preface to "Paradise Lost"* [London: Oxford University Press, 1942], pp. 131–32)

Although Lewis may not have intended it so, this argument is also directed against any attempt to discuss the psychological stream of consciousness. For the psychologist too depends heavily upon introspection for his knowledge of the stream of consciousness and must use language to describe his findings. And, indeed, many psychologists, impressed by the difficulties involved and fearful of possible resultant inaccuracies, avoid concepts like "consciousness" and "mind"; they prefer instead to adopt a behavioristic approach, discussing what they can see and measure. Many psychologists are not so behaviorist, however, and do deal directly with the stream of consciousness. We shall therefore examine what these psychologists have to say about both the components and the flow of the stream of consciousness, fully conscious of the possible distortion involved.

The problem of the distortion resulting from putting the stream of consciousness into words will be discussed later at some length, since it is an important difficulty in the simulation of the psychological stream of consciousness.

14. Vinacke, *Psychology of Thinking*, p. 47.

15. Warren, *Dictionary of Psychology*, pp. 245, 196, 131. For a fuller definition of image, see Alan Richardson, *Mental Imagery* (New York: Springer Publishing Co., 1969), pp. 1–12. Richardson's concise definition is: "Mental imagery refers to (1) all those quasi-sensory or quasi-perceptual experiences of which (2) we are self-consciously aware, and which (3) exist for us in the absence of those stimulus conditions that are known to produce their genuine sensory or perceptual counterparts, and which (4) may be expected to have different consequences from their sensory or perceptual counterparts" (pp. 2–3).

16. George A. Miller, *Language and Communication* (New York: McGraw-Hill, 1951), p. 225.

17. Edward G. Boring, *A History of Experimental Psychology* (New York: Appleton-Century-Crofts, 1957), pp. 642–43.

18. J. B. Watson, *Psychology from the Standpoint of a Behaviorist* (Philadelphia: J. B. Lippincott, 1924), p. 104.

19. David Katz, *Gestalt Psychology* (New York: Ronald Press, 1950), p. 55.

20. Ibid., p. 55.

21. Robert R. Holt, "Imagery: The Return of the Ostracized," *American Psychologist* 19 (1964): 257. There was, of course, some disagreement. Vinacke wrote, for example: "We may certainly accept the reality of images and at the same time accept the facts uncovered by the exponents of imageless thought. Both are necessary for an understanding of thought (*Psychology of Thinking*, p. 52). But many psychologists explained perception, thinking, and imagination largely without images. For example, a code theory was presented (R. W. Perry, "Neurology and the Mind-Brain Problem," *American Scientist* 40 [April 1952]:295) and a theory that "the entire output of our thinking machine consists of nothing but patterns of motor coordination" (pp. 297–98). Other psychologists argued that we think directly and not in terms of anything:

We perceive objects directly, not through the intermediary of "presentations," "ideas," or "sensations." Similarly, *we imagine objects directly,* not through the intermediary of images, though images are present as an important part of the whole activity. In each of these two cases, we may assign an important part, though not all, of the activity to one or other of the sensory modalities. *We may, however, think a proposition, or (draw) an inference . . . in such a way that the activity in question falls within none of the sensory modalities;* though in general such activity is accompanied by either perception or imagination. This would be a fair conclusion, stated in more modern terms, from the experiments of which those of the Würzburg school are typical (George Humphrey, *Thinking* [New York: John Wiley & Sons, 1951], p. 129)

Those psychologists who did not cast images "into outer darkness" tended not to find it profitable to do research on them or to include them in their systems or models.

22. Holt, "Imagery," pp. 254–64. Holt discusses the history of the banishment and factors in the reemergence of imagery as well as important studies of imagery and their implications for further research.

23. Jerome L. Singer, *Daydreaming* (New York: Random House, 1966), pp. 44, 57. Singer summarizes his own studies and studies of others and concludes with a full and useful bibliography.

24. Richardson, *Mental Imagery*, p. ix, also includes a full and useful bibliography.

25. Ibid., pp. 70, 80.

26. Peter McKellar, *Imagination and Thinking* (New York: Basic Books, 1957), p. 34; Lois J. Michael, "A Factor Analysis of Mental Imagery," *Dissertation Abstracts* 27 (1967): 3761A (Auburn University).

27. Richardson, *Mental Imagery*, p. 70.

28. Alfred Korzybski, *Science and Sanity*, 3rd ed. (Lakeville, Conn.: International Non-Aristotelian Library, 1948), p. 59.

29. Gotthold Ephraim Lessing, *Laokoon* (London: Bell, 1914), p. 101.

30. Benjamin Lee Whorf, "Language and Logic" (reprinted from *Technology Review* 43 [1941]: 250), in *Language, Thought and Reality,* ed. John B. Carroll (New York: Technology Press of M. I. T., 1956), pp. 240, 241, 242. One further quotation from Whorf containing examples may help the reader to understand specifically what he means:

In Nootka, a language of Vancouver Island, all words seem to us to be verbs . . . ; we have, as it were, a monistic view of nature that gives us only one class of word for all kinds of events. "A house occurs" or "it houses" is the way of saying "house," exactly like "a flame occurs" or "it burns." These terms seem to us like verbs because they are inflected for durational and temporal nuances, so that the suffixes of the word for house event make it mean long-lasting house, temporary house, future house,

house that used to be, what started out to be a house, and so on ("Science and Linguistics," reprinted from *Technology Review* 42 [1940]: 229, in *Language, Thought, and Reality*, pp. 215-16)

31. Lessing, *Laokoon*, p. 91.
32. Virginia Woolf, "Modern Fiction," *The Common Reader* (1925; reprint ed., New York: Harcourt, Brace, 1953), p. 155.
33. A. A. Mendilow, *Time and the Novel* (London: Peter Nevill, 1952), p. 80.
34. Aldous Huxley, *Brave New World* (1932; reprint ed., New York: Harper 1950), pp. 200-1.
35. Herbert J. Muller, *Science and Criticism* (New Haven: Yale University Press, 1950), p. 97.
36. James, *Principles*, pp. 224-25.
37. John Livingston Lowes, *The Road to Xanadu* (Boston: Houghton Mifflin, 1927), pp. 55-56, 405, 429-30. Lowes attributes this difficulty to "the limitations of our finite minds."
38. Korzybski, *Science and Sanity*, p. 179.
39. Mendilow, *Time and the Novel*, p. 81.
40. Gardner Murphy, *Personality* (New York: Harper, 1947), p. 353. Murphy says that "the thinker and the imaginer . . . can be understood in the same terms" (p. 391).
41. Vinacke, *Psychology of Thinking*, p. 160.
42. Ibid., pp. 218, 220, 233.
43. Singer, *Daydreaming*, pp. 77-78.
44. Murphy, *Personality*, pp. 998, 989, 991, 983, 996, 988.
45. Vinacke, *Psychology of Thinking*, pp. 19-20.
46. C. G. Jung, *Studies in Word-Association* (London: Heinemann, 1918), p. 167.
47. Fred Schwartz and Richard O. Rouse, "The Activation and Recovery of Associations," *Psychological Issues* 3, no. 1 (1961): 1-2.
48. H. A. Witkin et al., *Personality through Perception* (New York: Harper, 1954), p. 479.

O'Brien, PROUST CONFIRMED BY NEUROSURGERY

1. Mme. Elizabeth Czoniczer in her most stimulating book, *Quelques antécédants d'A la recherche du temps perdu* (Droz, 1956) argues cogently that Proust's father and brother, both medical doctors, must have left such texts throughout the apartment, where Marcel Proust could have absorbed their contents.
2. See "La Mémoire involontaire avant Marcel Proust" by Justin O'Brien in *Revue de Littérature Comparée* (March 1939).
3. *Journal* 1:785 (19 juin 1924).
4. *Proceedings of the National Academy of Sciences* 44 ii (15 Feb., 1958).

Leopold, SOME PROBLEMS OF TERMINOLOGY

1. L. E. Bowling, "What Is the Stream of Consciousness Technique?" *PMLA* 65 (1950): 337-45.
2. R. Humphrey, *Stream of Consciousness in the Modern Novel* (Berkeley: University of California Press, 1954).
3. M. J. Friedman, *Stream of Consciousness: A Study in Literary Method* (New Haven: Yale University Press, 1955).
4. Ibid., p. 21.
5. L. Edel, *The Psychological Novel, 1900-1950* (New York: Lippincott, 1955).
6. K. R. Meyer, *Zur erlebten Rede (The Interior Monologue) im englischen Roman des 20. Jahrhunderts* (Winterthur: Keller, 1957).
7. Ibid., p. 67.
8. G. Storz, "Uber den 'Monologue intérieur' oder die 'Erlebte Rede,'" *Der Deutschunterricht* 7 (1955): 41.

9.   W. Kayser, *Entstehung und Krise des modernen Romans* (Stuttgart: Metzler-sche Verlagsbuchhandlung, 1955), p. 31.
10.   E. Dujardin, *Le Monologue intérieur* (Paris: Messein, 1931).
11.   A. Warren & R. Wellek, *Theory of Literature* (London: Cape, 1954), p. 233.
12.   Friedman, op. cit., p. 3.
13.   The first use of the term in literary criticism is almost certainly by Valéry Larbaud in a lecture on James Joyce in 1921. The phrase "un monologue intérieur" is supposed to have been coined by Alexander Dumas. It occurs in *Vingt ans après*. (See Friedman, op. cit., p. 1.)
14.   Quoted by K. R. Meyer, op. cit., p. 67.
15.   Humphrey, op. cit., p. 2.
16.   Kayser, loc. cit.
17.   O. Funke, "Zur 'erlebten Rede' bei Galsworthy," *Englische Studien*, vol. 64, 1929. This term is taken over from Funke by K. R. Meyer.
18.   From Arnold Bennett's *Clayhanger*. Quoted by K. R. Meyer, op. cit., p. 14.
19.   From Dorothy Richardson's *The Tunnel*. Quoted by K. R. Meyer, op. cit., p. 81. [Dorothy Richardson, *The Tunnel*, in *Pilgrimage* (New York: Popular Library, 1976), p. 126.]
20.   According to E. Lerch, "Ursprung und Bedeutung der sog. 'Erlebten Rede,'" *GRM* 16 (1928): 462.
21.   G. O. Curme, *A Grammar of the German Language* (New York: Macmillan, 1905), p. 248.
22.   O. Jespersen, *The Philosophy of Grammar* (London: Allen & Unwin, 1951), p. 291.
23.   A. A. Mendilow, *Time and the Novel* (London: Nevill, 1952), p. 112.
24.   G. Von Wilpert, *Sachwörterbuch der Literatur* (Stuttgart: Kröner, 1955).
25.   Dujardin, op. cit., pp. 58f.
26.   J. Joyce, *Ulysses* (New York: Modern Library, 1946), p. 723.
27.   F. Stanzel, *Die typischen Erzählsituationen im Roman* (Vienna: Braumuller, 1955).

Steinberg, TECHNIQUE DEFINED

1.   Jacques Souvage, "The 'Dramatized' Novel," *An Introduction to the Study of the Novel* (Ghent: E. Story–Scientia P.V.B.A., 1965), p. 46. For this discussion, Souvage's sections "'Telling' versus 'Showing' in the Novel," "Point of View," and "Point of View and Other Types of Narration" are helpful (pp. 48–62). Souvage's quotation from Leon Edel comes from *The Psychological Novel, 1900-1950* (New York and Philadelphia: J. B. Lippincott, 1955), p. 83. As the spelling shows, Souvage used the British edition.
2.   Edouard Dujardin, *Le Monologue intérieur* (Paris: Albert Messein, 1931), p. 59.
3.   Ibid., p. 41.
4.   Frank Budgen, *James Joyce and the Making of "Ulysses"* (New York: Harri-son Smith and Robert Haas, 1934), p. 92; Djuna Barnes, "James Joyce," *Vanity Fair* 18, no. 2 (April 1922): 65, 104.
5.   Virginia Woolf, "Modern Fiction," *The Common Reader* (1925; reprint ed., New York: Harcourt, Brace, 1953), pp. 154–55.
6.   Lawrence E. Bowling, "What Is the Stream of Consciousness Technique?" *PMLA* 65 (1950): 345.
7.   Robert Humphrey, *Stream of Consciousness in the Modern Novel* (Berkeley: University of California Press, 1954), p. 4.
8.   Dujardin, *Le Monologue intérieur*, p. 58.
9.   James Joyce, *A Portrait of the Artist as a Young Man* (New York: Viking Press, 1968), p. 215.

10.   Alfred Korzybski, *Science and Sanity* (Lakeville, Conn.: International Non-Aristotelian Library, 1948), p. 179.
11.   Phyllis Bentley, *Some Observations on the Art of Narrative* (New York: Macmillan Co., 1947), p. 9.
12.   Edel, *The Psychological Novel*, p. 83. Edel does not use the concept of level of abstraction, but at the bottom of p. 84 he makes much the same point in other language.
13.   Humphrey, *Stream of Consciousness*, pp. 36, 26.
14.   Edel, *The Psychological Novel*, pp. 83, 23.
15.   Stuart Gilbert, *James Joyce's "Ulysses"* (New York: Alfred A. Knopf, 1952), p. 255.
16.   Dorrit Cohn, "Narrated Monologue: Definition of a Fictional Style," *Comparative Literature* 18 (1966): 97-98. Mrs. Cohn hesitates between "narrated consciousness" and "narrated monologue" as a translation for *erlebte Rede* and settles "tentatively" for "narrated monologue" (p. 104).
17.   Joyce, *A Portrait;* Cohn, "Narrated Monologue," p. 98. Mrs. Cohn added the italics to indicate *erlebte Rede.*
18.   Cohn, "Narrated Monologue," p. 98. "The deviation from past to conditional and pluperfect is explained in n. 23 [pp. 104-5 in Cohn]."
19.   Edel, *The Psychological Novel*, p. 47.
20.   Anthony Trollope, *Barchester Towers,* chap. 15; quoted by A. A. Mendilow in *Time and the Novel* (London: Peter Nevill, 1952), p. 101. For other discussions of the "intrusive author," see Mendilow's chapter by that title and Humphrey, *Stream of Consciousness.*
21.   The italics are added.
22.   Bentley, *Some Observations,* "Use of Summary."
23.   From Stuart Gilbert's translation, entitled *We'll to the Woods No More* (Norfolk, Conn.: New Directions, 1938), p. 6.
24.   For other attempts to sort out the various techniques generally lumped together by critics under the term "stream-of-consciousness technique," see Derek Bickerton, "Modes of Interior Monologue: A Formal Definition," *Modern Language Quarterly* 28 (1967): 229-39; Bickerton, "James Joyce and the Development of Interior Monologue," *Essays in Criticism* 18 (1968): 32-37; Bowling, "What Is the Stream of Consciousness Technique?" pp. 333-45; Liisa Dahl, *Linguistic Features of the Stream-of-Consciousness Technique in James Joyce, Virginia Woolf, and Eugene O'Neill* (Turku, Finland: University of Turku, 1970); Melvin J. Friedman, *Stream of Consciousness: A Study in Literary Method* (New Haven: Yale University Press, 1955); Norman Friedman, "Point of View in Fiction: The Development of the Critical Concept" *PMLA* 70 (1955): 1160-84; Humphrey, *Stream of Consciousness;* H. A. Kelly, "Consciousness in the Monologues of *Ulysses,*" *Modern Language Quarterly* 24 (1963): 3-12; Keith Leopold, "Some Problems of Terminology in the Analysis of the Stream of Consciousness Novel," *AUMLA* 13 (May 1960): 23-32; W. J. Lillyman, "The Interior Monologue in James Joyce and Otto Ludwig," *Comparative Literature* 23 (1971): 45-54; Robie Macauley and George Lanning, *Technique in Fiction* (New York: Harper & Row, 1964), pp. 88-94; John Spencer, "A Note on the 'Steady Monologuy of the Interiors,'" *Review of English Literature* 6 (1965): 32-41; William Flint Thrall and Addison Hibbard, *A Handbook to Literature,* rev. and enl. by C. Hugh Holman (New York: Odyssey Press, 1960), see "Interior Monologue" (p. 243) and "Stream-of-Consciousness Novel" (pp. 471-72).
        The continuum above maintains a perfect correlation between the level of abstraction and the intrusiveness of the author: the lower the level of abstraction, the less intrusive the author; the higher the level, the more obvious the manipulations and judgments of the author become.

Humphrey, THE RESULTS

1. (New York: Harcourt, Brace, 1946), p. 426.
2. (New York: Random House, 1950), p. 258.
3. Joseph Warren Beach in *The Twentieth Century Novel: Studies in Technique* (New York: D. Appleton-Century, 1932); Frederick J. Hoffman in *The Modern Novel in America, 1900--1950* (Chicago: Regnery, 1951).

ACKNOWLEDGMENTS

"The Stream-of-Consciousness Novel." From *A Handbook to Literature* by C. Hugh Holman, William Flint Thrall, and Addison Hibbard. Copyright © 1936, 1970 by The Odyssey Press. Copyright © 1972 by the Bobbs-Merril Company.

"Narrative Technique in the Novel: The Dramatized Novel and Point of View." From *An Introduction to the Study of the Novel* by Jacques Souvage. Copyright © 1965 by E. Story-Scientia P. V. B. A. By permission of the publisher.

"The Sources of the Stream," "The Psychological Stream of Consciousness," and "The Stream-of-Consciousness Technique Defined." From *The Stream of Consciousness and Beyond in ULYSSES* by Erwin R. Steinberg. Copyright © 1958, 1973 by Erwin R. Steinberg. Reprinted by permission of the University of Pittsburgh Press.

"This Moment." From *Conceptions of Modern Psychiatry* by Harry Stack Sullivan, M.D. Copyright © 1940, 1945, 1947, and 1953 by the William Alanson White Psychiatry Foundation. Excerpt is used with the permission of the publisher, W. W. Norton & Company, Inc., New York, N. Y.

"The Stream of Thought." From *The Principles of Psychology* by William James. Copyright © 1890 by Holt, Rinehart and Winston. Reprinted by permission of Holt, Rinehart and Winston.

"The Stream of Consciousness." From *Talks to Teachers on Psychology; and to Students on Some of Life's Ideals* by William James. Copyright © 1899, 1900 by Holt, Rinehart and Winston. Reprinted by permission of Holt, Rinehart and Winston.

"Free Association." From *The Complete Introductory Lectures on Psychoanalysis* by Sigmund Freud. Translated and edited by James Strachey. By permission of W. W. Norton & Company, Inc. Copyright © 1966 by W. W. Norton & Company, Inc. Copyright © 1965, 1964, 1963 by James Strachey. Copyright 1963 by Sigmund Freud. Copyright renewed 1961 by W. J. H. Sprott. Copyright 1920, 1935 by Edward L. Bernays.

"A Note on the Prehistory of the Technique of Analysis." From *Collected Papers,* by Sigmund Freud, edited by Ernest Jones, M.D., volume 5, edited by James Strachey. Published by Basic Books, Inc. by arrangement with The Hogarth Press, Ltd. and the Institute of Psycho-Analysis, London.

"Understanding Reality from Within." From *An Introduction to Metaphysics* by Henri Bergson. Copyright © 1913 by G. P. Putnam's Sons. By permission of G. P. Putnam's Sons.

"Duration." From *Creative Evolution* by Henri Bergson, Copyright © 1911 by Holt, Rinehart and Winston. Reprinted by permission of Holt, Rinehart and Winston.

"Modern Fiction." From *The Common Reader* by Virginia Woolf. Copyright 1925 by Harcourt Brace Jovanovich, Inc. Copyright 1953 by Leonard Woolf. Reprinted by permission of the publisher.

"On Dorothy Richardson, James Joyce, and *Ulysses.*" Excerpts from *A Writer's Diary* by Virginia Woolf. Copyright 1953, 1954 by Leonard Woolf. Reprinted by permission of Harcourt Brace Jovanovich, Inc.

"James Joyce on Modern Literature." From *Conversations with James Joyce* by Arthur Power, edited by Clive Hart. Copyright © 1974 by Barnes & Noble Books, a division of Harper & Row Publishers. Reprinted by permission of the publisher.

"On the Stream of Consciousness." Passage from the diary of Stanislaus Joyce, from *The Workshop of Daedalus* by Robert Scholes and Richard M. Kain. Published 1965 by Northwestern University Press, Evanston, Illinois. By permission of the publisher.

"Autobiographical Sketch," by Dorothy Richardson. From *Authors Today and Yesterday*. Copyright 1933 by the H. W. Wilson Company. Reprinted by permission of the H. W. Wilson Company, Bronx, New York.

Foreword to *Pilgrimage* by Dorothy Richardson. By permission of Alfred A. Knopf, Inc.

"A Little Cake Releases a Hidden Memory." From *Remembrance of Things Past,* by Marcel Proust, translated by C. K. Scott Moncrieff. Copyright 1928 and renewed 1956 by the Modern Library, Inc. Reprinted by permission of Random House, Inc.

"The Principle of Involuntary Memory." Prologue to *Contra Sainte-Beuve* by Marcel Proust, from *On Art and Literature* (New York: Meridan Books, 1958). Copyright © 1954 by Editions Gallimard. By permission of the publisher.

"The Novels of Dorothy Richardson." By May Sinclair, *The Egoist* 5 (April 1918): 57–59.

"The Break-Up of the Novel." From *Discoveries* by John Middleton Murry, published 1924 by W. W. Collins Sons. By permission from The Society of Authors as the literary representative of the Estate of John Middleton Murry.

"The Stream of Consciousness Novel," by Ethel Wallace Hawkins, *The Atlantic Monthly,* 138 (September 1926), pp. 356–360. Copyright © 1926 by The Atlantic Monthly Company, Boston, Mass. Reprinted with permission.

"A Survey of the Various Theories Advanced to Explain the Nature and Scope of the Stream-of-Consciousness Technique." Reprinted by permission of New York University Press from *Bergson and the Stream of Consciousness Novel* by Shiv K. Kumar, 1962.

"Proust Confirmed by Neurosurgery," by Justin O'Brien. Reprinted by permission of the Modern Language Association of America from *PMLA,* 85 (March 1970), pp. 295–297. Copyright © 1970, the Modern Language Association of America.

"Some Problems of Terminology in the Analysis of the Stream of Consciousness Novel," by Keith Leopold, *AUMLA,* No. 13 (May 1960), pp. 23–32. Copyright © 1960, *AUMLA*. By permission of the publisher.

"The Stream-of-Consciousness Techniques of Joyce, Woolf, and O'Neill," from *Linguistic Features of the Stream-of-Consciousness Techniques of James Joyce, Virginia Woolf, and Eugene O'Neill* by Liisa Dahl. (Turku, Finland: Turun Yliopisto, 1970). Copyright © 1970. By permission of Liisa Dahl.

"The Results," from *Stream of Consciousness in the Modern Novel* by Robert Humphrey. Copyright © 1954 by The Regents of the University of California; reprinted by permission of the University of California Press.